Quality Popular Television

Quality Popular Television

Cult TV, the Industry and Fans

Edited by
Mark Jancovich and James Lyons

 Publishing

First published in 2003 by the
British Film Institute
21 Stephen Street, London W1T 1LN

Reprinted 2004

The British Film Institute promotes greater understanding of,
and access to, film and moving image culture in the UK.

Cover design: Mark Swan

Set by Alden Bookset, Northampton
Printed by St Edmundsbury Press, Bury St Edmunds, Suffolk

British Library Cataloguing-in-Publication Data

A catalogue record for this book is available from the British Library
ISBN 0–85170–941–9 (pbk)
ISBN 0–85170–940–0 (hbk)

Contents

Afterword

Acknowledgments

This book is dedicated to Peter Krämer, who, as with most things, pointed the way forward. We would also like to thank Andrew Lockett for his patience and the contributors for their dedication and commitment. It is fair to say that without the above, this book would never have happened. We would also like to thank the following for their support, encouragement and inspiration across the years: Martin Barker, Ian F. A. Bell, Steve Cohan, Paul Grainge, Lee Grieveson, Ina Rae Hark, Henry Jenkins, Barbara Klinger, Peter Ling, Robert McMinn, Tara McPherson, Richard Maltby, Sharon Monteith, Geoff Mulgan, Tim O'Sullivan, Simon Philo, Karen Schneider, Bev Skeggs, Douglas Tallack and, of course, Karen Goldstein and Joanne Hollows.

Notes on Contributors

Ian Gordon is an associate professor in History and the Convenor of the American Studies Program at the National University of Singapore. He is currently researching visual stereotypes of Asians in America. His book *Comic Strips and Consumer Culture* was published by the Smithsonian Press in 1998 and his co-edited collection *Comics and Ideology* by Peter Lang in 2001. He is an International Contributing Editor to the *Journal of American History*. He is the managing editor of H-Amstdy the internet American Studies discussion list.

Sara Gwenllian Jones lectures in Film, Television and Digital Media at Cardiff University and is co-editor of *Intensities: the Journal of Cult Media* (*http://www.cult-media.com*). She is currently writing a book on cult television (Edward Arnold, 2002).

Jennifer Holt is a PhD candidate in the Department of Film and Digital Media at UCLA, where she is also a graduate teaching fellow in Critical Studies. Her work has been published in *Film Quarterly* and *Film and History*, and she is currently completing her dissertation, entitled *In Deregulation We Trust: Hollywood and Politics in the Reagan Era*.

Mark Jancovich is Reader and Director of the Institute of Film Studies at the University of Nottingham. He has written and edited several books, including: *Approaches to Popular Film* (with Joanne Hollows) (MUP, 1995); *Rational Fears: American Horror in the 1950s*; *The Film Studies Reader* (with Joanne Hollows and Peter Hutchings) (MUP, 1996); *Horror, The Film Reader* (Routledge, 2002); and *The Place of the Audience: Cultural Geographies of Film Consumption* (with Lucy Faire and Sarah Stubbings) (BFI, forthcoming). He is a founder member of *Scope: An Online Journal of Film Studies*; the series editor (with Eric Schaefer) of *Inside Popular Film*; and is currently working on *Sexual Tastes: A Cultural History of Playboy Magazine*.

James Lyons is a lecturer in film at the University of Exeter. He is currently completing a book on the meanings of Seattle. He is also the author of 'John Sayles: Independence, Integrity and the Borders of Identity' (co-written with Mark Jancovich, in Yvonne Tasker [ed.] *Fifty Contemporary Film Makers [Routledge, 2001]*); is a co-editor of *Defining Cult Movies: The Cultural Politics of Oppositional Taste* (MUP, forthcoming); and a member of the editorial advisory board of *Scope: An Online Journal of Film Studies*. His future research explores the impact of new media on American urban culture.

Anna McCarthy teaches in the department of Cinema Studies in the Tisch School of the Arts, New York University. She is the author of *Ambient Television: Visual Culture and Public Space* (Duke University Press, 2001).

Alan McKee was the cultural theorist on the Australian version of *Big Brother*, and has been cited with approval by Bert Newton. Apart from that, he teaches Media and Cultural Studies at the University of Queensland, is the author of *Australian Television: A Genealogy of Great Moments*, and has just submitted his seventh idea for a Doctor Who novel to the BBC. (The previous six have all been rejected).

John McMurria is a PhD candidate in the Department of Cinema Studies at New York University. His research investigates global dynamics in multi-channel television culture. He is co-author, with Toby Miller, Nitin Govil and Richard Maxwell of *Global Hollywood* (BFI, 2001).

Nancy San Martín is a doctoral candidate in History of Consciousness at the University of California, Santa Cruz, where she is completing her dissertation, *Queer TV: Framing Sexualities on US Network Television*.

Máire Messenger-Davies is a senior lecturer and Deputy Head of School in the School of Journalism, Media and Cultural Studies, Cardiff University. A former journalist, she has a BA from Trinity College Dublin and a PhD in psychology from the University of East London, where she studied audiences' cognitive responses to television. She is a former associate professor at Boston University College of Communication, and was an Annenberg Research Fellow at the University of Pennsylvania in 1993. Her most recent book is *Dear BBC: Children, Television-Storytelling and the Public Sphere*, published by Cambridge University Press, 2001. With Dr Roberta Pearson, she is writing a book for the University of California Press on *Star Trek* and Television Studies.

Lisa Parks is Assistant Professor of Film Studies and an Affiliate of Women's Studies at the University of California at Santa Barbara. Parks is the author of *Cultures in Orbit: Satellites and Televisual* (Duke University Press, forthcoming) and co-editor of *Planet TV: A Global Television Studies Reader* (NYU Press, 2002) and *Red Noise: Buffy the Vampire Slayer and Television Studies* (Duke University Press, forthcoming). She has also published articles in the journals *Screen, Television and New Media, Convergence, Ecumene* and *Social Identities*.

Roberta E. Pearson is a reader in the School of Journalism, Media and Cultural Studies, Cardiff University. She is the author, co-author and editor of numerous books and articles among which the most recent are *American Cultural Studies: A Reader* (Oxford University Press) and *The Critical Dictionary of Film and Television Theory* (Routledge). She and Máire Messenger-Davies are writing a book called *Small Screen, Big Universe: Star Trek and Television Studies* (University of California Press, forthcoming).

Paul Rixon is Principal Lecturer in Media Studies at Staffordshire University. His current research interests include the new media, the rise of the information city and the changing role of American programmes on British screens.

Andrew Willis is a lecturer in Media and Performance at the University of Salford. He is the co-author of *Media Studies: Texts, Institutions and Audiences* (Blackwell) with Lisa Taylor, and is currently editing three books: *Film Stars: Hollywood and Beyond* (MUP), *Defining Cult Movies: The Cultural Politics of Oppositional Taste* (MUP, with Mark Jancovich, Antonio Lazaro and Julian Stringer), and *Spanish Popular Film* (MUP, with Antonio Lazaro). He is also completing a manuscript entitled: *Violent Exchanges: Genre, Nation and Cultural Traffic* (MUP). He has published widely on martial arts movies and Spanish horror films.

I

Introduction

Mark Jancovich and James Lyons

In the mid-1990s, in a bar in Staffordshire, England, Peter Krämer made a heretical claim: American fictional television is now better than the movies! He therefore challenged anyone to name a detective film of the past fifteen years that was as good as an average episode of *NYPD Blue* or *Homicide: Life on the Streets*; a horror film that was as good as an average episode of *The X Files* or *Buffy the Vampire Slayer*; or a romantic comedy that was as good as any one of a score of television sitcoms. Many shows were now so compelling, he claimed, that 'a life is something you get when there is nothing on television'.

For Krämer, this situation could be linked to the demise of the 'classical' Hollywood studio system, and the emergence of a flexible mode of Hollywood film production (see Krämer, 1996, 1998, 2001; see also Neale and Smith, 1998). He suggested that while films are now usually made as one-off events, the regularised production of programming on television generated a wealth of rich, intertextual references not unlike the films of 'classical' Hollywood, and made the viewing of these shows essential and compulsive. For example, each minor event on *Buffy the Vampire Slayer* is contextualised with hours of prior narrative or 'backstory' that invests each moment, and the characters' responses within it, with a weight of nuance and significance.

Krämer is not alone in this celebration of contemporary television. Indeed, over the past twenty years television programmes, and the academic analysis of them, have undergone a discernible transformation. David Marc, for example, refers to the 'literate peak' of the sitcom genre, which he identifies with a series of shows from the 1970s such as *All in the Family* and *M*A*S*H*. While he concedes that these shows 'did not bring about the sitcom millennium' (Marc, 1989, p. 200), their influence has nevertheless been crucial, and none more so than *The Mary Tyler Moore Show*. *The Mary Tyler Moore Show* launched the production company MTM, which not only produced some of the most revered shows in Television Studies, shows such as *Lou Grant*, *St Elsewhere* and *Hill Street Blues*, but also created the template for many later shows (see Feuer, Kerr and Vahimagi, 1984). For example, MTM established the career of Steven Bochco, who would later produce *NYPD Blue* – itself a template for numerous other shows. Furthermore, genre redefining sitcoms such as *Taxi* and *Cheers* had 'production teams [that] were rife with MTM veterans' (Marc, 1989, p. 201).

Another key moment was the launch of David Lynch's *Twin Peaks*, a show that promised to 'change TV' (advert republished in Collins, 1992) and usher in the era of post-modern television (ibid.). In retrospect, *Twin Peaks* could be said to have transformed television, but not quite in the ways that were initially predicted. On the one hand, it created a transatlantic cycle of programmes about idiosyncratic communities that continues today and ranges from the sublime (*Northern Exposure, Picket Fences, Eerie, Indiana*) to the ridiculous (*Ballykissangel*). Perhaps more significantly, the show was instrumental in provoking television producers to rethink their relationship to fans and cult audiences. Rather than being simply oddities and nuisances, producers came to recognise that fans could be vital to the development of shows. Not only could fans generate a loyal audience base that might help a show avoid cancellation in its vulnerable early days, but they could also act as a source of additional revenue through merchandising. Indeed, commentators have noted the impact of *Twin Peaks* on subsequent shows such as *The X Files* (Lavery, Hague and Cartwright, 1996), and it is clear that the range of programmes directed at cult audiences has proliferated.

While television has traditionally been discussed in terms of habitual viewing and televisual 'flow' (Williams, 1974), the trends outlined above suggest that contemporary television has witnessed the emergence of 'must see TV', shows that are not simply part of a habitual flow of television programming but, either through design or audience response, have become 'essential viewing'. These programmes have also been referred to as 'date' or 'appointment' television, and they are distinguished by the compulsive viewing practices of dedicated audiences who organise their schedules around these shows.

As many readers will recognise, 'must see TV' was a phrase originally used by the American NBC network to promote its schedule and network brand, and this is important for a number of reasons. This book initially intended to incorporate the phrase in its title: the phrase 'must see TV' seemed to encapsulate particular trends in contemporary television. However, the title was later dropped to avoid any confusion between NBC's specific commercial use of the phrase and the book's own aims. Yet it is worth noting that many contributors still felt the need to negotiate their own position in relation to this phrase, and thus to wrest the meaning of 'must see TV' away from the circumscribed identity provided for it by NBC. It is also significant that popular opposition to the network has taken issue with the phrase, rebranding the network 'must flea TV'.

While the critical accounts of television outlined thus far have a certain appeal, this book is designed to question many of the assumptions that underpin them. Marc's analysis offers little in the way of explanation beyond a vaguely auteurist appraisal of creative individuals and their influences, while Feuer, Kerr and Vahimagi differ only in providing space for a more substantial institutional analysis. Nor is Peter Krämer's account fully satisfying. Indeed, we might suggest that, during the emergence of 'must see' television, the networks that produced these shows were going through a crisis in audience demographics not dissimilar to that which resulted in the production strategies of 'post-classical' Hollywood film-making. In other words, these shows emerged at the very moment when network audiences were declining. In this sense, these shows might be understood as akin to the blockbuster 'event' movies to which Hollywood turned in the post-war period (Schatz, 1993) rather than the regularised product that the studio system produced in the 1930s and 40s.

As a result, it is possible to argue for an alternative history of 'must see' television and one that is necessarily much less celebratory. As network audiences declined in the face of competition from the proliferation of cable and satellite channels in the 1980s, the networks became less concerned with attracting mass audiences and increasingly concerned with retaining the most *valuable* audiences: affluent viewers that advertisers were prepared to pay the highest rates to address. In other words, the compulsiveness of 'must see' television is designed to appeal to affluent, highly educated consumers who value the literary qualities of these programmes, and they are used by the networks to hook this valuable cohort of viewers into their schedules.

The other transition discernible here is the shift from networks as facilitators of a national public sphere to a situation in which these organisations are increasingly pre-occupied with garnering international niche audiences. Interestingly, this transition has also been instrumental in television's acquisition of greater cultural legitimacy. As Nicholas Garnham points out, the decline in the audience for a popular medium means that a taste for it becomes increasingly rare. The result is that the medium is then open to appropriation and legitimation by the middle classes (Garnham, 1990). Cinema's conversion from debased, popular entertainment to respected art form exemplifies this process, as does the establishment of academic Film Studies in the 1960s and 70s in the aftermath of the dramatic decline in the cinema audience. Similarly, while there is a long-standing tradition of work on the economics and politics of television, studies in television aesthetics emerged largely in the 1980s and 90s, the period in which terrestrial television was threatened by cable and satellite. In Britain, for example, the arrival of cable and satellite not only prompted a fear of 'wall-to-wall *Dallas*' (Webster, 1988; Morley and Robins, 1995) but also a defence of 'quality' television on the part of many critics for whom the notion would have been an oxymoron only twenty years earlier (for work on the quality television debate, see Brunsdon 1997; Mulgan, 1990).

Furthermore, while many 'must see' shows have been praised for their quality, they have also been criticised for displaying an overwhelming preoccupation with the white, affluent, urban middle classes. However, these are two sides of the same coin, since it is the celebrated formal features of such shows, rather than any troublesome content, that work to exclude sections of the viewing public. While the lack of interest in the textual analysis of television shows is rightly criticised in Alan McKee's contribution to this collection, critics need to remain mindful of the terms under which they turn to the analysis of lauded 'must see' shows – if only to recognise the cultural values and taste dispositions often inherent in such notions of 'quality' (Bourdieu, 1984).

The response to such shows should not be to reject them as narrow 'bourgeois' entertainment, but to be attentive to the various processes that work to produce them. As a result, the essays in this volume do not create a unitary viewpoint on the phenomenon of 'must see' television: on the contrary, the collection is designed to approach the topic from a range of perspectives. Some essays take a more unfavourable view of developments in contemporary television than others, but all generate intriguing analyses of

different aspects of the phenomenon. There is work here on the economics of the producing institutions, the scheduling strategies of networks and channels, the analysis of
formats and individual shows, and studies of audience activities. In the process, most –
if not all – of the essays also raise issues about the history of television.

For example, Jennifer Holt's essay examines the economic deregulation of television
in the 1980s and 90s, and explores how 'the current industrial economy of tightly diversified, vertically integrated entertainment conglomerates impact on programming
decisions'. She considers the effect of the liberalisation of regulations limiting the ownership of broadcasting companies in the 1980s, a move that allowed networks to be
absorbed into entertainment conglomerates. Holt notes that this coincided with a massive proliferation of cable channels requiring programming content. These new channels
transformed the meaning and value of media archives, but the networks were effectively
barred from exploiting this situation by the Financial Interest and Syndication rules that
prevented them from owning prime-time programming. In other words, 'Fin Syn' rules
limited the networks' capacity to reap profits from syndication and made them dependent on Hollywood studios for programming. The removal of these rules has significantly
changed the position of the networks, and has also had a profound impact upon the
nature of their programming. However, as Holt points out, it is still unclear whether 'the
networks [will] ever become the equivalent of the movie studios . . . the engines driving
an entire industry' or 'mere satellites, offshoots in a larger structure organised around
feature films and cable channels'.

If Holt examines the conditions that work to determine the production of programming, Nancy San Martín considers the ways in which shows are put together through
scheduling. 'Must see' shows might be unmissable events that stand out from the 'flow',
but they also function as 'anchors' that bring people to the network and extend the duration of their viewing loyalty. The key exemplar of this practice has been NBC's
Thursday-night scheduling. Martín therefore examines the use of *Friends* and *ER* as the
two great anchors of the network's Thursday-night schedule: rather than seeing them as
individual shows, she examines how they function within the evening's programming,
encouraging audiences to start the night with the former and stay with the channel
through a series of other shows in anticipation of the latter. The move from light comedy to realist drama is also read as 'a significant syntagmatic structure' that 'depends
upon a substantive move from the comedies' structuring homoerotic fantasies and playful sexual innuendo towards *ER*'s rigidly heteronormative, rightist, conservative
discourses of "family values" '.

While Martín's account describes NBC's scheduling of such shows, the American
network audience is only one of the markets for 'must see' programming. Paul Rixon's
essay therefore explores the use of American television shows by British broadcasters.
As we have seen, these shows are made increasingly with an emphasis upon international
rather than national audiences, but their meanings also change as they move to different channels with different schedules. Rixon gives an overview of the history of American
shows on British television. He points out that accounts of British broadcasting fail not
only to acknowledge the popularity of American shows with British audiences, but also

their influence in stimulating important trends in British television production. More-over, Rixon considers the crucial role of 'quality' American shows such as *Hill Street Blues*, *Cheers*, *NYPD Blue*, *Homicide*, *Friends* and most recently *Ally McBeal* and *The Sopranos* in establishing an audience for the British Channel 4 network in the 1990s. Although Channel 4 faced recent pressure from regulators to concentrate on home-produced shows, it has also launched a prestigious new cable channel, E4, which is sold almost entirely on its access to 'hot' American shows such as *Friends* and *Ally McBeal*.

If Rixon reminds us that American shows operate in complex ways as key elements of the programming schedules of broadcasters in other national contexts, John McMurria points out that supposedly 'American' shows are often actually transnational productions that bring together finance, personnel and locations from across the globe. McMurria examines recent developments in the production of 'long-format special-event' pro-grammes, such as *Scarlett* and *The Mists of Avalon*. He also considers the relationship of such shows to the increasingly crucial issue of network branding:

> Just as the television network moves from a space of transmission for collecting a national mass-audience to one focused on targeting more narrowly defined special interest groups, the long-format programming that drives network branding campaigns is ever-dependent on global audience reach.

In other words, McMurria demonstrates that 'US multi-channel television culture is intertwined in these post-national systems of global media production.'

McMurria's essay examines the ways in which the long-format special-event pro-gramming is the product of complex transnational broadcasting systems. Anna McCarthy's essay, however, looks at another aspect of 'event' television: special episodes in long-running series. In this particular case, McCarthy concentrates on the 'coming out' episode of *Ellen* in order to investigate the problematic relationship of visibility poli-tics and the serial form. Most accounts of the *Ellen* episode see it as either a brave move that 'opened up' possibilities for the representation of queer identities on mainstream television, or a failure that did queer politics no favours or was quickly silenced by pol-itical reaction. In contrast, McCarthy examines the way the event was placed within narratives of liberalisation and the ways in which the show itself explored these narra-tives. In the process, the essay considers the opportunities for the figuring of queer identities within the serial format of the sitcom.

Pearson and Messenger-Davies' essay also examines a serial format but it does so through a comparison with the blockbuster film. The comparison is focused through the use of the *Star Trek: The Next Generation* franchise in which the authors are able to exam-ine a range of formal differences between the television show and the *Star Trek* motion pictures. For example, they explore the difference in television and film's approach to notions of spectacle, action, narrative and character and they address the institutional and formal features that produce these differences. In this way, they detail many of the points that we discussed in relation to Krämer at the beginning of this introduction. The essay also provides a close and detailed reading of a classic of 'must see' television, a show that was not only a response to the fan culture organised around the original series, but has helped to launch another three series: *Star Trek: Deep Space 9*, *Star Trek: Voyager* and the forthcoming *Star Trek: Enterprise*.

It is this relationship between producers and fans that concerns Andrew Willis in his essay on *Martial Law*. Although it never commanded the audiences figures of *ER* or *Friends*, *Martial Law* had a solid fan following and was clearly produced with that audience in mind. As we have seen, one of the key problems for television producers is that the real profits are to be made from syndication and that to syndicate a show, it must run for at least two complete series. However, a huge number of shows are cancelled within their first season and, for this reason, many producers have turned to pre-existing cult materials. Shows developed in relation to pre-established fan cultures can use these audiences to guard against early cancellation and so establish a base from which to build a larger audience. As Willis demonstrates, *Martial Law* was developed after Jackie Chan was finally able to break through into the mainstream motion picture industry and, in its early stages, it was clearly designed to appeal to the established fan cultures surrounding Hong Kong martial arts stars such as Jackie Chan and its own lead, Sammo Hung. In this way, its comparison with early stages of martial arts television demonstrates how attitudes to fan audiences have changed within the industry, but it also reveals a tension within such projects. While *Martial Law* initially courted martial arts fans in order to establish an audience, the producers kept changing the identity of the show in an attempt to appeal to a broader, more mainstream, viewing public – a move that ended up failing to convince the targeted audience, alienating the existing fans and resulting in the cancellation of the series. As Willis shows, while fans may be valued as a way of launching a series, they are not always valued thereafter.

Fans of a series can even be refigured as a problem and, as Lisa Parks notes, in the aftermath of the murders at Columbine High School, *Buffy the Vampire Slayer* became the focus of concerns about violence on television. While the show was already 'must see' television for many of its fans, Lisa Parks reverses the logic of the debate over violence in *Buffy* to claim that the violence of this show is 'exactly the kind of TV violence that teens and parents need to see'. In other words, she examines the working of violence in the show to demonstrate the ways in which it explores and comments on violence within American culture, particularly within the lives of American teenagers. For example, *Buffy*'s teenage heroes spend most of their time combating authoritarian forms of violence within teenage culture, families and the institutions of local and national government, but the series has also examined the gendered and racial dynamics of violence. As Parks puts it:

> If Columbine has taught us anything, it's that disaffected white suburban kids are ticking time-bombs in the USA despite attempts over the past decade by political leaders, moral conservatives and news media to label African-American men as such.

Indeed, as she demonstrates, one of the episodes barred from broadcast on the show's WB Network in the aftermath of Columbine was concerned with the very pressures that lead teenagers to perform such violent acts.

Furthermore, while WB barred episodes of the show from broadcast, they nevertheless soon became available via the internet, a technology that has rapidly acquired major significance in the ways in which fans communicate with one another and organise themselves. As a result, like Lisa Parks' essay, Ian Gordon also provides a reading of a 'must see' show, *Lois & Clark* (a.k.a. *The New Adventures of Superman*), in which he not only explores the ways in which this product was developed out of the pre-existing property of *Superman*, but also the different receptions of the show by fans from around the world. In the process, he considers the specific uses of nostalgia to generate an audience for the show but, like Willis, he also details how many fans' investments in the show were frustrated in its search for a broader audience.

Sara Gwenllian Jones also considers the significance of the internet and issues of intellectual property in her account of the relationship between fans and the industry. However, rather than reproduce an uncritical celebration of fans as resistant and creative 'textual poachers' (Jenkins, 1992), Jones argues that distinctions 'between the so-called "general audience" and so-called "fandom" have become increasingly blurred as cult series become franchises' and industries are in no way averse to

> a significant following of fans so devoted that they will not only watch every episode but also tape and archive it *and* buy official video releases as well, who will purchase a range of spinoff products, and who will participate in loyal fan cultures that promote and 'support' the series in a variety of ways.

It is important to recognise that in rejecting the romanticisation of the fan in Cultural Studies, there is always the risk of simply inverting the problem, and presenting the fan as consumer dupe. To avoid such unfortunate reversals, one needs not only to examine the complex and situated encounters between fans and media industries but also the encounters between different fans. Fans or fan practices are not all the same and fandom is rife with internal struggle (Jancovich, 2000).

Finally, Alan McKee's essay provides a timely reminder that while recent changes in audience demographics and industry strategies might have produced 'must see' television, it would be wrong to see a clear distinction between a period in which television was organised around 'flow' and one in which it was organised around 'events'. As we saw in relation to Martín, the purpose of events is still to attract people to a station's schedule, and event shows are therefore elements within a 'syntagmatic structure'. However, as McKee demonstrates, the practice of using event shows to attract viewers is not unique to the 1980s and after. On the contrary, television has always produced event programming and McKee examines the ways in which several key shows from the period before the emergence of 'must see' television have come to be understood as 'classics'. Furthermore, he does so in order to examine the ways in which such 'must see' programming has been used to construct a 'public archive' of TV memories, and in ways that make important contributions to a sense of history and nationhood.

However, while this collection raises questions about the history and historicisation of television, its main focus is nevertheless upon transformations in contemporary television culture. If we have Peter Krämer's selfless devotion to American fictional programming to thank for our initial inspiration, then it is our contributors who demonstrate why it is essential that we continue to take a view on contemporary television and the processes that produce it.

Bibliography

Bourdieu, Pierre, *Distinction: A Social Critique of the Judgement of Taste* (London: Routledge, 1984).

Brunsdon, Charlotte, *Screen Tastes: Soap Operas to Satellite Dishes* (London: Routledge, 1997).

Collins, Jim, 'Postmodernism and Television', in Robert C. Allen (ed.), *Channels of Discourse Reassembled* (London: Routledge, 1992), pp. 327–53.

Feuer, Jane, Kerr, Paul and Vahimagi, Tise, *MtM: 'Quality Television'* (London: BFI, 1984).

Garnham, Nicholas, *Capitalism and Communication: Global Culture and the Economics of Information* (London: Sage, 1990).

Jancovich, Mark, 'A Real Shocker: Authenticity, Genre and the Struggle for Cultural Distinctions', *Continuum*, vol. 14, no. 1 (April 2000), pp. 23–35.

Jenkins, Henry, *Textual Poachers: Television, Fans and Participatory Culture* (New York: Routledge, 1992).

Krämer, Peter, 'The Lure of the Big Picture: Film, Television and Hollywood', in John Hill and Martin McLoone (eds), *Big Picture, Small Screen: The Relations between Film and Television* (Luton: John Libbey, 1996), pp. 9–46.

Krämer, Peter, 'Post-classical Hollywood', in John Hill and Pamela Church Gibson (eds), *The Oxford Guide to Film Studies* (Oxford: Oxford University Press, 1998), pp. 289–309.

Krämer, Peter, ' "It's aimed at kids – the kid in everybody": George Lucas, *Star Wars* and Children's Entertainment', in *Scope: An Online Journal of Film Studies* (December 2001), <www.nottingham.ac.uk/film/journal>.

Lavery, David, Hague, Angela and Cartwright, Marla (eds), *Deny All Knowledge: Reading The X Files* (London: Faber, 1996).

Marc, David, *Comic Vision: Television Comedy and American Culture* (Boston: Unwin Hyman, 1989).

Morley, David and Robins, Kevin, *Spaces of Identity: Global Media, Electronic Landscapes and Cultural Boundaries* (London: Routledge, 1995).

Mulgan, Geoff (ed.), *The Question of Quality* (London: BFI, 1990).

Neale, Steve and Smith, Murray (eds), *Contemporary Hollywood Cinema* (London: Routledge, 1998).

Schatz, Thomas, 'The New Hollywood', in Jim Collins, Hilary Radner and Ava Preacher Collins (eds), *Film Theory Goes to the Movies* (London: Routledge, 1993), pp. 8–36.

Webster, Duncan, *Looka Yonder! The Imaginary America of Populist Culture* (London: Comedia, 1988).

Williams, Raymond, *Television: Technology and Cultural Form* (London: Fontana, 1974).

Part One

Industries, Networks and Programming

2

Vertical Vision: Deregulation, Industrial Economy and Prime-time Design

Jennifer Holt

Introduction: what's on TV... and why?

With increasing mergers, acquisitions and takeovers, the American broadcast industry has become a complicated and tangled web of 'webs'. Since the mid-1980s, the playing field has been dramatically reconstructed – twice. Rivals in all facets of the business now find themselves under one vertically integrated corporate umbrella or another, rendered both competitors and collective assets by virtue of their parent companies' vast size. In light of this transformation, Peter Bart of *Variety* has noted that to survive in the present media marketplace, a major player must 'mobilize a vast array of global brands to command both content and distribution. Indeed, such an enterprise must be more than a company – it must be a virtual nation-state' (Bart, 1996, p. 10).

The companies that control the airwaves today are precisely that: a high-powered cabal of entertainment empires, dominating film, television, publishing, cable systems, home video, music, merchandising and theme parks – all at the same time. Consequently, to maintain their sovereignty, the CEOs of these conglomerates are constantly redefining the art of vertical integration in a new and paradoxical market – one that is simultaneously driven by segmentation and unified vision, broad range and specific demographics, localism and global scope, expansion and consolidation. Just a glimpse at their broadcast properties alone shows the principal TV players in the year 2000 (AOL Time Warner, Disney, Viacom and News Corp.) owning five of the six broadcast networks, eighty affiliates in major US cities, extensive distribution systems and the majority of programming being produced for air on these channels (see Compaine and Gomery, 2000).

The catalyst for this present industrial design has been the striking turn in the political philosophy behind broadcast regulation over the last twenty years. A frantic cycle of crisis and expansion that began in the 1980s coupled with a presidential administration devoted to deregulating the marketplace set the industry on its course. By the mid-1990s, with a new structural groundwork in place, the broadcast networks entered another phase of frenzied merger and acquisitions activity characterised by an unprecedented commitment to vertical integration and 'synergy'. In 1995 alone, Disney announced a $19 billion deal to buy ABC, Westinghouse acquired CBS in a $5.4 billion merger and two new networks were born, conceived by studio-based conglomerates in the throes of deregulation (Viacom's UPN and AOL Time Warner's WB).

This new state of affairs also requires a new manual for conducting business; as ownership has changed, so have the rules of the game and in turn, so have programming options. Boundaries between production, distribution and exhibition have collapsed to the point that the old edicts no longer apply. As a result, the industry is adapting to a new vision of television built largely on faith in a modern version of synergy that requires the vast media resources of entertainment conglomerates to feed off themselves, rendering industrial organisation a prominent factor in determining what's on TV. This concept of 'must see' TV in the literal sense raises powerful questions regarding the corporate structure of the American television industry and its effect on the television schedule. Primarily, how does the current industrial economy of tightly diversified, vertically integrated entertainment conglomerates impact programming decisions? Furthermore, how has regulation dictated the course of the relationships between networks, independent producers, Hollywood studios and their parent companies? Ultimately, I will argue that the concept of 'must see' can also be interpreted as a mandate of industrial economy and government regulation as opposed to solely a marketing design or textual paradigm.

'Television is just another appliance. It's a toaster with pictures.' Mark Fowler, FCC Chairman 1981–6

With President Reagan's appointment of Mark Fowler as chairman of the Federal Communications Commission (FCC) in 1981, the deregulatory swing that began during the late 1970s under such chairmen as Charles Ferris was institutionalised. Reagan and Fowler shared the common vision of an unfettered marketplace. Suddenly 'there was a sense that you could do whatever the hell you wanted' in the broadcast industry, according to then CBS News president, William Leonard (Hertsgaard, 1988, p. 180). It was during this period that the agency began to be described as the industry lap dog instead of the watchdog it was intended to be. Fowler became known as the darling of the broadcast industry with his mantra of 'Let the market prevail!' and he aggressively pursued a pro-network agenda throughout his term of office.

The eradication of structural and content regulations proceeded rapidly with Reagan's appointment of chairman Fowler, and the move towards a free broadcast market was underway. With it, came the FCC's emphasis on competition and profit as opposed to scheduling mandates or programming requirements. By the end of Fowler's first four years as chairman, the FCC had reviewed, changed or deleted 89 per cent of the agency's approximately 900 mass media rules (*Broadcasting*, 18 February 1985, p. 1).

Most notable about Fowler's tenure was the way that he challenged the basic and foundational assumptions of the regulatory agency he chaired: whether or not the FCC should police the airwaves and industry conduct in the name of the 'public interest'. Commissioner Dennis Patrick summed it up best when he said that the FCC's threshold question had become whether it should regulate at all, not what sort of regulation might be appropriate (ibid.). With this shift, Fowler changed the terms of the entire regulatory debate, equated the public interest with the profit interest and to some extent, even redefined the mandate of the FCC. Deregulation was officially sanctioned and as a result, the concept of the broadcaster as public trustee swiftly deteriorated and the airwaves became another commodity on the open market.

While they had historically been safeguarded by their relationship with the FCC, the networks were now being exposed to the vagaries of the changing marketplace. With the role of the commission changing, broadcasters could no longer rely on the FCC for a certain measure of security and protection and, as a result, were left quite vulnerable in an increasingly unstable industry. The aggressive competition signalled by a changing marketplace substantially reduced the networks' profits and threatened their livelihood. What ensued was a complicated battle over the business of home entertainment in the 1980s that fundamentally reshaped the structural foundation of the broadcast industry.

'It really all comes down to government regulations'. John Malone, President and CEO, TCI

The FCC under Fowler moved to dismantle numerous fundamental regulations in broadcasting. However, the complications of new technology, cable, a rapidly evolving corporate geography and the industry's renewed global emphasis had made maintaining a free, unregulated *and* profitable market very tricky. One of the FCC's most contentious campaigns was waged to raise the limits on ownership of broadcast properties from seven to twelve stations, which took effect in 1985. This was allowed with the provision that the twelve stations together reached no more than 25 per cent of the nation's homes. The newly established '12-12-12' law additionally contributed to the substantial increase in advertising ratings and station prices, as these perceived values skyrocketed along with demand.

The repeal of the 'anti-trafficking' provision was another move by the FCC that alerted potential players to sit up and take notice. Owners had been required to retain stations for three years before selling them, but the reversal of this law in 1982 eliminated that requirement altogether. This ruling subsequently encouraged the practice of 'flipping' stations for a profit and further inflated station values. After the FCC also decreased the processing time for broadcast licences and increased ownership limits, the industry was primed for corporate raiders. Station prices kept creeping higher, even as the broadcast playing field widened. This standard presented an invitation to well-bankrolled speculators and outside investors to buy up station properties to fortify their empire, similar in nature to the corporate takeovers in Hollywood during the late 1960s.

Essentially, the FCC's machinations introduced a crippling measure of instability to an industry that was already extremely vulnerable. By this time, the networks were facing a financial crisis (largely attributed to spiralling costs, poor management and growing competition from cable and home entertainment), stock prices were depressed and ratings were sliding. Thus, the combination of relaxed rules and abandoned regulations provided the crowning impetus for what was termed by the industry trades as 'merger mania' during the mid-1980s, as the FCC basically invited and encouraged more exchange and concentration of ownership.

The result was a brisk increase in station sales, the takeover of all three broadcast networks by new owners and the beginning of a fourth during Reagan's second term. Capital Cities bought ABC for $3.5 billion in 1985 and one month later, Rupert Murdoch purchased Metromedia's stations to launch the Fox Network. Loew's Corporation chairman Laurence Tisch became the controlling shareholder at CBS in 1986 and that same year, General Electric also acquired RCA (the parent company of NBC). Without the increase in station ownership limits and relaxed rules, such properties would have been less attractive, less accessible, and these transactions would have been quite unlikely.

These changes in ownership were just the beginning ... the real transformation would come when the FCC attended to the key piece of regulation that lingered: the Financial Interest and Syndication Laws ('Fin Syn'). Fowler's determination to eliminate these rules caused numerous clashes on Capitol Hill and Fin Syn would prove to be an albatross for the chairman and his commission throughout the 1980s. Ultimately, it was Fin Syn that provided the key to entirely new dimensions of industrial structure, efficiency and synergy in broadcasting.

Fin Syn

If the regulatory climate was the principal force shaping the blueprint of the broadcast industry over the last two decades, then the Financial Interest and Syndication rules served as the chief architect. The FCC instituted these rules in 1970 in order to increase diversity in programming and prevent the three networks from dominating the market through their control of the airwaves. Fin Syn prohibited the networks from having an ownership stake in their prime-time programming and severely restricted their participation in syndication, considerably eroding the network's control of their own industry and making them dependent on the Hollywood studios for product.

In 1970, the three broadcast networks had financial interest or syndication rights to 98 per cent of their programming and independent producers were practically shut out of the market (MacDonald, 1990, p. 186). The network power was such that there was nothing to challenge their control over the industry. Programme suppliers, mainly consisting of the Hollywood studios, were furious over the terms extracted by the networks for airing their products – often a stake in the profits or distribution rights for reruns in other markets. The FCC performed an exhaustive inquiry of the networks' monopolistic behaviour in the late 1960s and in response to the abuses of power that they perceived, the FCC established Fin Syn and the Prime Time Access Rule (PTAR) in tandem.

PTAR prohibited network-affiliated television stations in the top fifty television markets from broadcasting more than three hours of network or 'off-network' (i.e., rerun) programmes during the four prime-time viewing hours. It was intended as a means of promoting the growth of independent stations and was to be implemented in the Autumn 1971 season. The Financial Interest and Syndication rules were enacted with similar goals in mind: to loosen the grip of network power over the industry and also expand the market for independent producers. They were formulated largely as a response to insistent lobbying from the Hollywood studios, who were having serious troubles of their own in the late 1960s and were increasingly reliant on their revenues from television production.

Consent decrees between the Justice Department and the three networks, signed between 1976 and 1980, enforced and further solidified Fin Syn and also strictly limited the hours of 'in-house' prime-time programming the networks could produce. All of these restrictions prohibited the vertical integration of production, sale and distribution of programming, preventing the networks from creating a schedule that privileged their own products. It was further argued that separating the networks from syndication would strengthen independent stations, removing the networks' ability to stock-pile popular rerun material (second-run, off-network series) or funnel hits directly to their owned and operated affiliate stations.

In reality, however, the rules did not significantly tip the scales in favour of the independent sector. Some producers and affiliate stations did receive a boost, as the fortunes of independents such as Tandem, MTM and Lorimar can attest. First-run syndicators (producers of shows such as *Wheel of Fortune, Entertainment Tonight,* etc.) also flourished as syndication revenue spiked from about $520 million in 1980 to over $2 billion in 1994 (Harris, 1995, p. 86). Primarily, though, Fin Syn merely strengthened the position of the major Hollywood studios and solidified a specific political economy in the broadcast industry that was based on a delicate balance of two mighty forces: the studios and the broadcast networks. The net result for Hollywood was a secure position as the largest supplier of television shows as well as what looked to be permanent, guaranteed access to this all-important market.

As for the networks, Fin Syn seriously damaged their collective and competitive position. After all, only pockets as deep as the studios' are capable of enduring deficit financing (whereby the producer receives payment from the network that is far below cost during the programme's first run, gambling on the enormous potential windfall that syndication could bring). With the advent of cable, these rules were becoming even more profound in terms of their restrictions because cable introduced an expanding pool of riches that the networks were barred from earning as the market exploded. The channels that would require product – syndicated product – continued to grow and the networks were forced to watch the spoils go to the Hollywood studios.

Consequently, producers and distributors became instantly deadlocked, waging a lobbying war over Fin Syn's existence and legitimacy. As predicted by insiders, President Reagan ignored the momentum in Washington to repeal the laws and personally got involved. One day after a closed-door meeting with MCA/Universal chief Lew Wasserman – who was also his agent in Hollywood during his days as an actor and a personal friend – Reagan stepped in and overruled Fowler's commission. Suddenly, the hands-off President was in up to his elbows re-regulating the broadcast industry and directly contradicting his own FCC. In the end, Reagan's allegiance to the studios prevailed and he saw to it that the rules were not modified during his administration.

Post Fin Syn

The FCC again considered modifying Fin Syn at the end of Reagan's tenure, largely due to lobbying pressures by the networks and the undeniable changes in the industry that had taken place since the rules were implemented. By the late 1980s there was a fourth network settling into place and various new forms of competition (cable, home video, satellite services, pay-per-view movies, etc.) were steadily eroding the dominance of the broadcast networks. None of these elements represented any significant threat in 1970 when Fin Syn was enacted and the networks' combined share of the television audience was around 90 per cent (as opposed to the low of 57 per cent that would hit in the early 1990s). Furthermore, emerging media conglomerates were reaping the benefits of vertical integration in the cable landscape, but the broadcast networks were precluded from doing the same thing.

Initially, in light of the changing marketplace, Fin Syn was relaxed to allow each network to produce up to three hours of prime time in the 1986–7 season and up to five hours in the 1988–9 season. Gradual repeal finally began in 1991 and the Financial Interest and Syndication rules were officially repealed on 21 September 1995 – two months ahead of schedule. One year later, PTAR was also repealed.

The Telecommunications Act of 1996 also fed into this wave of deregulation by liberalising television station ownership limits. It eliminated the former ownership cap of twelve television stations altogether and increased the nationwide audience reach limitation from 25 per cent to 35 per cent. This change in the restrictions on national television ownership has enabled broadcast groups to considerably increase their television holdings. Since the passing of the 1996 act, networks have been furiously lobbying Congress to raise the number higher still, painting apocalyptic portraits of their demise in the face of cable competition. The speculation is that this cap will be the next restriction to go.

In anticipation of the Telecommunications Act, the industry began a flurry of merger activity: ABC announced it would merge with Disney and Westinghouse made a deal to acquire CBS before the ink was even dry. Further, Time Warner, perhaps the biggest media giant of all at the time, merged with Turner Broadcasting System and acquired Turner's immensely successful cable networks (TBS, TNN, TNT, etc.) as well as his massive film libraries. Meanwhile, Fox bought all of the stations formerly owned by New World, and Gannett TV Group merged with Multimedia.

Indisputably, the most significant outcome of deregulation in the broadcast industry (and specifically the repeal of Fin Syn) is the union of programme suppliers with programme distributors – namely, the Hollywood studios and the television networks. The fact that Fin Syn remained in place throughout the 1980s and early 90s ensured that while the industrial economy was shifting, the real seismic activity was yet to come. Once the rules were repealed, the earthquake would soon follow and the abrogation of Fin Syn would ignite the most important reorganisation of the corporate landscape in the industry's history. This was manifested in mergers, takeovers and new studio-based networks that would continue to ensure guaranteed distribution for Hollywood-produced television programming.

Now, networks are allowed to broadcast as much in-house programming as they like and retain the lucrative syndication rights as well. The percentage of programming produced in-house by the networks has steadily climbed ever since the repeal of Fin Syn. In 1995, the networks owned approximately 40 per cent of their schedules on average. By the start of the 2000 season, however, CBS had an interest in or owned outright

68 per cent of its prime-time schedule, including ten weekly entertainment series and Fox owned 71 per cent of its prime-time lineup (McClellan, 2000, p. 30). NBC aired seven shows produced in-house. In all, the six broadcast networks owned or co-owned more than half of their new shows, and three of them had a stake in more than 75 per cent of the 2000 schedules (Schneider and Adalian, 2000, p. 15).

'How can you go broke buying the Rembrandts of the programming business, when you are a programmer?' Ted Turner, Vice Chairman, AOL Time Warner

Ted Turner was not subject to the limitations of Fin Syn and consequently was well ahead of the pack in the frantic race to vertically integrate. Turner was one of the first New Hollywood moguls to have the vision, resources and drive to unite programme ownership and production with distribution. After entrenched network forces and FCC regulators thwarted his 1985 takeover attempt of CBS, Turner was stinging and anxious to become a major player in the media industry. At the time, Turner's broadcasting system was strapped for product and at the mercy of the major studios that were increasing the licensing fees for old films.

On 6 August 1985 Turner made a deal with Kerkorian to buy MGM/UA for $1.5 billion. For this, Turner received the studio, lot and library of 3,500 MGM films – including 750 pre-1948 Warner Bros. titles, 700 RKO features and numerous shorts, television series and specials (Hilmes, 1990, pp. 194–5). He now owned many of the most treasured titles in American cinema – *Gone with the Wind*, *Casablanca*, *Citizen Kane* and *The Wizard of Oz* to name a few. Yet, almost immediately a debt-ridden Turner was forced to sell all of the studio operations that he purchased in the MGM/UA deal right back to Kerkorian. However, the film library was the one asset that he retained. Turner proceeded to pump these films directly into his ever-expanding pipelines, beginning with WTBS and later funnelling them into TNT after its launch in 1988.

By 1989, the MGM library had become 'the core of both a syndication business *and* a successful new network – together worth a projected $1.6 billion by mid-1989' (Goldberg and Goldberg, 1995, p. 397). He bought Hanna-Barbera's library in late 1991 for $320 million. Turner immediately began showcasing these animated programmes on WTBS, TNT and eventually on his Cartoon Network, the first twenty-four-hour all-animation channel, after its launch in October 1992. Yet another outlet for his massive library was established in April 1994: Turner Classic Movies.

Turner even envisioned the Atlanta Braves and Atlanta Hawks as more programming inventory to plug into his distribution networks, even though he admitted that they were 'the world's worst two sports franchises' when he acquired them in 1976–7 (ibid., p. 194). Still, he could indefinitely broadcast the games on his superstation WTBS or sell the rights to other stations. This was part of Turner's approach to his business. As he told *Forbes* magazine, television is like chicken farming:

> Modern chicken farmers, they grind up the intestines to make dog food. The feathers go into pillows. Even the chicken manure they make into fertilizer. They use every bit of the chicken.

Well, that's what we try to do over here with television products, is use everything to its fullest extent.

Maney, 1995, p. 183

Time Warner announced its merger with Turner Communications just two days after the official repeal of Fin Syn in 1995. Eight months earlier, the conglomerate had launched the WB network. When the two companies finally came together in 1996, the result was a $7.6 billion colossus that encompassed a vast array of entertainment properties from Warner Bros. film and television production, HBO, CNN, TBS, TNT, and the WB Network to Warner Bros. Records, Time Life, Turner's world-class film library, the Atlanta Braves and Atlanta Hawks and Time Warner Cable. While this was less than half of the price of the Disney/ABC merger, it brought a much larger magnitude and range of assets under the same corporate insignia and far greater potential for vertical arrangements. Deregulation made the deal attractive and Turner's prescience and years of stealthy, strategic acquisitions made it irresistible. With AOL's purchase of the company in 2000, the largest internet service provider merged with the largest film and television producer as well as a host of cable systems and programmes that reach 20 per cent of American homes. At present, the marketplace has yet to return a verdict on whether or not such an expansive alliance can function efficiently and profitably.

Back when Turner was buying MGM/UA, Australian mogul Rupert Murdoch (Turner's archrival) was designing his own aggressive blueprint for vertical integration in American media. In 1985, Murdoch's News Corporation bought 20th Century-Fox from Marvin Davis. That same year, Murdoch made a deal to buy six stations from major group owner Metromedia – well-placed, independent, successful properties in Washington, DC, New York City, Chicago, Los Angeles, Houston and Dallas – and formed Fox Television Inc. to do so. His CEO, Barry Diller, had been cultivating the dream of a fourth network since his days at Paramount in the late 1970s and was deeply involved in the entire process. Since then, Murdoch has gone on to become the largest producer of prime-time television, set the standard for the vertically integrated global media giant and is widely regarded as one of the shrewdest strategists in the industry.

The timing for the new Fox network was in perfect synchronicity with the regulatory climate in Washington, DC, in the 1980s. At the onset of the Reagan administration, the Fowler FCC began immediately licensing new broadcast stations in unprecedented numbers and the industry began to change shape. Since most markets already had a full slate of network affiliates, the majority of these newer stations were independent. According to the Association of Independent Television Stations (INTV), the number of unaffiliated stations rose by 150 per cent in the first six years of the Reagan presidency, from 112 in 1980 to 272 in 1986 (Block, 1990, p. 125). Murdoch was able to take advantage of this development and in 1986, there were finally enough independent stations to support a fourth broadcast network.

Murdoch proceeded to combine his Metromedia purchases with product from his studio and launched the Fox Network, the first to rival ABC, CBS and NBC since the demise of DuMont, thirty years earlier. Fox began programming mainly in weekend prime-time hours. With the combination of cable TV technology (which made it poss-ible for UHF stations to find a viable audience), practically unlimited financing and resources available from his global media ventures, a government committed to dereg-ulation and a sympathetic FCC, Murdoch was primed to explore the possibilities of horizontal and vertical integration. Furthermore, the Fox target audience of young males spawned a new age of niche marketing in broadcasting and with it, a new universe of advertising capital and incentive for investors. Remaining below the fifteen hours per week of prime-time programming that defined a full-fledged network, Fox was also free to syndicate their hits and begin to mount a growing challenge to the established net-works in the face of widespread skepticism and doubt. Their surprisingly tremendous success (especially after adding twelve more affiliates in 1994, most from CBS when Fox acquired their rights to NFL football) inspired further expansion and similar strategic alliances. After the prescience of Turner and the trailblazing of Fox, there were two more studio-owned broadcast networks – UPN and WB – on air by 1995.

'I walk out the door each morning as a fully vertically integrated executive'. Robert Iger, President and COO, Walt Disney Co.

The quintessential New Hollywood marriage of product and pipeline was achieved in 1995 when Disney bought ABC for $19 billion. This was the first merger of the post-Fin Syn landscape between a studio and broadcast network (even though it was announced months before the official repeal of the rules) and in 1995, was the second largest cor-porate deal ever made. It occurred in the midst of unprecedented consolidation in the entertainment industry – worth more than $40 billion in 1995, with over $200 million more spent on severance packages to those who lost their jobs in the crunch (Eller and Hofmeister, 1995, p. 1). Disney was paying an exorbitant amount for the network (three times the price that Westinghouse paid for CBS that same year). Still, the press hailed the merger as 'the type of combination other media moguls dream about' and Wall St was lauding the deal as 'the benchmark for the rest of the industry' (Smith, 1999, p. 15). The announcement was impeccably timed, and Disney/ABC rode the crest of the Fin Syn repeal to a smooth FCC approval. At the time, the new conglomerate represented the promise of boundless synergy for a brave new Magic Kingdom.

ABC and Disney had both come a long way since the first time they combined forces in 1954, in order to create *Disneyland*. ABC, bought by Capital Cities in 1985, was the most profitable and highest-rated television network at the time, the majority owner of cable networks ESPN and ESPN2, and a partner in the A&E and Lifetime cable net-works. The company also owned ten TV stations, thirty radio stations and fed more than 200 affiliates on the ABC television network. The Disney studio was an immense global entertainment juggernaut of its own in 1995, a $12 billion dollar powerhouse engineered by Michael Eisner, Frank Wells and Jeffrey Katzenberg during the 1980s. The stealthy merger happened almost before anyone in the business realised what was occurring, unlike the CBS-Westinghouse buy, which was public for weeks before closing. However, the astronomical cost involved incited some skeptics to scoff at the potential upside for synergy in such an overloaded and expensive deal.

Nevertheless, CEO Michael Eisner was repeatedly quoted as being 'totally optimistic that one and one will add up to four in this situation' when explaining the deal to the press. 'There are synergies under every rock we turn over,' he beamed. Suddenly, vertical integration was resurrected from the list of taboo phrases in Hollywood ... it was widely discussed in the press as the strategy for the new millennium and became the buzzword on the lips of all merger-minded moguls. For its part, Disney was not at all shy about discussing the role vertical integration played in the ABC purchase.

> The purpose of the acquisition was to protect the mouse, to ensure that no other institution could block us from getting our shows access on the networks and on cable ... At Disney, we like to control our own destiny, and we concluded that the only way not to be at the mercy of other institutions ('gatekeepers') was to assure our own access.
>
> Mermigas, 1998a, p. 46

In 1999, Disney/ABC consolidated even further, combining Disney's TV production and ABC's prime-time programming division into a single entity known as ABC Entertainment Television Group. Suddenly, studio series production and network scheduling were not only under the same roof, they were merely separated by an adjoining door. The goal of capitalising on a vertically integrated entity in order to guarantee Disney access to ABC's prime-time hours was readily acknowledged and reported. For the first time, the threat of regulation was eliminated and there would be no secret of the preferential treatment that would be a foundation of this studio-network relationship. 'The aim,' ABC executives explained, 'is to streamline and to get more Disney-owned product on ABC's air' (Hofmeister, 1999, p. 5).

However, managing this synergy has not been a magic carpet ride for Disney ... it has been more of a stomach-churning roller-coaster. ABC experienced a dramatic ratings slide in prime-time and news programming after the takeover and languished in third place in the ratings race for years, nearly overtaken by fourth-place Fox for the first time ever. Numerous high-profile management shake-ups and personnel crises also plagued ABC; they were forced to fire 200 employees in 1997 and News Chairman Roone Arledge and Entertainment President Jamie Tarses both left the network. The success of *Who Wants to Be a Millionaire?* in 2000 resurrected the network from the ratings cellar but the long-term prospects for ABC are unsteady at best, presently resting on a very narrow strategy of reality-based programming. As analysts have noted that Disney/ABC's version of synergy is nothing more than cross-promotion, exploiting one idea or property in several channels of distribution rather than creating anything new. The company has yet to create any successful new ideas or visionary programming for their properties.

ABC represented just 8 per cent of Disney's corporate profits in 1997 (Mermigas, 1998a, p. 46), thus its significance has been largely as a distribution network and marketing tool for Disney's other products and subsidiaries. However, its importance to Disney's bottom line is growing, as broadcasting revenues were 24 per cent of Disney's empire at the start of the millennium (1999 Annual Report). Furthermore, as of the beginning of the 2000 season, ABC had an ownership stake in 44 per cent of their prime-time schedule, including six weekly entertainment series (McClellan, 2000, p. 30). The 1996–7 season was the first time Disney would have the opportunity to take advantage of their network assets, in light of year-long lead times for series development. In the three years immediately following, Disney launched only ten shows at ABC, five of which lasted one season (Schlosser, 1999, p. 23). Now that the company has taken steps to remedy the notoriously antagonistic relationship of studio and network executives, perhaps the wonderful world of synergy will be more promising for Disney. For the 2000–1 season, over half of the Disney-owned television productions have been sold directly to ABC (Producer Scorecard, 2000, p. 34).

The merger of Viacom and CBS was also a family reunion of sorts, made possible by the mid-1990s wave of deregulation. Viacom was once merely a small syndication company spawned by CBS in the wake of Fin Syn. However, after a long, steady diet of mergers, acquisitions and an expanding entertainment economy, the minnow returned and swallowed the whale whole with its $35 billion deal for CBS in 1999. It was the biggest entertainment industry conglomerate ever – for four months, until they dropped to second place in January 2000 when AOL Time Warner's $135 billion merger was announced.

The Viacom story is one of deregulation's great ironies. While attempting to harness network control, the FCC actually helped to usher a far more formidable power into the media landscape. Reminiscent of the way in which the government's forced breakup of John D. Rockefeller's Standard Oil led to the creation of two of the world's largest oil companies (Exxon and Mobil), Viacom's path also offers a revealing chart of America's intersecting regulatory cycles and political tides.

In 1970, when Fin Syn declared syndication revenues to be unlawful revenue for the major networks CBS formed Viacom Inc. in order to comply with federal regulations. CBS transferred its syndication operation and its programme library to Viacom by 1971. Now, the company that began life in order to separate a network from its programming library has not only turned the clock back by buying that network, but it had also bought the syndicated production that *all* of the networks were forced to divest after Fin Syn along the way. The pre-1973 television libraries of ABC, NBC and CBS are now under one roof, as part of Viacom's Paramount Domestic Television, offering CBS a mighty programming weapon. This gold mine includes 55,000 hours of programming and 180 different series such as CBS's *I Love Lucy* and *Perry Mason*, NBC's *Bonanza* and *Get Smart* and ABC's *The Fugitive* and *Mod Squad* (Spring, 1999, p. 3). In the end, the FCC helped to restore what it dismantled, effectively putting the pieces of Viacom and CBS back together with relaxed ownership rules and the repeal of Fin Syn.

The marriage of Viacom and CBS has also united two different corporate philosophies – that of Sumner Redstone, Chairman and CEO of Viacom whose mantra has always been 'content is king', and the 'distribution is king' approach as embraced by CBS. One look at the constitution of the New Hollywood royalty, however, and it is clear that entertainment conglomerates in the post-Fin Syn era no longer have to choose between the two. They can have it all in their vertically integrated media empires. Viacom-CBS owns a multitude of broadcast content (King World Productions,

Paramount Pictures, Paramount TV, CBS Prods., Spelling Entertainment), a tremendous distribution enterprise (CBS network and its chain of 212 TV affiliates, thirty-five TV stations, Infinity Broadcasting's 163 radio stations and UPN), as well as some of the top cable brands, such as MTV, VH1, BET, Nickelodeon, Country Music Television, Showtime and the Movie Channel. Additionally, the company's assets include Blockbuster Entertainment, billboards that sprawl across the nation, sizeable theatre chains and a commanding presence in the internet economy.

Under existing rules, Viacom will still have to sell several television stations as well as the UPN network to satisfy government regulations. The FCC still restricts any company from reaching more than 35 per cent of the nation's TV audience and with this merger, Viacom reaches 41 per cent. When asked how Viacom-CBS would remain within the 35 per cent cap when their holdings reveal a 41 per cent audience reach, CBS President Mel Karmazin responded, 'We believe that the 35 per cent cap is a very antiquated rule. We believe that the rule will go away' (Jessell and McClellan, 1999, p. 30). Karmazin's public confidence is instructive in the way that it belies a shifting balance of power in the regulatory arena. The industry's expanding sense of entitlement swells with each mega-merger, their security enshrined by the government's staunch reluctance to curtail the consolidation of the entertainment industry. As Patricia Aufderhide has noted, these companies 'no longer feel like they need to kiss Congress goodnight' (Aufderhide, 1997, p. 162).

True to Karmazin's prediction, the 35 per cent cap is actually quite likely to 'go away' under the stewardship of Bush administration FCC chief, Michael Powell. Powell is firmly committed to deregulation and perhaps the new bearer of the Fowler flame. He has already made his disdain for the ownership cap well known during his first month on the job, saying 'I am quite skeptical that anyone has any demonstrable case that such caps actually inure to the benefit of consumers in the form of greater and more diverse product' (Labaton, 2001, p. 1). The FCC approval of Fox's purchase of rival Chris-Craft Industries in 2001, which put Fox at a 40 per cent reach, eliminated any remaining doubts about the fate of present ownership caps.

Currently, both the FCC and the Department of Justice review all telecommunications mergers. (The Federal Trade Commission also has authority to review such mergers but rarely does, deferring instead to the Justice Department.) While each administration brings different appointees to those offices, partisan politics are no longer a reliable predictor of procedure in the broadcast arena. After all, it was the Department of Justice under Republican President Richard Nixon that mandated the split of CBS and Viacom, while President Clinton's activist Department of Justice was the one that approved the reunion merger. However, since the days of the Reagan administration, the Department of Justice has often regarded consolidation in the media as benign and even beneficial to surviving in the competitive global marketplace.

The FCC rules continue to bend capriciously in order to accommodate the changing parameters of the conglomerate structures, largely because the foundational principles of regulation are becoming increasingly irrelevant. The public interest standard, for example, is based on the notion of the broadcast spectrum's scarcity, but new technologies and global markets have rendered this model inadequate. The idea of the public interest itself has also been consistently redefined and does not have a definition that satisfies current conditions. Further, the FCC emphasis on localism and the community-oriented nature of broadcasting has also become quite ironic and hypocritical, since the commission is a centralised, federal agency regulating a profit-driven, global industry designed to appeal to the widest possible audience. In reality, the local market and the public interest have become nothing more than theoretical constructs, or figments of the regulatory imagination, left behind in all but the language of broadcast regulation.

'Selling movies to the networks is just not as much fun as it used to be.' John Dempsey, *Variety*, 2000

In the end, is it possible to discern how corporate holdings translate into an evening of entertainment and opportunity? Is a conglomerate built on the principle of synergy necessarily able to exploit that potential fully? Structural deregulation and consolidation have certainly helped to enhance those opportunities for the major players, especially with respect to their broadcast properties. Presently, Viacom and its subsidiaries have twenty-eight shows on the air in 2000–1 season, spread over all networks, with more than half (fifteen of them) broadcast on CBS. 20th Century-Fox has eighteen shows on the autumn schedules, ten of which air on its own network. Warner Bros. has sold eighteen shows, with seven of them airing on WB and Disney has produced nine programmes, five of which are on ABC.

In addition to servicing their own networks, the big four (AOL Time Warner, Fox, Viacom-CBS and Disney) are still making significant deals with their competitors for programming. For example, currently Warner Bros. (or a subsidiary) is producing *ER*, *Friends* and *The West Wing* for NBC rather than funnelling these programmes directly to their own WB Network. Fox Television produces two of ABC's most popular programmes, *Dharma & Greg* and *The Practice*, CBS's *Judging Amy*, as well as one of WB's flagship hits: *Buffy the Vampire Slayer*. (However, *Buffy* is a complicated example, as the show moved in 2001 to Viacom's UPN – a network in which Fox's parent company has a vested interest – after a high-profile bidding war.) Disney still sells *Felicity* and *Popular* to WB instead of to their subsidiary ABC, and Paramount Television is producing two hits for CBS rivals – *Frasier* for NBC and *Sabrina* for WB.

On the surface, these arrangements seem to undermine many of the strategies and inherent benefits of a carefully crafted entertainment conglomerate. After all, why would one of these companies put money directly into a competitor's pocket or send popular programming to a rival? News Corp.'s COO Peter Chernin points to the big picture and the personal relationships that drive business in Hollywood when he explains why Fox-produced shows air on rival networks.

> We would limit the creative talent we are in business with if we only produced for the Fox network ... There are plenty of profits to be derived at all different parts of this chain, and we don't have to control every piece of it.
>
> Hofmeister, 2001, p. C5

Another explanation can be found in the expanding docket of lawsuits starring some of TV's biggest profit participants who are accusing their parent corporations of 'self-dealing'. In a series of well-publicised cases (all settled out of court), prominent producers and actors have begun suing the owner/distributors of their programmes. They are charging their parent companies with selling programmes to their own subsidiaries at a bargain rate, which in turn significantly lowers the return from profit participation that the talent receives. The threat of these lawsuits has given conglomerates serious pause before engaging in 'sweetheart deals', throwing an enormous wrench into even the best-laid synergist plans. Fear of becoming embroiled in expensive and lengthy court battles that bring an avalanche of negative publicity has had a dramatic chilling effect, sabotaging many potential benefits that could be derived from a vertically integrated structure. As one industry executive has said, today's vertically integrated companies 'have to constantly remind themselves of the old adage that, like Caesar's wife, they have to be above suspicion' (Dempsey, 2000, p. 17).

The most notable examples of self-dealing conflicts have involved Disney, Fox and ABC. Fox was under the closest scrutiny because, until 2000, it was the conglomerate that supplied itself with the most home-grown product. Steven Bochco sued Fox in 1999 for negotiating what he saw as a cut-rate deal for syndicated episodes of *NYPD Blue* to air on one of Fox's cable channels, FX. Bochco claimed that Fox cheated him out of at least $15 million by selling reruns of his *NYPD Blue* series to the FX cable channel without seeking out any other offers. Bochco was again slighted by the system in 2000, this time by ABC, when the network moved *NYPD Blue* out of its time slot to make way for *Once and Again*, a new series produced by Disney-owned subsidiary, Touchstone Television.

David Duchovny also sued Fox in 1999 on a charge of self-dealing, accusing the company of cheating him out of at least $25 million by negotiating a significantly discounted rate for *The X Files* to play on its own networks. The star of the Fox series sued the show's distributor, 20th Century-Fox Television, for allegedly selling rerun rights to cable channel FX at below-market rates. Duchovny also charged that the sweetheart licensing terms that Fox has been offering to its affiliated stations has precluded higher bids from being seriously entertained, which in turn reduces the flow of the $800 million in profits back to him. The case was also settled out of court for a reported $20 million.

Fox was sued yet again by Alan Alda, who claimed the studio did not test the marketplace for *M*A*S*H* before selling the series to its in-house cable network FX at what Alda claimed was far below market price. The Alda suit was surprising, partly because the 255 half-hour episodes have been in syndication since the mid-1970s. This case was settled out of court on the eve of trial. The suit brought by Matt Williams and Wind Dancer Productions Group against Disney was another charge of self-dealing that was widely reported. The producers of *Home Improvement* sued Disney for failing to actively pursue a deal with networks besides ABC once their contract was up for renewal. Instead of seeking competitive bids from other networks, Disney merely renewed with their subsidiary, ABC.

Still, the self-dealing accusation with the most publicity and also the most at stake was undoubtedly Jeffrey Katzenberg's $580 million suit against Disney. Katzenberg alleged (among many other things) that Disney sold television rights to its movies at a high discount to its network subsidiary, ABC. Apparently, Disney was charging ABC a licence fee of about 4.2 per cent of box-office receipts for its animated features, as opposed to the going rate of 15 per cent (Ricker, 1999, p. 62). Katzenberg also charged Disney with taking less money for broadcast rights than ABC offered, and even giving the network free programming, in order to make ABC appear more profitable (Schneider, 1999, p. 4). After an embarrassing and lengthy court battle, Katzenberg's 1999 settlement was supposedly $250 million. Aside from being a deterrent, these lawsuits have also spawned a cottage industry of outside consultants examining the merits of intra-conglomerate deals for producers. The studios, on the other hand, are now increasingly inserting clauses (for their own 'protection') into contracts that allow them to do business with their subsidiaries without fear of reprisal by profit participants.

The self-dealing syndrome may also have cost Fox a boatload of money when it drastically underbid for the television rights to *Titanic*. The arrogance and carelessness marking their offer cost them dearly in untold sums of advertising revenue and missed opportunities for cross-promotion. As a co-production of 20th Century-Fox and Paramount, the Fox Network was given first crack at buying the TV rights. However, their $20 million bid was $10 million short of what NBC was happy to pay, and $40 million short of what Paramount and Fox officials later asserted would have been a fair price for the property. Instead, NBC's $30 million bought them exclusive rights to broadcast *Titanic* five times in five years, beginning in 2000. This record deal was made even before the film had finished its first run in theatres, demonstrating the pressure that spiralling costs have exerted on film-makers to find ways to offset their production expenses – and the attendant opportunities that such desperation breeds.

There are other reasons that can explain why self-contained entertainment conglomerates would go shopping elsewhere for programming, the primary one being the company's bottom line. For example, the $13 million per episode that NBC is paying Warner Bros. Television for *ER* is a far greater price than Warner Bros. could ever command from siphoning the hit show to its own fledgeling network, WB. With the repeal of Fin Syn and the growth of studio-network alliances, NBC got panicky about the competition in such a formidable landscape of rivals and began a hysterical odyssey of overbidding to retain the popular drama, much to Warner Bros.' delight.

Another important factor is that the networks have begun developing niche audiences much like cable stations, which limits the number of in-house productions that would be particularly appropriate for their target markets. WB, for instance, has conceived a strategy based on the eighteen- to twenty-five-year-old audience, while UPN caters more to a younger, more urban viewer. The programmes produced by Warner Bros., Paramount and their affiliated outfits are not all necessarily going to appeal to those markets, so they take their products to other buyers.

Consequently, the industry is not enjoying the incestuous programming free-for-all that would be expected now that production and distribution have been reunited. Conglomerates have learned that negotiating the terrain of this vertically integrated industry is truly a precarious sport. If a network allows a sister studio to pay less than market price for advertising time, or snubs an important outside customer to favour corporate holdings, then both units run the larger risk of losing their competitive edge. Overall, synergy works best when players combine their assets to originate new lines of business, creating instant economies of scale. Turner Classic Movies is a perfect example; the values of both the MGM library and a cable channel catering to cinephiles instantly skyrocketed once they were brought together. By putting them under the same roof, Ted Turner enhanced both properties and created a huge revenue stream that might never have been realised had they remained independent of one another. News Corp.'s marriage of Metromedia's underperforming UHF television stations and the ailing Fox studio jump-started the creation of the new Fox Television network.

'Content is King'
'Distribution is King'
'The King is Dead! Long Live the King!'

Just as the great merger wave triggered by the Industrial Revolution was sparked by the desire to capitalise on efficiencies of scale and be more competitive in a transforming economy, the wholesale consolidation in the broadcast industry was motivated by similar incentives. Deregulation and technological change served as supreme catalysts to enact a sweeping realignment of corporate terrain. Longstanding safety shields that protected broadcasters from takeovers fostered new competition and threatened their livelihood. Ultimately, the process paved the way for the global media expansion and the intensive conglomerate consolidation that characterises the entertainment industry today, perhaps giving the networks a second lease of life.

It was also the power of deregulation that propelled the broadcast landscape from one paradigm to another in a span of just thirty years. The industry shifted from one largely run by the men who founded their networks (i.e., William Paley at CBS, Leonard Goldenson at ABC) to one cog in the machine of multimedia empires envisioning networks as part-time promotional vehicles for their web portals. Will the networks ever become the equivalent of the movie studios in the corporate paradigm, the engines driving an entire industry or setting an agenda for an entertainment conglomerate? Or are they now reduced to mere satellites, offshoots in a larger structure organised around feature films and cable channels? Regulation will surely play a role in determining whether broadcasting will become the tail or the dog, a central focus or mere ancillary distribution form.

Still, it is important to remember that most regulatory guidelines for broadcasting were not designed with an internet economy, 500 channels or a global audience in mind. It is increasingly clear that current standards cannot accommodate the complexities and vagaries of the present market. As a result, particularly since the Viacom-CBS and AOL Time Warner deals, the system seems to be driven from the bottom up; the size and scope of mergers has put regulators in the back seat, following the lead of market activity rather than setting the pace. Consequently, the new reality of broadcast regulation is one in which the industrial economy has essentially outgrown the dimensions and arbiters of current policy. How that continues to influence the corporate landscape and what becomes 'must see TV' will undoubtedly be a fascinating drama to watch unfold.

Timeline

1970   Financial Interest and Syndication laws enacted along with the Prime Time Access Rule (PTAR)
        Viacom created when CBS is forced to divest its syndication operation

1976   Department of Justice files suit against NBC, CBS and ABC which results in consent decrees being signed with all networks by 1980. They mirror Fin Syn restrictions and impose further limitations on the number of prime-time hours the networks are allowed to produce

1981   Marvin Davis, Denver oilman, buys 20th Century-Fox Film Corp. for $720 million

1984   Kirk Kerkorian buys MGM/UA
        May: Barry Diller leaves Paramount and becomes Chairman/CEO of Fox
        22 September: Michael Eisner and Frank Wells become Chairman and President of Walt Disney Productions, Jeffrey Katzenberg named Motion Picture President in October
        ABC buys ESPN ($227 million deal)

1985   FCC increases station ownership limits
        Rupert Murdoch buys Fox for $575 million
        March: Capital Cities Communications Inc. announces deal to buy ABC for $3.5 billion (deal is official in January 1986)
        6 May: Fox announces deal to buy six of Metromedia's seven television stations (Los Angeles, Chicago, Dallas-Ft Worth, Houston, Washington, DC, and New York City) for $1.85 billion. These stations would form the core of the fourth broadcasting network
        6 August: Turner buys MGM/UA for $1.5 billion

1986   3 January: Capital Cities Communications Inc. purchases ABC for $3.5 billion
        9 June: GE buys RCA Corp., parent company of NBC, for $6.4 billion
        News Corp. launches Fox, the fourth broadcast network
        September: Laurence Tisch and his Loews Corp. gain control of CBS

1989   June: Time Inc. acquires Warner Communications Inc. for $14 billion to form Time Warner after forestalling hostile bid by Paramount

1993   12 September: Sumner Redstone announces Viacom will acquire Paramount for $8.2 billion
        Barry Diller leaves Fox

1994   7 July: Viacom Inc. buys Paramount Communications Inc. for $10 billion

29 September: Viacom Inc. announces $8 billion deal for Blockbuster Entertainment Corp.

1995   January: launch of UPN (Viacom/Chris-Craft) and WB (Time Warner) networks
31 July: Disney announces deal to buy Capital Cities Communications Inc./ABC for $19 billion
1 August: Westinghouse announces deal to acquire CBS Inc. for $5.4 billion
21 September: Official repeal of the Financial Interest and Syndication rules
23 September: Time Warner announces merger with Turner, $7.6 billion deal
24 November: Westinghouse $5.4 billion deal for CBS Inc. approved by FCC

1996   8 February: President Clinton signs the Telecommunications Act into law
30 August: Prime Time Access Rule expires
11 October: Time Warner and Turner Broadcasting System complete $7.6 billion merger

1997   December: Westinghouse becomes CBS Inc.
News Corp. becomes the largest owner of TV stations in the USA after purchasing the rest of New World Communications group

1999   1 April: CBS announces deal to buy leading syndicator King World Prods. Inc. for $2.5 billion
September: Viacom buys Spelling outright, after owning 80 per cent of stock
7 September: Viacom Inc. announces deal to buy CBS Corp. for $34.5 billion

2000   10 January: America Online Inc. announces deal to buy Time Warner Inc. in $135 billion merger agreement, largest combination ever in media history
3 May: FCC approves transfer of control of the CBS Corp. to Viacom Inc., including approval of the transfer of thirty-eight television stations, 162 radio stations, several translator and satellite stations

2001   25 July: FCC approves News Corp.'s purchase of rival broadcaster Chris-Craft Industries for $5.4 billion. This deal gives Murdoch two major stations in Los Angeles and New York City, as well as a total of thirty-three stations reaching 41 per cent of the national audience

Sources:
Variety, *New York Times*, *Los Angeles Times*, *The Wall Street Journal*, *Fortune* and Benjamin Compaine and Douglas Gomery, *Who Owns the Media?*

Bibliography

Aufderhide, Patricia, 'Telecommunications and the Public Interest', in Erik Barnouw (ed.), *Conglomerates and the Media* (New York: The New Press, 1997), pp. 157–72.

Auletta, Ken, *Three Blind Mice: How the TV Networks Lost Their Way* (New York: Vintage Books, 1992).

Auletta, Ken, *The Highwaymen* (San Diego: Harcourt Brace & Company, 1998).

Balio, Tino, 'A Major Presence in All of the World's Important Markets', in Steve Neale and Murray Smith (eds), *Contemporary Hollywood Cinema* (New York: Routledge, 1998), pp. 58–73.

Bart, Peter, 'Vertical Disintegration', *Variety* (6–12 May 1996), p. 10.

Block, Alex Ben, *Outfoxed* (New York: St Martin's Press, 1990).

Compaine, Benjamin and Gomery, Douglas, *Who Owns the Media?* (3rd Edition) (London: Lawrence Erlbaum Associates, 2000).

Dempsey, John, 'Studio Sibs Parry Perils of Pix Pacts', *Variety* (24–30 July 2000), p. 17.

Eller, Claudia and Hofmeister, Sallie, 'Hollywood's Wildest Ride', *Los Angeles Times* (29 December 1995), p. D1.

Ferguson, Douglas and Walker, James, *The Broadcast Television Industry* (Boston, MA: Allyn and Bacon, 1998).

Galbraith, Jane, 'Turner Keeps Pics, Drops Rest of MGM', *Variety* (11 June 1986), p. 3.

Goldberg, Robert and Goldberg, Gerald Jay, *Citizen Turner: The Wild Rise of an American Tycoon* (New York: Harcourt Brace & Company, 1995).

Gomery, Douglas, 'Disney's Business History: A Reinterpretation', in Eric Smoodin (ed.), *Disney Discourse* (New York: Routledge, 1994) pp. 71–86.

Harris, Kathryn, 'Lights! Camera! Regulation!', *Fortune* (4 September 1995), pp. 83–6.

Herskovitz, Marc L., 'The Repeal of the Financial Interest and Syndication Rules', *Cardozo Arts & Entertainment Law Journal*, no. 177, (1997), p. 15.

Hertsgaard, Mark, *On Bended Knee: The Press and the Reagan Presidency* (New York: Ferrar Straus Giroux, 1988).

Hilmes, Michele, *Hollywood and Broadcasting: From Radio to Cable* (Chicago: University of Illinois Press, 1990).

Hofmeister, Sallie, 'Disney Combining Network TV Operations into One ABC Unit', *Los Angeles Times* (9 July 1999), p. C5.

Hofmeister, Sallie, 'Q&A: Murdoch Empire's Chief Engineer', *Los Angeles Times* (2 September 2001), pp. C1, C5.

Horwitz, Robert Britt, *The Irony of Regulatory Reform* (New York: Oxford University Press, 1989).

Jessell, Harry and McClellan, Steve, 'The Viacom Vision', *Electronic Media* (15 November 1999), pp. 28–37.

Kidder, Rushworth M., 'FCC's Fowler: Free Market "Ideologue" or Free-Speech Champion?', *Christian Science Monitor* (20 May 1985), National, p. 1.

Koch, Neal, 'Television's Independents: Working on a Slippery Slope', *New York Times* (30 September 1990), p. C10.

Labaton, Stephen, 'New FCC Chief Would Curb Agency Reach', *New York Times* (7 February 2001), p. C1.

Lewis, Jon, 'Disney After Disney', in Eric Smoodin (ed.), *Disney Discourse* (New York: Routledge, 1994), pp. 87–105.

Liebowitz, Dennis H., 'The Networks Go Hollywood', *New York Law Journal* (26 June 1998), p. 5.

Lyons, Charles, 'Peter's Principle', *Daily Variety* (12 October 2000), p. 1.

MacDonald, J. Fred, *One Nation under Television* (Chicago: Nelson-Hall, 1990).

MacLachlan, Claudia, 'TV Deregulation Is Driving the Deals', *The National Law Journal* (14 August 1995), p. B1.

McClellan, Steve, 'Fin Syn', *Broadcasting and Cable* (24 January 2000), pp. 30ff.

McConville, Jim, Halonen, Doug, Wang, Karissa S., Lafayette, John and Mermigas Diane, 'The Insider', *Electronic Media* (22 November 1999), p. 8.

Maney, Kevin, *Megamedia Shakeout* (New York: John Wiley, 1995).

Mayer, Caroline E., 'FCC Chief's Fears' *Washington Post* (6 February 1983), pp. K1ff.

Mermigas, Diane, 'Eisner Justifies ABC Purchase', *Electronic Media* (12 January 1998a), p. 46.

Mermigas, Diane, 'Can the Old Networks Survive in a New Era?', *Electronic Media* (27 July 1998b), p. 1.

Nossiter, Bernard D., 'The FCC's Big Giveaway Show', *The Nation* (26 October 1985), pp. 402–4.

Orwall, Bruce and Pope, Kyle, 'Disney-ABC Merger Has Yet to Add Up', *Houston Chronicle* (18 May 1997), Business, p. 4.

Powell, Bill, Smith, Vern E. and McAlevey, Peter, 'Turner's Windless Sails', *Newsweek* (9 February 1987), p. 46.

Prince, Stephen, *A New Pot of Gold: Hollywood under the Electronic Rainbow, 1980–1989* (New York: Charles Scribner's Sons, 2000).

Producer Scorecard, *Hollywood Reporter 2000–01 Guide to the Fall TV Season* (September 2000), p. 34.

Ricker, Di Mari, 'X Files' Star David Duchovny's Suit Seeks Answers to How Hollywood Keeps Its Books', *Legal Times* (27 September 1999), p. 62.

Schlosser, Joe, 'A Mouse In-House', *Broadcasting & Cable* (29 November 1999), pp. 22–30.

Schneider, Michael, 'Vertical Disintegration', *Electronic Media* (10 May 1999), p. 4.

Schneider, Michael and Adalian, Josef, 'Nets Get It Together', *Variety* (22–28 May 2000), p. 15.

Shawcross, William, *Murdoch* (New York: Simon and Schuster, 1992).

Smith, Roger, 'It's Only Money', *Daily Variety* (13 October 1999), p. 15.

Spring, Greg, 'Paramount's Syndication Nation', *Electronic Media* (2 August 1999), p. 3.

Broadcasting magazine articles – no author given

'Down to the Wire on Fin-Syn' (24 October 1983), pp. 27–9.

'Valenti Repeats Criticism of Fin-Syn Repeal' (17 October 1983), p. 54.

'Ganging up on the Networks RE Fin-Syn' (7 November 1983), pp. 31–5.

'The Bittersweet Chairmanship of Mark S. Fowler' (18 February, 1985), pp. 1, 41–3.

'The Lobbyists' (25 February 1985).

Comments of the staff of the Bureau of Economics of the Federal Trade Commission before the Federal Communications Commission, Washington, DC. In RE: Review of the Prime Time Access Rule, Section 73.658(k) of the Commission's Rules MM Docket no. 94-123, 7 March 1995.

FEDERAL REGISTER vol. 60, no. 167, Rules and Regulations, Federal Communications
    Commission, 47 CFR Part 73 [MM Docket no. 94-123; FCC 95-314] Radio Broadcast
    Services; Television Program Practices 60 FR 44773, 29 August 1995.

FEDERAL REGISTER vol. 58, no. 94, Rules and Regulations, Federal Communications
    Commission, 47 CFR Part 73 [MM Docket no. 90-162; FCC 93-179] Broadcast Services;
    Syndication and Financial Interest Rules 58 FR 28927, 18 May 1993, Final Rule.

FEDERAL REGISTER vol. 65, no. 135, Notices, Federal Communications Commission
    [MM Docket no. 98-35; FCC 00-191] Broadcast Services; Radio Stations, Television
    Stations, 65 FR 43333, 13 July 2000, Notice.

Standard & Poor's Industry Surveys: *Broadcasting/Media*, 1980–90.

74667

3

'Must See TV': Programming Identity on NBC Thursdays

Nancy San Martín

What else would we do on Thursday nights?

Trying to capture the wistful tone of a home movie, the promotional campaign for the new autumn season of programming that aired during prime-time broadcasts of the 2000 Summer Olympics featured backstage footage of the casts of 'must see TV' shows, the staple of 1990s weeknight programming on the National Broadcasting Company (NBC). In these ads, actors from Thursdays' *Friends*, *Will & Grace*, and *ER* greet one another and get reacquainted with production crews. The ads' only sound is voice-over of an announcer promising a post-Olympic Thursday – 'a night when America has always come together' (NBC, 2000b). Just as this campaign portrays actors happily looking forward to their return to work, so it envisions audiences eagerly awaiting the chance to reaffirm their identity as 'Americans' by watching together on Thursday nights. NBC, Thursday nights and 'America', it seems, fit together neatly.

For NBC, the prime-time Thursday schedule has been inordinately important since the early 1980s, when the network first developed its ' "best night of television on television" ' tag-line (Thompson, 1996, p. 67). Thursday nights typically produce more than one-third of the network's revenues ('*Frasier* vs.', 1999) with signature hit series like *Hill Street Blues* (1980–7), *Cheers* (1982–93), *The Cosby Show* (1984–93), *Seinfeld* (1990–8) and, most recently, *Friends* and *ER*. By the mid-1990s, NBC was the top network in the US, garnering millions of viewers and consistently earning record-breaking advertising dollars (Brockington, 1998; Coe, 1996; Gay, 1986; Mandese, 1995b; Schmuckler, 1993, 1994; Sharkey, 1998). Since 1994, NBC's Thursday block has consisted of four comedies that set up the ten o'clock medical drama *ER* . Though 'must see' has since become the slogan for most NBC weeknight programming, it came into use soon enough after *Friends* and *ER*'s 1994 premieres as to be linked inextricably with these shows – 'must see' 'building blocks' (Mandese, 1995a, p. 3). NBC relies heavily on the draw of *Friends* in particular, lengthening the show as needed in order to compete with other networks, airing first-run episodes at 8pm and reruns at 8.30, or airing reruns or rebroadcasts on other weeknights. The comedy in the 9pm anchor slot tends to stay the same throughout the season: *Seinfeld*, *Frasier* and *Will & Grace* have anchored the block since 1994. In contrast, the 8.30 and 9.30 hammock slots typically house a variety of similarly written and set comedies with nearly entirely white casts, but most of these shows have experienced short runs or early cancellation. Thus, *Friends*' malleability and *ER*'s consistency are central to understanding NBC's Thursday-night block.

The 'must see' fictions are typically set in metropolises that index the larger nation – *Friends*, *Just Shoot Me* and *Will & Grace*'s New York, *Frasier*'s Seattle, *ER*'s Chicago. Resisting ambiguous, fictional, isolated, or fantastical settings, 'must see TV' codifies urban centres as microcosms of the USA. The viewer courted and imagined by NBC closely resembles the average character on a given Thursday-night comedy – that is to say, an employed, white, (ostensibly) straight twenty- to thirty-year-old with money to spend in the big city (Gunther, 1997). Thus, on *Just Shoot Me*, ultra-hip fashion editor Nina Van Horne is appalled at a boyfriend's suggestion that they settle down in Tennessee: 'Tennessee?!' she exclaims in horror, 'Who lives in Tennessee??' Similarly, a test of the *Friends*' geography skills – they must name as many US states as they can in twelve minutes – elicits some telling omissions. Monica forgets fourteen states: 'Nobody cares about the Dakotas!' she yells indignantly. Following what Todd Gitlin (2000) has termed situation comedy's move into urban space, 'must see' absents poorer, isolated, or rural regions, a rejection informed perhaps by the network's desire to disassociate itself from the provinciality, backwardness, or cultural homogeneity it associates with then displaces onto these regions. Ironically, 'must see TV''s preponderance of affluent, well-appointed white bodies produces just such an erasure of difference in its appeal to and reliance upon that elusive 'hip, urban sensibility' (Stanley, 1996b, p. 28) that characterises 1990s US network programming. This sensibility makes it safe for 'America' to 'come together' in viewership through an appeal to white audiences that whitewashes urban and sexual subcultures.

While I reject the ease with which NBC deploys 'America' as a code word for privileged identities and subject positions, 'must see TV''s unprecedented success, its widespread cultural currency, and its significant influence on the landscape of US network television demand critical attention. The viewer-citizen by turns imagined, courted, represented and created by the networks is mapped upon temporal, national, corporate and representational terrains in multiple and often contradictory ways. Consequently, the ideological investments narrativised on NBC's incredibly successful Thursdays draw from complex, often competing discourses of identity – sexuality and race, in particular. I maintain that 'must see TV' Thursdays' particular conflation of sexuality, race and citizenship has refashioned weeknight network broadcasting, shaping new ways through which to understand how television programming is identified, structured and sold. Drawing methodologically from cultural studies, queer theory, narrative theory and televisual industry analysis, I explore how identificatory practices and identities – particularly in the domains of sexuality and race – are programmed and narrativised in 'must see TV' Thursdays' serial fictions.

Programming identity

Organisationally, the 'comedy juggernaut that begins with *Friends* ... and flows into the drama of *ER*' (Sharkey, 1997, p. 30) naturalises and reinforces a traditional narrative order – providing a readily discernible beginning, middle and end. Apart from selling products and services to those demographically desirable populations charged with standing in for the nation, NBC's mandate – '(you) must see TV'!! – presupposes and instructs not only that we watch, but that we watch four comedies set up a drama, in that order, over and over, on almost every weeknight. Of course, NBC executives understand that viewing patterns have changed dramatically in the post-network era (Dubow, 1999; McClellan, 1998; Saenz, 1994; Sharkey, 1998). Nevertheless, blocking remains a common, effective strategy that determines, in large part, how and when certain identities – sexual, racial, normative, non-normative – are featured, obscured, or excluded.

'Must see TV' 's comedy-foursome-plus-drama block is linked by a series of structuring devices and intertextualities – intersecting, multi-episode storylines; ensemble casting; casting crossovers; cross-show promotional campaigns; uniformly high production values; a self-reflexive pastiche of popular culture references; and similar direction, editing and writing – that reward viewers for watching the block in order in its entirety (Marin, 1996; Owen, 1997; Stark, 1997; Stempel, 1992). These strategies blur the generic distinctions between and among the block's programmes, commercials, trailers, credits and station identifications (Owen, 1997; Ross, 1998; Sharkey, 1998; Taylor, 1996). In short, 'must see' juxtaposes same with same: every image, every narrative is a paean to urban sophistication. 'Must see TV' repackages and reiterates the same sounds and images in a clearly demarcated three-hour story, one told in a series of similar vignettes that constantly call attention to the conditions of their own production. There is, in other words, a built-in homo-sensibility to 'must see' 's scheduling practices. 'Must see' 's iterations of sameness produce a kind of representational flattening that makes this block a serial narrative form in its own right, much in the way that successive instalments of a weekly show constitute a serial narrative. Yet, why should comedy so consistently precede drama in the prime-time schedule (and, almost always in the USA, lead up to the late-night 'real' drama of the eleven o'clock local news)? Indeed, it seems almost unnatural – queer? – that viewers should expect drama to precede comedy. But why? After all, the unpleasant complex of feelings engendered by *ER* and other 10pm dramas – fear, abjection, disgust, sadness, fury, paranoia, ambivalence – seem rather unpalatable beforebed fodder. Nevertheless, the larger sequence is so entrenched in turn-of-the-century programming practices as to constitute a significant syntagmatic structure.

'Must see' 's comedy-foursome-plus-drama syntax is unified by a normalising drive that pushes away from a celebration of liminal or non-normative identities. Fundamentally sexualised, this drive depends upon a substantive move from the comedies' structuring homoerotic fantasies and playful sexual innuendo towards *ER*'s rigidly heteronormative, rightist, conservative discourses of 'family values'. In positing drive as an organising metaphor, I presume that television's syntagmatic patterns are not natural but naturalised through a narratological impetus towards sexualised catharsis. In other words, 'must see TV' Thursdays strive to mimic the heterosexual sex act: if titillation is aroused by the homoerotic foreplay of *Friends* or *Will & Grace*, *ER*'s climax depends upon straight sex, the kind that produces 'normal' families.

The drive is fundamentally unidirectional. Ads and trailers only ever reference what is upcoming. Moreover, it is teleological: *Friends*, *Will & Grace*, and the hammock comedies move the viewer towards a definite endpoint, *ER* . The high-end products routinely advertised during the block help sustain the drive, promising fast cars, speedy travel, expedient software and internet connections, and ever-more efficient communications and messaging systems. Industry analysts have picked up on and contributed to 'must see''s motor-driven sense of urgency. The Thursday shows have been variously called NBC's 'power plant' (Coe, 1996, p. 26), its 'Cape Canaveral' (Lesly, 1997, p. 119), not only its 'engine' but 'the whole car' (Schmuckler, 1994, p. 21). Furthermore, throughout the evening, trailers for *ER* – more and more as the night progresses – repeatedly remind viewers that *ER* is coming up tonight, later, next, now. The most anticipated (moving, surprising, shocking, star-studded, riveting, unforgettable) *ER* is always just ahead, promised by trailers featuring tantalising clips, expectant music and sound effects, and fevered voice-overs. *ER* is always just coming.

The 5 November 1998 block exemplifies what I read as the teleological drive towards heteronormativity that organises NBC's Thursday nights. In 'The One with the Yeti', *Friends* begins that evening's programming by pitting five of the friends against Ross, whose impromptu marriage to his girlfriend Emily threatens the group dynamic. The friends dutifully try to hide their reservations about Ross' being on the rebound (from his on-again, off-again relationship with Rachel) and Emily's increasingly unreasonable demands. After Ross mistakenly utters Rachel's name instead of Emily's during his vows, the two become estranged. In order to save their marriage, Emily demands that he move out of his apartment, sell all his belongings and avoid Rachel and all her friends (i.e., all his friends). Finally, the friends confront Ross after Joey exclaims, 'We all hate Emily!' and Monica pleads, 'We just think that you're having to sacrifice a whole lot to make her happy'. With uncharacteristically explosive anger, Ross defends the controls of heterosexual marriage: 'You have no idea what it takes to make a marriage work! It's not all laughing, happy, candy in the sky, drinking coffee at Central Perk all the time. It's real life, okay. It's what *grown-ups* do'. By the end of the episode, though, the 'friends as family device' (Owen, 1997, p. 47) is recuperated from the threat of 'real life', the code word for heteronormativity.

Heteronormativity and its attenuating structures of control – jealousy, surveillance, suburbia – are displaced onto Emily and summarily excised. Emily, whose difference from the group is manifested by her British nationality and accent, is physically isolated from the group at this point, repeatedly calling from England to check on Ross. The editing alienates Emily: she is framed alone, holding a receiver, never sharing even a split-screen with Ross. Subsequently, mistrustful Emily's expectation that marital bliss take precedence over erotic friendship ultimately proves too much for Ross. The episode ends with a typical shot of the six hugging and comforting one another, promising to reintegrate Ross into the group and to help him cope with the end of another marriage. Marriage may be what other grown-ups do, but it's what these friends repeatedly fail at, reject, or substitute with homoerotic friendships and casual flings (at least for the show's first seven seasons). At this point, the shrewish and untenably jealous Emily is written off, and fans are heartened by the homoerotic possibilities presaged by Ross' moving into Joey and Chandler's apartment, possibilities drawn out in subsequent episodes.

That same night, *ER*'s 'Stuck on You' explores male homoeroticism and homosexual desire through the story of teen prostitute Kevin Delaney. Kevin spends his stay at the ER flirting with Dr Mark Greene, who has rescued him from the streets after Kevin is badly beaten by a trick. Kevin is obviously attracted to Mark: he makes explicit sexual references – 'customers like it better when they can ride me bareback' – and invites Mark to join him for a shower. In contrast to most gay, lesbian, transsexual, or intersexed patients brought into the ER, Kevin is not unconscious, anesthetised, or so near death as to be rendered non-threatening. The teen's rescue and subsequent interactions between doctor and patient become the talk of the ER. Even Mark's interest seems piqued, if only for a moment. However, even though Kevin troubles the ER with his explicitly (homo)sexualised presence, homosex is linked with death throughout this episode. Kevin is multiply threatening: he violates doctor/patient boundaries, seeks sex in a public place and proves unwilling to give up prostitution. Kevin is multiply threatened: he arrives in the ER bruised and bloodied; he suffers a bleeding disorder; he is exposed to HIV and other sexually transmitted diseases. The potentially lethal combination of prescription blood thinners, drugs and alcohol, rough sex and gay-bashing makes his very existence seem untenable.

Should viewers somehow miss the preponderance of threats that Kevin embodies, into the ER comes a particularly memorable trauma that presents yet another metaphor for the deathly potentialities of male same-sex desire. Paramedics bring in the Leahys, carpet layers who have become literally cemented together in a grotesque full-body embrace after a freak traffic accident. The force of the accident is so massive that it flings carpet cement into the truck cab, engulfs the 'two wacko brothers' in cement, forcibly intertwines them and projects a sharp carpet-laying tool into one brother with near-fatal force. Not even a fraternal relationship mitigates the remarkable overdetermination of this symbolism. When one of the brothers begins to bleed from the gut, Dr Kerry Weaver's diagnosis is 'an impalement of some kind' brought upon by 'some kind of tool with sharp prongs'. This image of male–male sex gone very wrong echoes Kevin's daily brushes with mortality in more ways than one. The mutually imbricated threats of contagious homosexuality and homosexuality as contagion are underscored as more and more of the doctors, including Elizabeth Corday and John Carter, become physically cemented to the brothers, too. (In fact, Carter must shave off his beard in order to extricate himself.)

The Leahy trauma begins with all the makings of sitcom slapstick and sight gags. Before one of them is rendered unconscious, the brothers bicker and thrash, and medical equipment is rendered useless as sticky glue spreads everywhere. This scene could just as easily happen on *Friends* or *Seinfeld*, where the physical comedy of contorted bodies – for instance, Joey wearing all of Chandler's clothes at once or Phoebe straining to scratch a boyfriend's itchy chicken pox blisters – nearly always presages erotic possibilities. Nevertheless, that this trauma draws from the tropes of physical comedy matters little, for the humorously bizarre and highly improbable scenario works in tandem with Kevin's tragedy. Just as the Leahy brothers spread their cement contaminant throughout the trauma room, the promise of Kevin's eager young flesh threatens Mark (and other patients and staff) with its sickly sharp embrace.

Though drive allows for eroticised, often sexualised same-sex pairings in the 'must see' comedies, it leads purposefully to the ER, where homoeroticism and homosexuality are disavowed, introduced as freak accidents (freaks of nature), or punished severely. *ER* pathologises what *Friends* takes pleasure in celebrating. Perhaps because it envisions a community where citizenship and belonging do not exclude non-normatively desiring subjects, *Friends* has been celebrated as the most 'humane' comedy of the 1990s, a show with a 'heart' (Medhurst, 1996, p. 17). *ER*'s heart, though, is tempered by a 'moral compass' (Bianco, 2000, p. 1D) and a 'moral center' (Brophy, 1999, p. 17): appropriately enough these are references to happily-ever-after heterosexual couple Carol Hathaway and Doug Ross. Its didactic, moralising force weighs down heavily upon non-normative bodies, desires and identities. Ever imminent, *ER* is coming, but it's coming to show viewers how non-normative bodies and desires will be punished for contributing to the loss of idealised heteronormative nuclear families.

All in the family

The majority of US comedies that ran from the late-70s to the mid-90s by and large omitted any references to or representations of non-normative sexualities, interracial sex and desire, abortion, pregnancy, childbirth, infidelity, polyamory, sexwork, pornography, or anything remotely understood as sexual themes. Almost twenty years of shows like *Family Matters* and *Family Ties* emblematised David Grote's theory of sitcom as a genre in which 'property is sacred, the family is eternal, the parents are always right, and authority always wins' (1983, p. 169). Indeed, the assumption that two parents of opposite sexes would be watching television alongside their traditionally biologically garnered offspring of not-indeterminate sex or gender became the *sine qua non* of early prime-time programming. Representations of the family in comedy – and to a large extent in the movie specials, mini-series and prime-time soap operas of this period – both signified and assumed an idealised, unproblematised heteronormativity. In stark contrast, *Friends* presents a laughably troubled heterosexuality. The six close-knit, sexually active and actively sexually fantasising friends trouble the (mythical) heteronormative family that networks had both presumed and represented. Furthermore, *Friends* redefines the kinds of representations of sex and sexuality deemed acceptable for newly organised television audiences, explicitly linking situation comedy and sex. In the wake of *Friends*, 8–9pm has become one of the most contentious hours on prime time.

Ken Tucker's review of *Friends* suggests that it 'trades on regular Do It jokes' (1997, p. 106), a fair enough charge. More significantly, *Friends*' major contribution to the genre is that it proffers multiple ways of understanding what 'doing it' might mean and who should get to 'do it' with whom. Largely disavowing that old standby – monogamous, heterosexual, procreative 'doing it' – it explores love and relationships in the contexts of lesbianism, homoeroticism, oral sex, non-genital erotic contact, voyeurism, pornography, multiple concurrent sex partners, public sex, group sex, masturbation, role-play and sexual fantasy. Understood neither as deviant aberrations nor passing stages in a heteronormative telos, *Friends*' playful explorations of homoeroticism as well as heteroeroticism and heterosociality undergird its rethinkings of family and kinship.

The eroticisation of commitment, intimacy, betrayal and emotional and financial support manifested in various same-sex dyads – Joey/Chandler and Rachel/Monica especially – and the ease with which men and women negotiate heteroerotic friendships in this series consistently challenge and trouble heteronormativity.[1] Divorcing family from hierarchically organised biological affiliations, *Friends* posits that fluidly erotic same-sex relationships and straight friendships with benefits can constitute desirable, fulfilling and enduring families and communities.

Routinely, *Friends* rejects the celebration or romanticisation of heteronormatively conceived families. It scoffs at the traditions and conventions like shopping for bridal gowns and planning wedding receptions. Its characters' relationships with their families of origin are troubled and marginalised even when their relatives are a bit queer themselves. For example, the occasionally featured Gellers make no secret of their preference for their son Ross over his sister, Monica. Chandler is haunted by that traumatic Thanksgiving when his father came out and ran away with the pool boy, and Ross's son is being raised by lesbian parents. While biological relatives come and go, erotic friendships see the characters through everything. *Friends* sets up multiple and interrelated homoeroticisms and invests even non-erotic storylines with sexual innuendo, consistently producing comedy that allows a safe space for male and female homoeroticisms. Examples abound. In 'The One with the Breast Milk', Ross and his ex-wife's new partner, Susan, battle over tasting Carol's breast milk. In 'The One with Rachel's Inadvertent Kiss', Monica and Phoebe get increasingly angry and aroused as they compete over who can have the most sex with her respective boyfriend. Joey and Chandler pick out furniture for their apartment and raise a pet duck and chicken. Joey's moving out of their apartment is presented as a messy breakup in 'The One Where Joey Moves Out'. In 'The One with all the Haste', Chandler and Joey simultaneously masturbate after Rachel and Monica make out (both of which happen, sadly, off-camera). Het lovers come and go, but the *Friends* stay connected.

Not only is heteronormativity indefinitely deferred through the show's caricatures of marriage and parenting, but *Friends* cannot understand kinship and community apart from friendships heartened by desire and lust. Whereas homoeroticism and heterosociality often function as place-holders for the reinstitution of heteronorms in comedy, on *Friends*, they lead at best to heteroambivalence. *Friends'* rewriting of family comes close to the kind of post-modern gay social organisation Kath Weston has termed 'families we choose'. Instead of considering friendship and kinship 'as competitors or assimilating friendships to biogenetic relationships regarded as somehow more fundamental' (1991, p. 118), these arrangements resist the impulse to frame heterosexual marriage and children as central. If, as Grote maintains, 'there is a strong sense in all the sit-coms of circling the wagons and fighting off the savages who want to upset the world' (1983, p. 83), the circle of friends guards against the wounding rigidity of heteronormative families. Though the show strives for an amoral economy with 'no lessons learned' (Owen, 1997, p. 113), *Friends* does teach that the families we create supersede blood ties.

Like all popular culture phenomena in the USA, the *Friends* formula has been widely copied, becoming 'the building block for almost every sitcom' (ibid., p. 115) introduced in 1995 (Auster, 1996; Bellafante, 1995; Gunther, 1997; Heuton, 1995; Lowry, 1995). Many of these shows rely on the types and tropes that fashion *Friends'* structuring homoeroticisms. For instance, the *Friends* clones often try to recapture Chandler, the sardonic, ambiguously heterosexual male who must repeatedly convince friends, family and coworkers that he really is straight.[2] Moreover, many of the *Friends* clones make use of a trope first used on *Frasier*, the recurring figure of the invisible spouse. Spoofing straight couplings by absenting one partner entirely, the invisible spouse enacts a kind of presence of absence, becoming the butt of running jokes but never appearing on screen. For instance, Stan, Karen's sugar-daddy husband on *Will & Grace* is only ever shot as a disembodied arm reaching for Karen's breast. Karen's invisible, unrecognisable husband enacts clearly the rejection of heteronorms that *Friends* has made conventional in the genre.

The fluidity that characterises representations of sexuality and family in the 'must see' comedies speaks to NBC's promotions and advertising practices as well. NBC sells the Thursday-night block as a family of shows that are home to a family of actors. In addition, the promotional stills released for print ad campaigns often look like family portraits. *Entertainment Weekly*'s advertising spread promoting the 2000–1 season, for instance, includes a fold-out display that celebrates NBC's growing family of 'more and more' quality shows (NBC, 2000a). The page devoted to *Will & Grace* employs NBC's rainbow logo, a stylised peacock's tail, to suggest a non-threatening (though certainly profit-driven) appeal to glbtq communities and families familiar with the semiotics of the rainbow flag. It's all in the family at NBC, as shows are united, indeed related, by programming strategies like theme nights such as Blackout Thursday (1994), Super Star Thursday (2000) and SuperSize Thursday (2001). It's all in the family at NBC when shows exchange principals and draw from the same stable of actors and guest actors who are cast in similar or crossover roles.

Friends' overwhelming popularity and the success of its many clones spurred a rash of popular and industry articles concerning the 'must see' comedies' treatment of non-normative sex and sexuality, what Brian Lowry has termed 'critical crankiness' (1995, p. 21) about 'musty', 'must flee', or 'must fix' TV's licentiousness and vapidity (Auster, 1996; Bianco, 2000; Lowry, 1995; Marin, 1995; Scott, 1994; Zoglin, 1995). Numerous industry analysts examine how other networks' counterprogramming courts conservative viewers supposedly off-put by 'must see' (Adalian, 1999; Bellafante, 1998; Rice, 1997; Sellers, 1999; Sharkey, 1997; Stanley, 1996a; Tobenkin, 1996). While the concept briefly considered by Fox for a show called *Enemies* (Robins, 1996) seems humorously to typify such counterprogramming trends, industry analysts suggest that the demographic, ideological and conceptual opposite of *Friends* is not enemies, but 'family'. For example, Marc Gunther fumes: 'it's likely that millions are fed up with *Friends* clones and ready to embrace that prime-time staple, the family sitcom' (1997, p. 28). Ironically, Gunther reflects just the kinds of conservative investments at work in *ER*'s interpretations of US families and urban communities. Industry critics' furious efforts to chastise NBC for its 'anti-family' representations overlook the 'must see' block's drive towards *ER*'s sustained, scathing critique of non-normative sexualities and redefinitions of the family.

The Thursday-night climax/conclusion coincides with *ER*'s mourning the loss of the heterosexual couple and grieving the disintegration of patriarchal, heteronormative families.

ER's vision of troubled urban communities is emblematised in its workplace family, which is as numerous and ever-shifting as *ER*'s large ensemble cast and as unstable and unruly as the families it treats and (sometimes) heals. Both the ER staff and the diseased, often broken, families that visit the ER require constant surveillance by hospital administrators, psychiatrists, psychologists, social workers, police, courts and the scolding voices of firm father figures (like chief-of-staff Donald Anspaugh) or even errant fathers (like scofflaw Doug Ross). *ER* consistently works towards what Lauren Berlant (1997) terms an infantilised public space, one made safe for babies and children – how *ER* dotes on them – at the expense of non-normative bodies and desires. Week after week, a plethora of social ills – including, but not limited to, drug use, teenage promiscuity and pregnancy, urban unrest, domestic violence and the mutually imbricated dangers of homosexuality and (HIV) contagion – are effected by heteronormativity gone awry.

ER's 'All in the Family' episode, the second of a two-part sequence set on Valentine's Day 2000 that began with 'Be Still My Heart', shows how *ER*'s families suffer the consequences of failed heteronormativity. One of numerous episodes in which Mark plays father to Carter and medical student Lucy Knight, 'Be Still My Heart' deals with Carter and Lucy's disagreement over the treatment of a white male patient. Both episodes draw on the competing registers of Lucy and Carter's relationship in the *ER* family: they are alternately depicted as quarrelling lovers and bickering siblings. 'Be Still My Heart' ends with Carter's being stabbed from behind in a darkened exam room and falling to the floor in agony. Before passing out, he sees that Lucy is also lying on the ground, bleeding profusely just feet away. The fact that Carter and Lucy wind up alone, wounded and near death suggests that neither their relationship as siblings or potential lovers is working. Replete with haunting instrumental music, images of inappropriate penetration and pools of spilled red blood, this grotesque caricature of Valentine's Day tropes clearly enacts 'the message of *ER* that things weren't working the way television had once taught us they should' (Stark, 1997, p. 293). The image of an oblivious, revelling staff enjoying a Valentine's Day party that ends 'Be Still My Heart' and begins 'All in the Family' eulogises the romantic sexual interlude between Carter and Lucy that could have been: significantly, the only other time they share the ER floor is during a failed attempt at impromptu sex. 'All in the Family' features practically the entire ER staff trying to save the two. Lucy dies while awaiting surgery. Her death – figured both as the loss of a child and as the severing of a potentially fruitful heterosex pairing – demonstrates how *ER* tirelessly mourns the heteronormativity irreverently deconstructed in the comedies that precede it.

Saving race

The 'must see' comedies, *Friends* in particular, have been the subject of extensive criticism for their portrayal of the urban centre as a 'totally sanitized bohemia ... without any poor, or the ethnic and racial tensions that plague the city' (Auster, 1996, p. 6). The comedies' treatment of non-normative sexualities occurs concomitantly with the presumption of whiteness as an unmarked category of racial identity. Mutually imbricated with 'must see''s drive towards heteronormativity is a concomitant drive towards racial and ethnic inclusiveness. By 10pm, it seems, the clean, safe and unnaturally pale comedic urban utopia is overrun by people of colour, the urban poor and homeless, and immigrants from a variety of nations speaking a variety of languages with various accents. With lead actors Eriq LaSalle (Peter Benton), Michael Michele (Cleo Finch) and Ming-Na (Jing-Mei Chen) – a host of people of colour in recurring roles – and weekly appearances by guest actors of colour, ER seems actively to work against civil rights groups' condemnations of the networks' lack of representational diversity (Collier, 1999; Gray, 1999; Lowry, 2000; 'New Study', 2000; Zook, 1999). It would seem that the ER symbolises an all-encompassing, multicultural and benevolent 'America'. Yet, such overdetermined diversity only underscores the fact that ER's 'family values' contain, infantilise and punish bodies and identities mapped as othered (either sexually or racially). Many plots involving Greene, Benton and Romano explore such racially charged issues as tokenism in hiring; however, ER's treatment of race and ethnicity assumes a level playing field that flattens the socioeconomic disparities, power differentials and experiences of lived racism that inform the interactions between and among differently empowered groups in the USA. In stark contrast to the comedies, ER does confront and engage with whiteness as a racial category, but it does so primarily through the beleaguered bodies of victimised white men. To watch the show on a regular basis is to bear witness to an almost genocidal assault upon white masculinity carried out through the strictures of bureaucracy, the castrating presence of women in power and, in large part, the malicious, usually unprovoked, violence of black men.

The horrific coupling of Carter and Lucy effected by Paul's butcher knife in 'Be Still My Heart' and 'All in the Family' makes plain ER's position that urban dangers unduly threaten white men and their (real or potential) families. An unsophisticated accounting of acts of violence in the ER would suggest that Paul's attack balances out, say, Mark's beating on the men's room floor by an unidentified black man in the 1997 episode 'Random Acts'. However, violence wreaked by white men takes on a very different valence than that caused by black men. 'All in the Family' mitigates and apologises for Paul's actions in 'Be Still My Heart', revealing that his violent behaviour results from the onset of debilitating paranoid schizophrenia. We know Paul is really just another victimised white male because he is situated within various registers of identity: unlike Mark's anonymous attacker, Paul has a name, a career, a pregnant wife and a chronic disease. In other words, Paul's violence is not his fault.[3]

Paul haunts the ER in more ways than one. He ends Lucy's life, and the stabbing results in Carter's post-traumatic stress disorder and drug addiction. The spectre of a successful white man losing control of his faculties through no fault of his own is revisited through the revelation that Mark has a brain tumour that threatens not only his life, but his speech, self-esteem and professional credibility. Because ER's conceptualisation of heterosexuality is intrinsically tied to its concerns for the safety of white racial identity, the tumour threatens another budding family: Mark's lover, Corday, is also pregnant. That Mark is merely one synaptic blip away from a complete loss of control evidences the vulnerability mapped onto the white male body and, by extension, onto heteronormativity. After all, even before the tumour forces Mark to be examined, probed, irradiated and cut open, he is already the epitome of beleaguered white masculinity: Mark has been naked, impotent, beaten, mutilated, bloodied, caught with his pants down (literally, while being fellated) and dropped from the sky in a helicopter accident.

Sally Robinson has argued that the marking of whiteness and masculinity does not necessarily 'erode their power' (2000, p. 3). Robinson's contention is supported by the way in which *ER*'s epidemic of tormented (innocent) white masculinity necessitates that (guilty) black masculinity be repeatedly associated with gang-banging and other kinds of urban violence. While Paul is recuperated from the role of vicious criminal by his illness, Mark's unknown attacker remains a threat. Because any black man could have attacked Mark, every black man who comes into the ER is suspect. The fact that many who do conceal weapons emblematises how racial difference threatens the physical integrity of white bodies and communities. Even Benton, *ER*'s version of the black male as 'ethical principle' (Appiah, 1993) is sullied by the taint of race, for his nephew dies in a gang-banging, and Benton himself is prone to violent and unpredictable behaviour.

Certainly *ER*'s setting delimits to some degree how and why certain stories get told: injury, illness, accidents and seeping bodies are inescapable. Regardless, certain identities are routinely mapped onto predictably stereotypical pathologies. Most young black men who visit this ER do not have toothaches: they have oozing bullet wounds. Similarly, most gay male patients – always white – suffer from AIDS or HIV-related opportunist diseases, never a less-value-laden diagnosis of, say, appendicitis. 'Must see' 's drive towards greater representational multiplicity moves forth at the expense of those hybrid identities that threaten the fixed categories required to sustain such racist narratives. Thus, the mixed-raced children who come to the ER for treatment are inevitably diagnosed with rare genetic disorders. The only exception is Chen's mixed-race child, Michael, whom she gives up for adoption ostensibly because of her parents' racism – a charge that displaces the burden of racism onto yet another marginalised group, Chinese Americans. (Significantly, Michael is adopted by an Asian/black straight couple so as not to introduce any further racial mixing.) If the ER works to stabilise bodies in distress, *ER* endeavours to prevent the violation of those boundaries that safeguard its structuring dichotomies. The blurring of fixed categories – inside/out, male/female, straight/gay, black/white, urban/rural, life/death – only ever produces devastating, deadly tensions.

During a given Thursday-night block, the composite serial narrative that *Friends* introduces and *ER* concludes charts a path towards proper heteronormativity that tolerates racial difference only insofar as it can contain the threat of miscegenation. It is uniquely convenient, then, that liminal spaces of interracial identity have been denounced publicly by LaSalle, the longest running person of colour lead on the show. LaSalle asked *ER*'s producers to end his character's interracial love affair with Corday, a white British woman, because of his concern about the dearth of positive media images of black heterosexual relationships: 'Hollywood has historically shown that it's neither comfortable with nor interested in Black sensuality or Black-on-Black relationships. ...We don't just have sex and father a bunch of illegitimate children' (see Collier, 1999, p. 52). Who can argue with such a position, particularly given *ER*'s own paternalistic relationship with regard to African-Americans and birth control, abortion, child abuse and even reproduction itself? However, Benton's 'illegitimate' child comes from his relationship with Carla Reese, a black woman. He and Corday have no children. Still, it is Benton's interracial relationship that bears the brunt of LaSalle's criticism:

> I feel it's a shame we can't point to a positive, three-dimensional, fully developed Black-on-Black relationship in recent memory. As a Black artist and as a Black man, I do have a responsibility to my community not to perpetuate things that are detrimental to my community and myself.
>
> See Collier, 1999, p. 52

This criticism is informed by the historically troubled collision of race and gender manifested in pairings of white women and black men that suggest, in racist fashion, that black men have only 'arrived' when they can procure white women. After Benton and Corday's breakup, Benton is paired with Cleo, a biracial character played by a light-skinned biracial actor. Though largely an underdeveloped character, Cleo frequently remarks upon instances of racism and racial tension in the ER, yet Benton routinely disregards or belittles her well-articulated indignation, ever angry at Cleo's trying to teach him how 'to be black'. The widespread publicity and credit garnered by LaSalle's taking on the role of 'race man' (Carby, 1998) in his critique of *ER* both subverts and facilitates the show's efforts to contain his character within familiar racist paradigms – albeit at the expense of interracial desire – and keeps in check the burdens and complexities of racial representation by consigning them onto 'individual difference rather than ... historic and contemporary structured social inequality' (Gray, 1995, p. 166). That the condemnation of interracial relationships and miscegenation can be displaced onto a black male actor participates in 'the maintenance and protection of existing structures and relations of power in terms of class, racial, and gender inequality' (ibid.).

Clearly, *ER* leaves little room for the destabilisation of racial categories. Furthermore, when racial difference and non-normative sexuality are considered together on *ER*, twice as much difference produces exponentially greater dis-ease. In 'The Healers', *ER*'s only recurring gay character of colour, firefighter Raúl Meléndez (Carlos Gómez), for example, is fatally injured in a fiery explosion that highlights how *ER* draws from and contributes to the kinds of rhetoric that pathologise difference and liminality. Suffering burns over 85 per cent of his body, Raúl, at once martyr, monster and pariah, is paraded through the halls of the ER as fellow firefighters look on in horror. That he dies after trying to save two children trapped in a burning building by no means cancels out the image of divine retribution for same-sex desire.

Burns and fire plague *ER*'s considerations of same-sex desire. In the 2000 season, this association recurs, albeit in displaced fashion, when Kerry explores a lesbian relationship. Even before she becomes the vehicle through which *ER* tries to make room for homosex, Kerry is lesbian-coded in stereotypically derogatory ways. Manipulatively pursuing promotion after promotion in medical administration, Kerry epitomises the castrating bitch, a woman empowered with dangerous phallic symbols – the cane she uses to walk (and, occasionally, defend herself) and the sternal saw she brandishes in the ER much to the consternation of her (mostly male) colleagues in surgery. When Kerry first meets Kim Legaspi, their relationship is strained because Kerry thinks they are just friends while Kim obviously wants more. Finally, Kerry gives in and sleeps with Kim. In 'Surrender', Kerry and Kim's first day as lovers frames a story involving Guatemalan factory workers. After Kerry decides – against the advice of a colleague – to report what she suspects are unsafe working conditions, many of the workers, all illegal immigrants, are trapped in the sweatshop after it has been abandoned, locked and set ablaze by unseen proprietors fearing a government raid. Many die in the sweatshop while others suffering electrical, chemical and thermal burns are brought into the ER. Towards the end of 'Surrender', shots of a child left orphaned by the fire and a dying husband are intercut with those of a tortured Kerry, framed amid the chaos of burned bodies. Though Kerry herself does not suffer the consequences of ER's fire-and-brimstone view of gay sex and desire as does Raúl, her desire, nevertheless, has consequences. The persecution of the sweatshop workers, and by extension people of colour, is mapped onto one individual in this community – one whose newly discovered same-sex desire becomes the repository for blame that belongs instead to larger networks of power, namely the exploitative and racist practices of big business and a government bent on curtailing the immigration of undesirably racialised bodies.

Because the 'must see' Thursday block knots sexuality and race in such disquieting ways, it seems unbefitting, at the very least, to celebrate this storyline as an achievement for same-sex representation (Champagne, 2000). Of course, it is pleasurable to witness the infrequent instances during which ER makes representational space for same-sex desire. However, the drive towards heteronormativity enacted every Thursday night cannot be readily undone by Kerry and Kim's awkward kisses or longing glances. More significantly, the drive that pushes to reinstitute heteronormativity – or, at the very least, mourn its demise – laments perceived assaults upon white masculinity and white families, celebrates racial purity and proscribes miscegenation. Furthermore, 'must see''s condemnation of non-normative desires and identities is enacted not only by the drive that sustains and manages one Thursday's viewing but by a similar impetus in larger sequences like November, February and May sweeps; the episodes leading up to season premieres and finales; and the scheduling of reruns. However tenuous or guilty the pleasure the average queer or queer-identified viewer obtains from Friends and manages to hold onto during ER, those pleasurable investments are routinely and crudely crushed when these larger drives not only defer visual pleasure but actively remind viewers of ER's punitive didacticism. 'What's going to happen now that Kim came out to Kerry?' read the various excited e-mails I received from friends and colleagues at the beginning of this much-anticipated storyline. The network rebroadcast 'All in the Family'. That Lucy's bruised, mutilated corpse punctuates Kerry and Kim's blossoming affair makes manifest the ways in which 'must see TV' encourages viewers to 'come together' to bear witness to a nation besieged by the mutually imbricated threats of non-normative identities and desires.

Notes

1. In addition, the show often plays with eroticised triangulations and other polymorphously perverse erotic combinations. For instance, the sexual relationship between Monica and Chandler that began in 1997 has, in some ways, fomented the continuing exploration of Joey and Chandler's erotic friendship. At one point, when Chandler and Monica talk about their possible future together, Chandler envisions a house, children and a room for Joey.

2. I would resist being unduly celebratory of *Friends'* treatment of coming out, particularly since this trope so effortlessly masks the very dangerous realities that public avowal of queer identity entails.

3. Additionally, Paul's attack and paranoia seem precipitated by Carter's painfully cruel and unnecessary spinal tap, another image of inappropriate, (homo)sexualised penetration.

Bibliography

Adalian, Josef, 'Challenge to Keep Peacock Strutting', *Variety* (22 November 1999), p. L18.

Appiah, K. Anthony, ' "No Bad Nigger": Blacks as the Ethical Principle in the Movies', in Marjorie Garber, Jann Matlock and Rebecca L. Walkowitz (eds), *Media Spectacles* (New York: Routledge, 1993), pp. 77–90.

Auster, Albert, 'It's *Friendship...*', *Television Quarterly*, vol. 28, no. 3 (1996) pp. 2–7.

Bellafante, Ginia, 'It's a Friendly Fall', *Time* (11 September 1995), pp. 74–6.

Bellafante, Ginia, 'Meet the Post-*Ally* Women', *Time* (15 February 1998), pp. 70–2.

Berlant, Lauren, *The Queen of America Goes to Washington City: Essays on Sex and Citizenship* (Durham: Duke University Press, 1997).

Bianco, Robert, ' "ER" Lifesaver Exits with a Piece of Our Heart', *USA Today* (11 May 2000), pp. 1Aff.

Brockington, Langdon, '*Seinfeld* Could Hit $2 Mil', *Mediaweek* (9 February 1998), p. 5.

Brophy, Beth, 'The Doctor Is Out', *TV Guide* (6–12 February 1999), pp. 16ff.

Carby, Hazel V., *Race Men: The W. E. B. DuBois Lectures* (Cambridge: Harvard University Press, 1998).

Champagne, Christine, 'Lesbians to *ER* Code Red!', *Gaywatch* (2000), <content.gay.com/channels/arts/gaywatch/er_legaspi.html> (16 February 2001).

Cheers, Video Recording, NBC Television, (1982–93).

Coe, Steve, 'NBC Preens in Prime Time', *Broadcasting & Cable* (26 February 1996), pp. 26–8.

Collier, Aldore D., '*ER* Star Eriq LaSalle', *Ebony* (August 1999), p. 52.

The Cosby Show, Video Recording, NBC Television, (1984–93).

Dubow, Charles, 'Prime Time Anytime', *Forbes.com* (6 April 1999) <forbes.com/1999/04/06/feat> (16 February 2001).

ER, Video Recording, NBC Television, (1994–present).

Family Matters, Video Recording, ABC Television and CBS Television, (1989–98).

Family Ties, Video Recording, NBC Television, (1982–9).

Frasier, Video Recording, NBC television, (1993–present).

'*Frasier* vs. "Stone Cold" Steve?', *Business Week* (6 September 1999), p. 38.

Friends, Video Recording, NBC Television, (1994–present).

Gay, Verne, 'Thursday Payday at NBC', *Advertising Age* (16 June 1986).

Gitlin, Todd, *Inside Prime Time* (Revised Edition) (Berkeley and Los Angeles: University of California Press, 2000).

Gray, Herman, *Watching Race: Television and the Struggle for 'Blackness'* (Minneapolis: University of Minnesota Press, 1995).

Gray, Herman, 'Identities in Crisis: The Politics of Representation in Post-Network American Television', Plenary Presented at the Society for Cinema Studies Convention, West Palm Beach, Florida (15 April 1999).

Grote, David, *The End of Comedy: The Sit-Com and the Comedic Tradition* (Hamden, CT: Archon, 1983).

Gunther, Marc, 'Yo, NBC: Enough Already!', *Fortune* (26 May 1997), pp. 24ff.

Heuton, Cheryl, 'Summertime Blues', *Mediaweek* (21 August 1995), p. 13.

Hill Street Blues, Video Recording, NBC Television, (1980–7).

Just Shoot Me, Video Recording, NBC Television, (1997–present).

Lesly, Elizabeth, '*Seinfeld* : The Economics of a TV Supershow and What It Means for NBC and the Industry', *Business Week* (2 June 1997), pp. 116–21.

Lowry, Brian, 'Sitcom Cloning Makes No "Friends" among Crix', *Variety* (31 July–6 August 1995), pp. 21ff.

Lowry, Brian, 'NBC: Last-Minute Deal Locks in *Friends* for Fall', *Los Angeles Times* (15 May 2000), n. pag. Electronic.

Mandese, Joe, ' "ER" Resuscitates NBC in Prime Time', *Advertising Age* (1 May 1995a), pp. 3ff.

Mandese, Joe, 'Seinfeld Is NBC's $1M/Minute-Man', *Advertising Age* (18 September 1995b), pp. 1ff.

Marin, Rick, 'Triumph of a Coffee Bar Hamlet', *Newsweek* (24 April 1995), pp. 68–9.

Marin, Rick. 'Let the Backlash Begin!', *Newsweek* (12 February 1996), p. 77.

McClellan, Steve, 'Feeding the Peacock', *Broadcasting & Cable* (9 February 1998), pp. 22–7.

Medhurst, Andy, '*Friends* of Yours', *Sight and Sound*, vol. 6, no. 10 (1996), pp. 16–18.

NBC, 'Print Advertisement', *Entertainment Weekly* (29 September 2000a), pp. 2–5.

NBC, 'Video Recorded Advertisement', NBC Television (27 September 2000b).

'New Study by the Screen Actors Guild Found That African Americans on Television Are "Ghettoized" and Underrepresented on Both Fox and NBC', *Broadcasting & Cable* (28 February 2000), p. 69.

Owen, Rob, *Gen X TV: The Brady Bunch to Melrose Place* (New York: Syracuse University Press, 1997).

Rice, Lynette, 'Comedies Focus on Family', *Broadcasting & Cable* (3 March 1997), pp. 24–5.

Robins, J. Max, 'Mad Ave. Mad about NBC', *Variety* (1–7 April 1996), pp. 37ff.

Robinson, Sally, *Marked Men: White Masculinity in Crisis* (New York: Columbia University Press, 2000).

Ross, Chuck, 'NBC Mulls Fewer, Longer Ad Breaks', *Advertising Age* (13 April 1998), p. 4.

Saenz, Michael K., 'Television Viewing as a Cultural Practice', in Horace Newcomb (ed.), *Television: the Critical View* (5th edn) (New York: Oxford University Press, 1994), pp. 573–86.

Schlosser, Joe, 'NBC Heavies up on Drama', *Broadcasting & Cable* (22 November 1999), p. 28.

Schmuckler, Eric, 'NBC Eyes Thursday', *Mediaweek* (4 January 1993).

Schmuckler, Eric, 'NBC: An Owner's Manual', *Mediaweek* (26 September 1994), pp. 18–23.

Scott, Tony, 'Rev. of *Friends*', *Variety* (19–25 September 1994), p. 50.

Seinfeld, Video Recording, NBC Television, (1989–98).

Sellers, John, 'Remote Possibilities: The Big TV Turn-ons, and Turnoffs, of 99', *Us* (October 1999), pp. 83–8.

Sharkey, Betsy, 'Sink-or-Swim Time', *Mediaweek* (22 September 1997), pp. 25–30.

Sharkey, Betsy, 'Master of His Domain', *Brandweek* (1 June 1998), pp. U26–U37.

Stanley, T. L., 'Must-Flee TV', *Mediaweek* (8 April 1996a), pp. 9ff.

Stanley, T. L., 'The *Single Guy* Guy', *Mediaweek* (18 November 1996b), pp. 28ff.

Stark, Steven D., *Glued to the Set: The 60 Television Shows and Events That Made Us Who We Are Today* (New York: Free, 1997).

Stempel, Tom, *Storytellers to the Nation: A History of American Television Writing* (New York: Continuum, 1992).

Taylor, Cathy, 'Tube Watchers, Unite', *Mediaweek* (11 November 1996), pp. 32–3.

Thompson, Robert J., *Television's Second Golden Age: From* Hill Street Blues *to* ER (New York: Continuum, 1996).

Tobenkin, David, 'It's All in the Family TV', *Broadcasting & Cable* (3 June 1996), pp. 24ff.

Tucker, Ken, 'Rev. of *Friends*', *Entertainment Weekly* (21 November 1997), p. 106.

Weston, Kath, *Families We Choose: Lesbians, Gays, Kinship* (New York: Columbia University Press, 1991).

Will & Grace, Video Recording, NBC Television, (1998–present).

Zoglin, Richard, '*Friends* and Layabouts', *Time* (20 March 1995), p. 74.

Zook, Kristal Brent, *Color by Fox: The Fox Network and the Revolution in Black Television* (New York: Oxford University Press, 1999).

4

The Changing Face of American Television Programmes on British Screens

Paul Rixon

[Imports are] seen as alien, to a large degree, and looked down on ... I think it's bad because there is a perception ... that if it's American it's crap.

Programme buyer, BBC (1993)

Introduction

With the coming of commercial television in the 1950s American programmes began to appear on British screens in larger numbers than ever before. On Independent Television (ITV) these imports, interlaced and cut apart by advertisements, danced to a modern upbeat commercial rhythm; on the BBC, while adverts were absent the rhythm remained exposing the slowness of existing fare. These were shows offering a glimpse of a more prosperous consumerist future, one that had, seemingly, arrived across the Atlantic. American shows, like *I Love Lucy*, *Dragnet*, *Gunsmoke* and *Highway Patrol* that spoke in a more 'universal', populist Americanised voice, quickly dominated the ratings. In 1955 a love affair between the British public and American programmes began; a love affair that, even with its ups and downs, has influenced much of the television that we have watched and enjoyed over the last forty-five years.

However, such programmes have not been without their critics; over time they have been lambasted for their violence, simplicity, vacuity and commercialism. Indeed for some they are 'televisual polyfiller', filling the gaps between quality domestic programmes with any signs of popularity being viewed in a derogatory fashion; a sign of programmes built to pander to the needs of the lowest common denominator. The establishment view has been one of British television as the best in the world with American programmes appearing mostly for cost reasons. By the 1990s, with few American programmes appearing in the top 100-rated programmes, some felt that the love affair was finally over and British audiences were now bored of US imports (Phillips, 1997; *The Times*, 1995).

I would like to argue in this chapter that American programmes, though not always visible in either the rating charts or prime time, are an important part of British television. They have, since the 1950s, coaxed British producers to learn 'from American technical innovations and from American talents in winning consenting audiences' (Marwick, 1991, p. 87). They have helped innovate and create new forms of genre and provide models for more streamlined forms of production (Segrave, 1998, p. 219). While encouraging British television to change American programmes have, in their own right, been popular with the general public and fans alike (Strinati and Wagg, 1992, p. 59). Over time they have become fixtures in the schedules, sometimes playing in prime time, sometimes in the off-peak hours. Indeed, some US imports have now become 'must see' programmes. It would seem, as Jeremy Tunstall points out, that American programmes have had a role that is greater than often assumed (1977, p. 271).

While American programmes have become part of our television culture, their role and importance has been hidden, dismissed and much maligned by the dominant historical, popular and critical discourses. Such approaches have mostly focused on the workings of the indigenous broadcasting system and its output with little regard to the way imported programmes become part of the British schedules. Before I go on to explore the changing face of American programmes on our screens, I will first argue the need for a new understanding of their role.

Broadcasting as British; television as programmes

In the seminal histories of the BBC and ITV written, respectively, by Asa Briggs (1961, 1965, 1970, 1979, 1995) (soon to be continued by Jean Seaton), Bernard Sendall (1982, 1983) and later Jeremy Potter (1989, 1990) and Paul Bonner and Lesley Aston (1998), the coverage of American programmes on British screens is minimal. Where reference is made it is often only as a name check, as part of a programme list and, occasionally, for the more well-known works such as *I Love Lucy*, with small descriptions. For example Briggs, in Volume V of his work on the BBC (1995), makes only two references to *Dr Kildare,* though in the early 1960s it was one of the rare BBC programmes in the top twenty; likewise *Star Trek*, a programme that came to be a staple diet of audiences from the 1960s onwards, gets one mention in relation to the home-grown sci-fi series *Dr Who* (p. 417). In a similar way Sendall, in Volume I of his history of ITV (1982), makes scant reference to American imports, for example three minor references to *I Love Lucy* whose star, Lucille Ball, was to become, 'a fixture on ... ITV or BBC for many years to come' (p. 322). Where Sendall does touch on such imports in more detail it is mostly dealing with quotas or their supposed societal effects (1983, pp. 98–102). Programmes that often topped the ratings, that were often the leading draws of their time, which stayed on our screens for years if not decades, are often only covered as footnotes – if at all. The stress throughout such historical works is on British productions, those such as *Hancock's Half Hour, That Was the Week That Was (TW3), Morecambe and Wise, Z Cars, The Ten O' Clock News, The Jewel in the Crown,* etc. It is as if domestically made programmes are British television while American programmes are mere interlopers.

Other more critical and analytical accounts that touch directly or indirectly on the relationship between British television and US imports have also often tended to view and dismiss American programmes in a derogatory way. The mass media discourse, appearing in the early part of the last century, has generally been concerned with how Americanisation and commercialisation, the two are usually conflated, are eroding our national culture – whether in terms of an élite or common culture (for a debate on the discourse around this issue, see Hebdige, 1989). Likewise media and cultural imperialism approaches view the influx of American cultural products as leading to cultural domination and an undermining of the local culture and identity (Dunkley, 1985; Schiller, 1969; Tunstall, 1977). Such discourses seem to suggest that there is some form of essential national television culture, one constituted by indigenous productions that American programmes are endangering.

In reaction to these accounts and their presumption of media effects, 'recent' audience work has sought to explore how audiences actually read imported television texts (two American soaps most famously focused on have been *Dallas* and *Dynasty*: Ang, 1985; Gripsrud, 1995; Katz and Liebes, 1985). While they have shown television texts to be polysemic, stressing the importance of the local cultural and social context of reception in the meaning produced, they have focused on the reading experience of identifiable programmes. They have mostly looked at discreet texts outside the schedule or programme 'flow' within which they are experienced. Those that have touched on what has been referred to as the super-text and mega-text that exists around such programmes have often argued that, at the end of the day, these can be, and should be, stripped away allowing analysis of the 'program proper' (Gripsrud, 1995, pp. 131–3).

Few have looked at the role and use of American programmes on our screens, the selective view they give of American culture, the way they affect the other programmes around them and how they become part of our whole cultural experience of television (one useful exception being Geoffrey Lealand [1984] who focuses on the way British audiences view American programmes on British screens). There has been little attempt to explore how American programmes have become a part of a site where the 'nation is constructed for its members' (Hartley, 1978, p. 124). Indeed, it could be argued that the question should not be one of an alien culture invading our screens, but how American programmes work as part of our television culture; how they merge, conflate and exist in the flow of programmes that make up the 'national' schedule; as Morley and Robins suggest, 'perhaps America is now within, now part of a European cultural repertoire, part of European identity' (1995, p. 57).

There are, however, some who have at a theoretical level, taken up and developed the notion of television as a form of flow, whether a flow structured by broadcasters into a schedule or flows as experienced by audiences, though there are differences in their accounts (Ellis, 1982, 2000; Paterson, 1990; Williams, 1978). These works stress the experience of watching television not as one of discrete programmes but, instead, as one of different types of narrative flows within and between programmes, trailers, adverts and channels. While some have criticised the lack of precision of this concept (Corner, 1999, pp. 60–9) this does not lessen the need for an approach that can begin to help conceptualise how and why television is constructed as it is and the way it is experienced, whether or not the programmes are domestic productions or acquired.

As Ellis notes:

> the factors that make every nation's television specific are ... not just to do with individual quirks ... so much as with the architecture of the entire output. As such, they are not easily amenable to the traditional forms of content analysis which privilege the systems of particular texts. Instead, they are produced and reproduced within the dynamic process of scheduling.
>
> Ellis, 2000, p. 36

A new approach

Any new approach must move away from the crude rather stilted view of imports as pernicious flows across borders offering little to the recipient nation; it must be able to help us understand how domestic and foreign programmes – acquired and commissioned – are shaped and placed in such a way to work dynamically together on our screens. This approach will have to be able to take account of the processes at work at three interconnecting levels: at the macro, focusing on the international flows of programmes and the changing relationships between national systems, broadcasters and producers; at the meso level (middle), where the focus will be on the schedule, the flow of programmes as constructed by particular organisations and broadcasters; and at the last level will be the micro – here there is a need to understand how different textual devices operate within programmes and the flow of programmes and how the viewer watches, experiences and makes sense of television (a similar approach to that outlined by Sepstrup, 1989).

In the remaining pages I will begin to explore aspects of the second level, the meso. I want to begin by sketching out the changing contours of American programmes on our screens over the last fifty-five years, looking at what was shown, when and its apparent popularity (this work will pull from an analysis of rating material and television schedules of the time). I will follow this by exploring, through a series of interviews with programme buyers, the way they actively shape the face of American programmes appearing on our screens (note that I will concentrate on TV programmes, series and serials, and will ignore American films because of the limits of space and the slightly different processes at work). This work, hopefully, will be a tentative first step in exploring how the national schedule is constructed and how any 'imported show is inserted into this context of scheduling and its cultural identity is significantly altered as a result' (Ellis, 2000, p. 36).

Changing contours

It was with the coming of ITV in 1955 that American television programmes first found a major place on UK screens. The reason for this was linked to a number of factors: the need to quickly fill hours before the ITV production base was fully developed; the appearance of a tradeable object when American television networks started to use filmed product (Anderson, 1994); the push to sell American programmes by US distributors; a need to attract audiences; the initial lack of advertising revenue; and demands by audiences to watch something less edifying than the programmes provided by the BBC (Segrave, 1998, pp. 49–53).

Within the first full year of operation ITV dominated all the places in the top twenty rating chart for London, its initial area of operation: of these five were US imports (*Dragnet*, *Gun Law* [a.k.a *Gunsmoke*], *Frontier Doctor*, *Fairbanks Presents* [NBC-commissioned programme made in the UK] and *Assignment Foreign Legion*) and four British series based on US game-show formats including *The $64,000 Question* and *Double Your Money* (Harbord and Wright, 1992, p. 1). Though some have pointed out that the poor showing by the BBC was not just related to its programmes, many of these were popular with audiences, but how it scheduled these; programmes would often fall indiscriminately next to each other driving viewers to turn to ITV (Crisell, 1997, p. 88).

Initially the BBC and ITV found themselves struggling to produce programmes that could stand up to many of those being imported from the USA: 'British television could produce nothing to approach them [American comedy shows] for style or suitability to television' (Goddard, 1991, p. 77). To compete the BBC joined in, on a lesser scale than ITV, buying in American comedy, police and cowboy programmes, often in sizeable numbers (Segrave, 1998, p. 27). Indeed, for a number of months in the early 1960s it was *Dr Kildare*, a US import, which was the most watched BBC programme (December 1961 and January 1962). However, the annual ratings for the period 1957–64 give the impression that there were only two huge American hits, *Wagon Train* and *Rawhide*; it might therefore seem as if the initial rush of American imports was short lived. Though, if one looks at schedules from the time one can see that ITV, the channel dominating the ratings in this period, was not networking all its prime-time shows, thus the regional popularity of some American shows was not always translated into national viewing figures. Popularity for American imports had not so much waned as been hidden by the nature of the domestic television system.

During the 1960s the relationship between ITV and BBC stabilised producing a period known as the duopoly – where competition occurred less over audiences than over the programmes being produced. Production facilities had now been built, advertising and licence fee income was rising and money was being spent to create more populist domestic programmes. The system had over the years learned how to create product that could, in some way, substitute for some of the bought-in programming. For example, *Z Cars*, a popular hit of the 1960s, was in some ways, inspired by *Highway Patrol* (Laing, 1991, p. 127); comedies began to experiment with the sitcom format often measuring themselves against the slick American imports, for example *Hancock's Half-Hour* (Goddard, 1991, pp. 75–89). Indeed, following on from the early success of *Robin Hood*, ATV began to create American-style shows that were successful on both sides of the Atlantic (often referred to as mid-Atlantic shows) such as *The Avengers* and *Danger Man*. Many of the prime-time American shows were increasingly displaced by domestic productions. Indeed, at the very moment that ITV began to sort out its national network schedule (Sendall, 1983, pp. 225–55) the prime-time slots available for American shows were shrinking (Segrave, 1998, p. 146).

American programmes now had a new role, to fill up the outer reaches of the growing schedule (the hours broadcast increased from the 1950s onwards with all government restrictions ending in 1972, see Sendall, 1989, pp. 70–1) and building lead-in audiences for domestic productions. Between the years 1965 and 1975 no US programmes appeared in the annual top twenty rated programmes, though when American shows were occasionally shown in peak slots they made the monthly charts. *A Man Called Ironside*, for example was one of the higher-placed BBC programmes in the late 1960s and early 70s.

From the mid-1970s to the early 80s, as the country faced an economic recession (Goodwin, 1998, p. 3), there was a renaissance of American programmes. Led by the likes of *Charlie's Angels, Fame, Cagney and Lacey, Hart to Hart, Dallas, The Six Million Dollar Man, Starsky and Hutch* and *The A-team,* American programmes again appeared in prime-time slots and the annual and monthly top twenty rating charts. Indeed, for some of the months they were the most watched, for example *Dallas* was number one in April 1980. Between 1980 and 1984 American programmes shown on British screens took two of the top twenty positions in the annual rating charts. For the BBC the position was more striking, with some months' American programmes providing their highest placing in the charts: in January 1978 *Starsky and Hutch* was nineteenth with 14.1 million viewers, the only BBC programme in the top twenty for that month (Harbord and Wright, 1992). It is interesting to note that in 1982 some 26 per cent of the BBC's prime time was American-sourced (Segrave, 1998, p. 202).

It would seem that for the period 1975–85, when provided peak-time slots some American shows were able to attract large audiences. These were programmes that had content, a style, a form and a cultural cache that were popular at this time. While there were British productions of the same genre that could compete and provide similar forms of entertainment, such as *The Sweeney* and *The Professionals*, many programmes were not as glossy and as fast paced as the American programmes nor made in the huge numbers that gave them a sustained presence; such programmes could also be obtained more cheaply than being produced domestically. In many ways the British broadcasters were still caught up in a system that privileged serious programming – single author texts, short serials and historical drama – often made in short runs with a form of realism that was not, at the time, that appealing (Paterson, 1998, p. 59). Far from American shows being unable to compete against domestic equivalents, as some suggest (ibid., p. 58), it would appear that, if given the right slot, they could. However, as Tunstall points out, imports were often not placed in the most advantageous position for attracting audiences:

> Most broadcast schedulers want to demonstrate that domestic programming gets the highest figures – and, even though this might well happen anyway, it can be made certain through scheduling. Often the most popular imports are not quite so popular as the local imitations of them; but the imports may be scheduled for different purposes – to attract advertisers into particular commercial breaks, or to build up the early evening audience for peak-time local product.
>
> Tunstall, 1977, p. 275

As the 1980s progressed the duopoly ended with the coming of Channel 4, Sky and BSB (now merged into BSkyB), followed more recently by Channel 5. As production costs rose, as hours broadcast and competition increased, American programmes took on new roles. While the two main channels, ITV and BBC, competed in the peak hours with domestically produced programmes, especially in terms of popular drama, American product was used to help fill some off-peak slots; for example ITV used American material to help fill its new twenty-four-hour schedule. The smaller channels, BBC2 and Channel 4, however, used some American material as important scheduling cornerstones attracting minority niche audiences, including the use of sci-fi series such as *Star Trek* and US films in the DEF II youth slot; while new satellite and cable channels often with few resources and even fewer viewers than their terrestrial competitors used substantial amounts of American material throughout the schedule.

Channel 4, in particular, followed a strategy of marketing and advertising a number of American programmes, building up the profile of these shows to attract a younger, more affluent audience (fifteen- to thirty-five-year-olds mostly in the ABC1 category). Helped by the appearance of new 'quality' productions, such as *Hill Street Blues*, Channel 4 began to refine the image and appeal of American programmes. Soon American programmes, partly helped by Channel 4's use of them within its schedule and partly by the start of the so-called second golden age of television in the USA, were sought-after programmes – by some viewers and broadcasters. Indeed, the television critics, once dismissive of American imports (Strinati and Wagg, 1992, p. 72), slowly came to praise them (see Collins, 2000). These programmes shown on Channel 4 (and on BBC2) in and around prime time were, for some, 'must see' programmes (Crisell, 1997, pp. 238–9; Segrave, 1998, p. 157).

In the 1990s while American programmes were increasingly banished on the two main terrestrial channels, ITV and BBC1, to the afternoon, early-morning and late-night slots, on BBC2 and Channel 4 American programmes continued to play a small but important role, supporting the schedule and attracting sought-after audiences. For example *The Simpsons*, *Star Ship Voyager* and *Buffy the Vampire Slayer* are often the most viewed programmes for BBC2, while *Friends* and *ER* frequently appear in Channel 4's most viewed list (Broadcasters Audience Research Board). For satellite and cable channels they are often the mainstay of the output: for most of 1999–2000 Sky One's top-viewed programmes were dominated by the *The Simpsons*, *Buffy the Vampire Slayer* and various sci-fi programmes. However, it must be noted, that some satellite and cable channels have appeared acting as second-run channels showing repeats of old British favourites, such as UK Gold, and that channels like Sky One are moving slowly into making more domestic product, including *The Sight*, *Harry Enfield's Brand Spanking New Show* and *Time Gentlemen Please*. Also some domestic productions have appeared that seem, in style and content, to have continued to learn from American programmes: *This Life* and *Cold Feet*, with their fast-paced, young casts and witty tight scripts could be viewed as responses to US programmes such as *Friends* and *thirtysomething*.

By the 1990s, because of Channel 4's continued financial success and, for some, their over-dependence on a large number of US imports, the Independent Television Commission (ITC) moved to force Channel 4 to use more domestic productions (Beavis and Ahmed, 1998). However, at the start of 2001, at the very moment that Channel 4 moved to reduce its reliance on bought-in programmes, it started a new digital channel, E4, that used many of its successful US imports as a draw (Collins, 2001). Programmes such as *Ally McBeal*, *ER* and *Friends,* initially made popular on Channel 4, now have their first run on E4; in many ways Channel 4 is now partly, in American television parlance, a second-run channel. It would seem that American programmes are now attractions in their own right; they have become the reason to subscribe to a channel and no longer just 'televisual polyfiller' (Brown, 2000).

The account above suggests that the role of American programmes on British screens is not simple and in continual decline – instead it is changeable and dynamic. While American programmes since the 1960s have often been side-lined to off-peak slots on the main TV channels, as the competitive environment has changed so the profile and use of American programmes by different channels has taken new paths. While on some channels they are still mostly banished to the late-night or daytime slots, on some they are presented and used as important 'must-see' programmes in the schedule and with new cable and satellite channels they often occupy much of their prime time. And where US imports have been displaced from prime time it is often by similar domestic productions.

I now wish to explore the relationship between the needs of the 'national' schedules and the supply of US programmes further, indeed to focus on the process by which programmes are selected and bought. This I will do by analysing a series of interviews with those who were acquiring programmes for the main UK channels (BBC, ITV, Channel 4 and Sky) during the 1990s.

Television's gatekeepers

Sitting between the national and international regime, between American programme distributors and British schedules, are programme buyers. They, along with the schedulers, are the guardians of our screens, selecting, filtering and buying American programmes for the national schedules. I will now explore the dynamic role they play in buying programmes that suit the changing needs and profiles of the different national channels.

Currently the actual amount of prime-time material used by ITV and BBC1 is limited as many of the slots are filled by domestic product. This the buyers put down to two main reasons: first, the lack of US material that could play at this time: 'Nothing is coming out of America that can play ... and get a good audience in these prime-time slots'; second, that domestic programmes help make a channel distinctive: 'you can't ... be distinctive if you're filling your schedules with exactly the same programming that BSkyB has' (Buyer, BBC). Though one buyer did note that, 'if something appeared on American television that had all the signs of being a huge hit ... [BBC1] would obviously be interested' – a programme like *The X Files* that has played in the 9.30 slot on BBC1 might well fall into this category. However, all buyers noted that with the huge number of slots available throughout the whole schedule there is always a need for acquired material.

For BBC2 and Channel 4 the needs are different: 'The real quality shows you actually target on BBC2 and Channel 4, not on the main channels.' Here 'quirky' American shows such as *Buffy the Vampire Slayer* and *Roswell High,* have helped BBC2 gain 'a certain profile' with particular audiences (Buyer, BBC); likewise Channel 4 has marketed and used 'quality' shows such as *Frasier, Friends, Homicide, The Sopranos* and *ER* to help create a reputation of showing cutting-edge home-grown and imported drama and comedy. For Sky One, with a heavy reliance on American imports, the question has been more one of balance: 'within the schedule you [need] a mix ... it is quite difficult to have undigested American programming spewing at the audience without a levelling of ... Britishness' (Buyer, Sky One).

It was suggested that the job of acquired material was threefold: to release funds for domestic productions, to help support domestic productions and to attract audiences, '... if we were to fully finance everything that we showed our money would not stretch to 6,000 hours a year' (Buyer, Channel 4), though the strategies followed differ between broadcasters. For the larger channels, BBC1 and ITV, imports are now mostly used to fill late-night and daytime hours, with a few exceptions, such as *The X Files*; on the smaller channels – for example Sky One, BBC2 and Channel 4 – American programmes occasionally play an important role in their own right helping to provide a cornerstone for building the schedule around or in helping to create niche blocks targeted at particular audiences for which enough suitable programme material is not always available – 'the [US] comedies are in a sense building blocks ... it is in fact a combination of American and British comedies [that play] ... on Friday' (Buyer, Channel 4).

The buyers do not just purchase good-looking material; they have to select the right programme for the profile of the channel, the audience aimed for, and the domestic programmes being shown around that slot. The aim is to purchase programmes that add something to the channel:

> ... the important thing is to find programming which has a quality profile that fits the channel, whether it's BBC1 or BBC2 may affect that, but it has to have the feel that is appropriate and suitable for the channel ... and is likely to draw a good audience.
>
> Buyer, BBC

With competition around certain films and programme series distributors have increasingly sold sought-after programmes in large packages or, as Segrave notes (1998, p. 172), in volume, a practice that has been going on for some time. The hope for distributors is twofold: to get a showing for such programmes to stimulate later sales and to off-load material that might not otherwise find a buyer. This can lead to a situation of programmes being bought and never shown, sometimes for competitive reasons and sometimes because of scheduling problems (for example *Millennium* was bought by ITV but, because of the violence, some of the episodes could not be broadcast in a commercial slot [Phillips, 1997, p. 30]), or programmes shown that were never wanted in the first place – in some ways going against the view of buyers as the all-powerful guardians of our screens:

> Some of the deals done to pick up the long-established comedies involve taking other material at the same time they are sold as a package. In order to get *Cosby* picked up, or *Roseanne*, I might pick whatever Viacom has produced as a new series. Because there is no way I'm going to say 'sorry Viacom I don't want *Cosby* or *Roseanne* this year if you want us to take all that new stuff you've made this year'. And they know that, so we actually get material that, in an ideal world, I wouldn't have bought.
>
> Buyer, Channel 4

Many purchasers noted that, as new competition weakened their position of strength in the marketplace, there was an increased need to be aware of what was happening in America. For example, to keep abreast of how well a possible future purchase is doing in America, its reception by the critics and press and whether or not it might be cancelled (when *Baywatch* was cancelled by US networks ITV and other European broadcasters quickly stepped in to keep it in production: Bonner and Aston, 1998, pp. 105–7), indeed to keep an eye out for the next big thing. One strategy buyers have taken on is waiting to see how a series is playing before purchasing it:

> What we did last year was rather than go in May (to Los Angeles), we [BBC] and ITV actually went in November … this allowed us to see more episodes of the show that made it onto the full schedule, which also allowed us to assess how the shows were doing.
>
> Buyer, BBC

As competition in the American broadcasting market has increased, as new networks and TV channels have appeared, indeed as the internet cuts into television audiences, so the product being made has changed: many of the buyers noted the appearance of programmes aimed at a younger audience;

> … the trend at this moment is definitely towards a youth/younger audience. Now that's been partly brought about by the rising profile of Fox Broadcasting … they have made a very definite play for a younger audience, and that is reflected in the kinds of shows they have.
>
> Buyer, BBC

Such programmes that have appeared in the 1990s include the rather sassy, knowing *Buffy the Vampire Slayer*, *Angel*, *Dawson's Creek*, *Roswell High* and *Popular* that explore teenage angst in a number of different contexts. These programmes have managed to cater to the desires of both teenagers and the ageing 'youth' markets still wishing to live out their teenage fantasies. Other more adult-oriented drama, attracting the older ABC1 grouping, has developed with programmes such as *Homicide*, *NYPD Blue*, *ER* and *The Sopranos* following on in the tradition of *Hill Street Blues*. These present large ensemble casts in well-crafted multi-layered narratives that explore a side of American society missing from the early formulaic action series like *Starsky and Hutch* or *Kojak* (Thompson, 1997). Others, like the sci-fi genre, have become more refined and specialised for fans, often appearing in blocks or with associated programmes in the schedule or on specialised channels, for example programmes like *Babylon 5* and channels such as the Sci-Fi Channel. Cartoons series like *Bob and God*, *The Simpsons*, *South Park* and *King of the Hill* have appeared that, in various ways, critique American culture and society in a way alien to the earlier cartoons more specifically aimed at children, such as *Scooby Doo* and *Tom and Jerry*. There have also been programmes harder to pigeonhole, programmes such as *Oz*, *Ally McBeal* and *Sex in the City*, which, following on from the reflexive 1980s series *Moonlighting*, present rather surreal views of life in America, often touching on once taboo TV subjects such as fellatio, S&M and sodomy.

Where *Dallas* and the like once rode high in the ratings and were popular with mass audiences, many of the new successful US programmes are mostly 'must see' for smaller audience groups who have to search out these programmes. For example *The Sopranos*, a series much praised by critics, has been shown at 10.30 on Channel 4 with an expectation that an audience will seek it out. However, while small audiences do seek out American programmes placed in late-night slots, many feel that such programmes are being wasted, indeed treated with disrespect:

> It was last week when I could stand it no longer. I put in a call to BBC2 and hit them with four words they fear most, 'I'm calling about *Seinfeld*.' I know, and they know (and they know I know) that they have handled their scheduling of this prince among sitcoms shamefully, kicking it around the schedules like an old tin can, so that even dedicated fans can't find it.
>
> Kelner, 2000

Seemingly while American product attracts sizeable audiences, and dedicated audiences at that, it is still viewed and used by many in the industry as 'cement to fill in the cracks between ... fine domestic output' (ibid.). What is important for the broadcaster is still its domestic product. Even Channel 4, a channel that has built its success and indeed identity on some American programmes, has sometimes treated US series in a derogatory fashion. For example, Channel 4 moved the multi-Emmy-award-winning programme *The West Wing* to what has been described as a graveyard slot at 11.05pm (*The Guardian*, 2001).

As much as the domestic environment has changed leading to different requirements and uses of American programmes, so too has American programming. Sometimes the two are in tune with America producing what the buyers are looking for, and sometimes not. Sometimes the material bought can play prime time and attract an audience and sometimes it cannot. Recently American producers have created programmes that, with the right slots and marketing, are very popular with sections of the audience that British broadcasters are keen to attract; these 'must see' programmes while not watched by all, and while not riding high in the rating charts, have become well known to those that watch them, and even to the British public as a whole. Sitting at the gateway between the US producers and British screens have been the buyers, it is they that have, since the 1950s, dynamically shaped the face of American programmes on our screens, seeking programmes that fit the different needs of the channels and schedules for which they work.

Conclusion

As has been argued above, to truly understand British television, the shape and form it has taken over the last fifty-five years, requires an understanding of the dynamic role taken by American programmes: how and where they played in our schedules, how they influenced domestic productions and widened the experiences of viewers and broadcasters alike. However, as we look to the future we must accept that the gatekeeping roles exercised by national channels in shaping the American programmes we view will lessen; with direct links to American networks and programme producers a possibility (via satellite, cable or the internet) (Segrave, 1998, pp. 213–39), with the appearance of themed channels, pay-TV and the introduction of technologies like TiVo (a personal video recorder) [PVR] able to seek out and record programmes according to a user's personal profile) the way we experience and watch American programmes will change. Once we watched the cream of American television, encased and infused within our national schedules; soon it will be possible to experience it in a more unmediated fashion, warts and all. However, while American programmes are popular there is evidence that audiences do not want to watch undiluted American programmes (see Lealand, 1984).

Once a few broadcasters determined the type and amount of American programmes on our screens, from which audiences selected their viewing, but as the gateways open up it will be the viewer who will increasingly determine what to watch and when. It might, however, be that the audience, though differentiated in what they will view, will be as selective as current programme buyers. Perhaps the important shift will not be towards the end of gatekeepers, but towards viewers being their own gatekeepers, actively selecting and constructing their own personal schedules, seeking out the well-advertised and marketed product, whether from home or abroad, often highlighted by critics as the 'must see' programmes of a new era.

Bibliography

Anderson, Christopher, *Hollywood TV: The Studio System in the Fifties* (Austin: University of Texas Press, 1994).

Ang, Ien, *Watching Dallas: Soap Opera and the Melodramatic Imagination* (London: Methuen, 1985).

Beavis, Simon and Ahmed, Kamal, 'ITV stations hit out at Channel 4's "populism"', *The Guardian* (20 January 1998).

Bonner, Paul and Aston, Lesley, *Independent Television in Britain*, vol. 5 (London: Macmillan, 1998).

Briggs, Asa, *The History of Broadcasting in the United Kingdom*, vols I–V (Oxford: Oxford University Press, 1961, 1965, 1970, 1979, 1995).

Brown, Maggie, 'With Friends Like These ...', *The Guardian* (6 November 2000).

Buscombe, Edward, 'All Bark and No Bite: The Film Industry's Response to Television', in John Corner (ed.), *Popular Television in Britain* (London: BFI, 1991), pp. 197–207.

Caughie, John, 'Before the Golden Age: Early Television Drama', in John Corner (ed.), *Popular Television in Britain* (London: BFI, 1991), pp. 22–41.

Collins, Andrew, 'TV duel: may the best family win', *The Guardian* (15 October 2000).

Collins, Andrew, 'Can you tell your E4 from your C4?', *The Guardian* (7 January 2001).

Collins, Richard, *Television: Policy and Culture* (London: Unwin Hyman, 1990).

Corner, John (ed.), *Popular Television in Britain* (London: BFI, 1991).

Corner, John, *Critical Ideas in Television Studies* (Oxford: Clarendon Press, 1999).

Crisell, Andrew, *An Introductory History of British Broadcasting* (London: Routledge, 1997).

Dunkley, Christopher, *Wall-to-Wall Dallas* (London: Penguin, 1985).

Ellis, John, *Visible Fictions* (London: Routledge and Kegan Paul, 1982).

Ellis, John, 'Scheduling: the last creative act in television?', *Media, Culture and Society*, vol. 22 (2000), pp. 25–38.

Goddard, Peter, ' "Hancock's Half Hour": A Watershed in British Television Comedy', in John Corner (ed.), *Popular Television in Britain* (London: BFI, 1991), pp. 75–89.

Goodwin, Peter, *Television under the Tories: Broadcasting Policy 1979–1997* (London: BFI, 1998).

Gripsrud, Jostein, *The Dynasty Years: Hollywood Television and Critical Media Studies* (London: Routledge, 1995).

The Guardian, 'Screen Grabs: Coming to a box near you' (23 April 2001).

Harbord, Jane and Wright, Jeff, *40 Years of British Television* (London: Boxtree, 1992).

Hartley, John, 'Invisible fictions', *Textual Practice*, vol. 1, no. 2 (1978), pp. 121–38.

Hebdige, Dick, *Hiding in the Light* (London: Routledge, 1989).

Hoggart, Richard, *The Uses of Literacy* (London: Pelican, 1965).

Katz, Elihu and Liebes, Tamar, 'Mutual Aid in the Decoding of *Dallas*: Preliminary Notes from a Cross-Cultural Study', in Peter Drummond and Richard Paterson (eds), *Television in Transition: Papers from the First International Television Studies Conference* (London: BFI, 1985).

Kelner, Martin, 'King of New York', *The Guardian* (10 October 2000).

Laing, Stuart, 'Banging in Some Reality: The Original "Z Cars", in John Corner (ed.), *Popular Television in Britain* (London: BFI, 1991), pp. 125–44.

Lawson, Mark, 'Why Don't We Love *Seinfeld?*', *The Guardian* (20 September 1999).

Lealand, Geoffrey, *American Television Programmes on British Screens* (London: BFI, 1984).

Marwick, Arthur, *Culture in Britain since 1945* (London: Blackwell, 1991).

Morley, David and Robins, Kevin, *Spaces of Identity: Global Media, Electronic Landscapes and Cultural Boundaries* (London: Routledge, 1995).

Paterson, Richard, 'A Suitable Schedule for the Family', in Andrew Goodwin and Garry Whannel (eds), *Understanding Television* (London: Routledge, 1990), pp. 30–41.

Paterson, Richard, 'Drama and Entertainment', in Anthony Smith (ed.), *Television: An International History* (Oxford: Oxford University Press, 1998), pp. 57–68.

Phillips, William, 'Bored with the USA?', *Broadcast* (10 January 1997), p. 30.

Potter, Jeremy, *Independent Television in Britain*, vols III and IV (London: Macmillan, 1989, 1990).

Ritchie, Michael, *Please Stand By: A Prehistory of Television* (New York: Overlook Press, 1995).

Schiller, Herbert, *Mass Communications and American Empire* (New York: A. M. Kelley, 1969).

Segrave, Kerry, *American Television Abroad: Hollywood's Attempt to Dominate World Television* (Jefferson, NC: McFarland, 1998).

Sendall, Bernard, *Independent Television in Britain*, vols I and II (London: Macmillan, 1982, 1983).

Sepstrup, Preben, 'Research into International TV Flows', *European Journal of Communication*, vol. 4, no. 4 (1989), pp. 393–408.

Strinati, Dominic and Wagg, Stephen (eds), *Come on Down? Popular Media Culture in Post-war Britain* (London: Routledge, 1992).

Thompson, Robert J., *From* Hill Street Blues *to* ER: *Television's Second Golden Age* (New York: Syracuse University Press, 1997).

The Times, 'Home Is Best', (1 November 1995).

Tunstall, Jeremy, *The Media Are American* (London: Constable, 1977).

Williams, Raymond, *Television: Technology and Cultural Form* (Glasgow: Fontana/Collins, 1978).

PART TWO

'Content is King': Formats, Shows and Events

5

Long-format TV: Globalisation and Network Branding in a Multi-Channel Era

John McMurria

On 13 November 1994, the eight-hour television mini-series *Scarlett*, adapted from the novel by Alexandra Ripley, the sequel to Margaret Mitchell's *Gone with the Wind*, premiered in prime time in nineteen national broadcasting markets including Italy, Spain, Germany, Sweden, Japan and the USA, and soon after in over 100 broadcasting markets world-wide (Carter, 1994; Tran, 1994). *Scarlett* is the product of an international consortium of European and US media companies, assembled by the independent TV producer Robert Halmi Sr, including three of Europe's largest media conglomerates, the German Kirch Group, the Italian commercial broadcaster Silvio Berlusconi Communications and Rupert Murdoch's UK satellite platform BSkyB, as well as several growing commercial television networks including the French channel TF1, Spain's Antena 3, the US network CBS and Austria's public channel ORF. The deal began four years earlier when Halmi outbid a gallery of mainly European media groups for the rights to the novel, paying $9 million, almost four times the highest price ever paid for rights to a literary property. A representative from the William Morris Agency, the auction broker, remarked 'it sold at this price because it's a huge bestseller, the international market is expanding and numerous international conglomerates saw this as a way of getting into the international TV and motion-picture markets with a big splash'. Halmi claimed to have sold $36 million in international distribution rights the day he purchased the book rights, not including the $20 million CBS later contributed to the $45 million production costs (Bowes, 1994; Carugati, 1994; Weinraub, 1991).

With 200 speaking roles, 2,000 extras, and filmed in fifty-three locations from London to Dublin to Charleston, *Scarlett* was a 'must see' event of exceptional scale. Berlusconi production head Riccardo Tozzi commented, 'the importance of the mega-event goes beyond the airing itself or the rating it obtains. What is important is the status it gives the network, the audience appreciation, the attention of the press and the anticipation it generates.' Ludwig zu Salm, in charge of creative development at Kirch's BetaFilm division added, 'mega-productions act as locomotives for the rest of our distribution activities'. Upon acquiring the rights to *Scarlett* in 1991, Halmi predicted

> the European marketplace in 1992 will be bigger than the United States for movies of the week. I can envision a time when we'll be making movies for the European market and selling the back-end rights to the United States.

However exaggerated this promotional rhetoric may be, *Scarlett* was a huge rating success in Europe, but failed to reach projections on CBS, leading Halmi to respond, 'here it is, the quintessential American product, and it's outside the US where everybody embraces it in a huge way. That's why we're gearing more and more of what we do for the international marketplace' (Coe, 1991; Lowry, 1994; Lowry and Robinsbrian 1994; Tran, 1994).

The television landscape, once a province of nationally organised systems of dissemination, regulation, finance, production and consumption, is increasingly contoured by national industry deregulation and global media conglomeration. This essay examines long-format television (TV movies and mini-series) such as *Scarlett* within the complex and rapid global transformations in the culture industries over the past decade. As the comments from industry executives above reveal, these 'must see' special-event television productions serve more than just to gain audience ratings on a given television evening. They are strategic attention-grabbing nodal points within increasingly crowded television schedules that are now 'geared' for international audiences. By tracing the economic and cultural contexts of these 'locomotives of distribution' we interface with key transformations in the culture industries including the rise of transnational cable and satellite channels, the privatisation and growth of European television, the international conglomeration of ownership in the audiovisual industries, and the continuing international geographic dispersal of English-language television production.

During a period when the US broadcast networks lost the majority of their viewers to cable, and the bar of success for cable ratings lowered to 2 per cent of households, the costs of these long-format originals continued to climb. Made-for-TV movies, once priced under $1 million, now commonly approach $4–6 million, and mini-series such as *The Odyssey* (1997) and *Gulliver's Travels* (1996) approach $40 million. As the difference between domestic licence fees and programme costs expands, international syndication revenues have become more integral to programme development. Halmi claimed that foreign broadcasters are getting 'far pickier about what they want' as broadcasters produce more local programming, and that 'there is a whole genre of American programming that cannot work overseas. It is too headline-oriented: the sickness of the month, the murder of the month. That is simply not translatable.' Rather, 'the trick is now to come up with a *Gulliver's Travels* or *The Odyssey* that every country can claim as its own' (Fabrikant, 1997).

While these Euro-centric claims of western canonical universalism invoke the ongoing legacies of cultural imperialism, TV movies in the post-network era have migrated away from the issues-oriented women-centred genres that often tapped into national headline news topics. Now more common on pay-TV than free-to-air broadcast channels, TV movies and mini-series captured seven of the top ten-rated cable programmes in 1999. As the low-budget 'disease-of-the-week' movies have given way to star-driven special effects-enhanced literary adaptations and action/mystery/Western genres, TV movies often seem closer to their feature film cousins than to their made-for-TV ancestors (McConville, 1999; Schneider, 1999). Just as the Hollywood studios for decades have been financed by international capital with a creative imperative to sell to global audiences, we also need to conceptualise the US television landscape within a global framework.

Long-format TV has seen a strategic value shift from ratings winners in critical 'sweeps' months on the broadcast networks, to prestigious 'must see' events on cable channels. As programming networks vie for space within a multi-channel environment, high-profile original movies and mini-series are used to attract new viewers and build network brand identities. This essay argues that these branding strategies construct the programming networks as new commodity forms. These branding campaigns derive less from viewer demands for more cohesive programming than from new initiatives to regulate programming streams and to facilitate relationships among industry gatekeepers. While much of US television programming remains firmly anchored in national and local contexts of regulation, dissemination and symbolic register, the high costs of these brand locomotives has meant most are filmed outside the USA to cut costs, are financed through international consortiums, and are often designed to circulate across national borders. If Hollywood has maintained cartel-like control over international theatrical distribution, independent producers and international distributors have established a dominant position in the TV movie business through ties to European commercial broadcasters and global advertising agencies.

Much scholarly attention to the internationalisation of television has focused on the US domination of programme flows (Varis, 1984; Wildman, 1988). Statistics continue to provide good reason for the relevancy of this focus. In 1997 the US still comprised 70 per cent of all international programme exports, although US programming internationally has seen a shift out of prime-time schedules as national broadcasters increase in-house and locally commissioned production (*Screen Digest*, 2000, p. 117). Flow models often consider the viewer effects of US cultural export, from cultural imperialist models which claim lasting negative impacts an ideal-volatile world viewing subjects (Schiller, 1969; Tunstall, 1977), to active viewer approaches which find a variety of viewer appropriation within a diversity of everyday lived contexts (Gripsrud, 1995; Liebes and Katz, 1990). But conceptual measures of trade and flow codify 'national' indices of cultural description and fail to account for either non-US television exporters, or the growth of transnational media conglomerates and their impact on transformations in US television culture. Other institutionally oriented studies focus on how transnational media organisations operate within (inter)national regulatory climates which consider the strategic power of primary 'gatekeepers' in the television industries, such as media owners, managers and programme buyers (Sinclair, Jacka and Cunningham, 1996, p. 17). This essay considers these institutional dynamics as it considers: first, the emergence of TV movies within national broadcasting institutions; second, long-format transformations within a multi-channel environment; third, the international conglomeration of long-format production/distribution; fourth, the relocation of labour; and fifth, the international expansion of branded programming networks.

Genre emergence in the network era

Made-for-TV movies emerged within the network era of broadcasting where three nationally networked channels vied for a majority of the US mass audience. With budgets typically under $1 million, often less than the licence fee for features, made-for-TV movies became a mainstay of network programming in the 1970s, and by 1983, occupied 20 per cent of the prime-time schedule (Lafferty, 1990, pp. 235–49). Networks scheduled these high-profile and heavily advertised original movies as counterprogramming to competitors' top-rated shows, and as valuable ratings winners in the important triennial sweeps months. Laurie Schulze found that because TV movies aired only once, the marketing imperatives to promote a film in a few short lines in TV-guide privileged made-for-TV subjects with 'hot concepts' and 'sensational' stories, often taken from magazine covers, talk shows or news headlines, and that tapped into national *Zeitgeist* topics or the 'standard issue of the week'. These stories often addressed social issues like alcohol abuse or domestic violence, and served a 'pedagogic function' with follow-up programmes that addressed real-world problems (1994, pp. 354–8). TV movies provided a national public space for grappling with contemporary issues in a way that feature films did not. Elayne Rapping, in her excellent study of the made-for-TV movie found that most TV movies of the 1970s and 80s featured women in central roles, and focused stories on issues of domestic violence, women's illness, or issues involving children, creating a discursive space for negotiating women's experience, but one that more often than not locked women into traditional roles in the domestic sphere as wives and mothers (1992, pp. xl–xli, 56–64, 95–7).

But advertiser interests and network decision-makers delimited the sphere of national social issues within the confines of commercial network television. In the early 1980s the networks still held an oligopoly over the airwaves, and although the Financial and Syndication rules of 1972 prevented the networks from owning the programmes they aired, the networks financed more made-for-TV movies in this period than all of the Hollywood studios combined. The network TV movie department heads served as 'gatekeepers' who took pitches from forty or fifty independent producers, and considered advertiser interests, the advice of insurance liability attorneys regarding controversial programming, and their own sensibilities for predicting the interests of a nationwide audience. Guided by pragmatic risk-reducing strategies, these gatekeepers avoided stories of racial conflict or political controversy in favour of stories pitched to the centre of a mass audience conceived as white, middle class and Protestant (Gitlin, 1983, pp. 157–200).

The networks' control over made-for-TV movies, and national television transmission in general, loosened when in the 1970s the FCC lifted rules that had insulated the network oligopoly under the banner of protecting 'local' broadcasting. The FCC approved applications for the launching of domestic communication satellites and initiated rules that facilitated the national networking of cable channels. By the mid-1970s satellite-relayed cable television opened up competition for nationwide television delivery to new corporate competitors from publishers, regional broadcasters, multi-system cable operators and the Hollywood studios. By 1983, cable television reached 35 per cent of all TV households in the USA, and by the end of the decade, began scheduling original movies and mini-series (Curtin, 1996, p. 186; Parsons and Frieden, 1998, pp. 47–56).

But as the television market moved from a broadcast oligopoly that targeted a national mass audience, to a fragmented multi-channel environment of competing cable/satellite channels, long-format television carried a strategic value beyond high-concept, headline-driven content designed to win an evening's rating. Cable networks called on original movies and mini-series to distinguish network identities with prestigious and so-called 'evergreen' content that could be repeated within more flexible scheduling practices. But multi-channel television emerged within a period of media deregulation and corporate conglomeration on a global scale. Michael Curtin, following global economy theories, has situated this transition from the network era to a multi-channel television environment within broader fundamental changes in global capitalism. The network era formed within a 'Fordist' economic system where large centralised firms mass produced standardised goods for consumers who had stable incomes won by the collective bargaining efforts of labour unions, and secured through New Deal social welfare measures. While the Hollywood studios established national theatre chains to circulate a standardised product, the feature film, under a centralised, factory-like L.A.-based studio system, radio and television developed through a state-regulated oligopoly that favoured national networks and advertiser interests over local and regional alternatives (1996, pp. 181–6; Puttnam, 2000).

In the post-war years, saturated markets and stagnant rates of productivity marked a period of reorganisation that called on more flexible procedures for meeting the needs of segmented local markets in the short term. These economic shifts, particularly in the 1970s, transformed labour practices as corporations increasingly used subcontractors and part-time employees, and the global dispersal of production created new international divisions of labour. The state responded with deregulation and privatisation policies that facilitated ongoing waves of transnational corporate mergers. Curtin describes the current economic organisation of the culture industries as neo-Fordist, in that the 'Fordist principles of mass production, mass marketing, and mass consumption exist side-by-side with emerging forms of flexible accumulation.' The large integrated conglomerates that have come to dominate the media industries, such as AOL Time Warner, Disney and Viacom, exemplify this as each controls an increasingly dispersed array of programming produced through numerous decentralised production facilities and by way of a proliferation of distribution channels including multiplex theatres, video, cable/satellite television and the internet. These conglomerates seek to profit from a broad array of cultural forms from mass-oriented Hollywood feature films and terrestrial network broadcasting programmes which are typically non-controversial and apolitical, to those that are more niche-oriented and target special-interest groups with programmes that offer more intense appeal such as the youth-oriented MTV (1996, pp. 186–98).

Situated within these dual movements of global conglomeration and flexible production/distribution, long-format television is produced by transnational organisations for multinational audiences, just as they serve to differentiate more niche-oriented channels through building brand prestige and awareness. We turn now to the strategic value of long-format television with a multi-channel TV era.

Multi-channel television and network branding

Table 5.1 illustrates that in 1998–9, cable networks scheduled almost twice the number of TV movies and mini-series as did the terrestrial networks. CBS was the only network

Table 5.1 TV movies and mini-series, orders for 1998–9

US broadcast networks	Number of movies or mini-series	US cable networks	Number of movies or mini-series
CBS	50	A&E	30
NBC	24	Showtime	30
ABC	19	The Movie Channel	24
Fox	4	USA Network	19
UPN	0	TNT	14
WB	0	The Disney Channel	12
		HBO	12
		Lifetime	12
		Fox Family Channel	5
		FX	4
		VH1	4
Total	97	Total	166

Data compiled from *Video Age International*, vol. 6, no. 18, (October 1998), p. 1.

broadcaster that maintained a heavy schedule of TV movies with two nights per week devoted to the genre, while in the late 1990s, NBC dropped its Sunday-, Monday- and Friday-night movie slots, and in 1999 ABC dropped its Thursday-night movie slot. Of the basic cable networks, the general-interest channels A&E, USA and TNT ordered more originals than the special-interest channels Lifetime and VH1, but these and other niche channels such as E! Entertainment, Black Entertainment Television and the Sci-Fi Network added original movies and mini-series in the 1999–2000 season (McConville, 1999). So while the broadcast networks were scheduling fewer original movies and mini-series, the cable channels grew increasingly dependent on them for weekly programme scheduling and channel promotion.

As stated above, FCC legislation in the 1970s fostered the growth of nationwide cable programming networks, following what Thomas Streeter has called a 'corporate liberal' mode of industry regulation that sought to 'stabilize, organize, and protect' the growth of the industry as a whole. The 1984 Cable Communications Act did so by shifting regulatory authority for cable systems away from hundreds of local municipalities to the FCC by sanctifying the monopoly status of the capital-intensive cable operators who were building their wired infrastructures, but prohibiting cities from regulating programme content and subscription fees, and capping local franchise fees at 5 per cent (1996, pp. 177–8). This facilitated the national integration of hundreds of small cable systems through mergers that produced large multi-system cable operators (MSOs).

Increasing ties were created between system operators and programming networks. In 1995, forty-one of the sixty-five top programming networks had vertical ties to MSOs, and for thirty-one of these sixty-five, a cable operator was involved in the network's launch. The ten most widely distributed basic cable channels accounted for three-quarters of total revenues for all fifty-one basic channels, and seven of these ten had vertical ties to MSOs. TCI and Time Warner together controlled 42 per cent of basic subscribers. In the ten years that followed the 1984 Cable Communications Act, TCI and Time Warner launched or acquired thirty-seven of their forty-one vertically affiliated programming networks. Similar vertical integration and concentration existed for the premium channels where the four channels with vertical ties accounted for three-quarters of total subscriptions. To address this rapid concentration of power, the 1992 Cable Television Consumer Protection and Competition Act limited the percentage of programming networks an MSO may own to 40 per cent, and capped the percentage of national households reached at 30 per cent. None the less, studies have shown that affiliated programming networks have higher carriage rates and receive more favourable promotions, channel position and pricing than do unaffiliated networks (Waterman and Weiss, 1997, pp. 13–15, 23, 39–41, 93–8).

While the most widely available channels are partially owned by cable system operators, other top-rated channels such as ESPN and the Disney Channel are unaffiliated. The Viacom-owned programming networks Showtime, Nickelodeon, MTV, VH1, the Sci-Fi Channel and USA Network that were either launched or strengthened by their affiliation with Viacom-owned cable systems, became unaffiliated when Viacom sold its cable systems to TCI in 1996, signalling a shift in strategy away from distribution to programme packaging. That year television distributors (local stations and cable operators) collected 65 per cent of total profits in the industry, while broadcast and cable networks earned 20 per cent, and producers just 15 per cent. But the average asset-based profit *margins* for cable networks between 1993 and 1996 were 16.2 per cent, compared to just 5 per cent for cable system operators. At the dawn of the 'digital age' where new technologies are proliferating the channels of television distribution, some industry observers see the beginning of a 'great value shift' away from distribution, which formerly capitalised on inhabiting the 'bottleneck' of programme delivery, and towards branded programming networks which 'package content' (Todreas, 1999, pp. 41, 56, 97–104). The value of the programming network brand has been voiced by Viacom chairman Sumner Redstone:

> As I see the world developing – particularly in a world of a lot of fragmentation, a lot of choices – strong, powerful branded content, like MTV and Nickelodeon, will remain the first choice. And, indeed, those powerful brands give us a lot of leverage in dealing with contemporaries around the world.
>
> Mahoney, 1999, p. 9

So while vertical ownership between coaxial cable systems and content producers facilitated the launching and promotion of the integrated programming networks, affiliated and unaffiliated networks sought strong network brands to create leverage in negotiating distribution contracts with MSOs. In a multi-channel television environment, the branded programming network itself is a commodity form in three ways: first, as a licensed property to cable systems; second, as either a basic or premium channel sold to individual viewers via subscription; and third, as a collector of audiences for sale to advertisers. The programming networks are both the standardised commodity of multi-channel television, a means of organising ongoing streams of audiovisual programmes, and, through branded programming, a differentiated product from other channels. Cable systems seek strongly branded networks to differentiate and diversify their basic and premium services, and advertisers look to place their ads in branding environments that add either credibility, prestige, quality, zest, or other sought-after attributes for their products. But as Mica Nava has argued, 'advertising is as much about promoting the corporate image of a company (or institution) to its rivals, clients and employees as it is about selling commodities to the consumer' (1997, p. 40). So network branding campaigns are less informational services for viewers as they are promotional campaigns that facilitate these economic relationships among the gatekeepers of the networks, distributors and advertisers. But empirical research also suggests that while viewers continue to channel surf in a much more unruly fashion, most tend to watch between five and ten channels regularly (Parsons and Frieden, 1998, p. 247). Internet usage has also seen similar patterns where web users visited half as many different sites in 2001 as they did in 2000, and 72 per cent of visitors to news sites chose just three web sources, MSNBC, CNN and the *New York Times* (Harmon, 2001). Important here is that branding practices define commodity processes that guide the decisions of cable systems, programming networks and advertisers in selecting, scheduling, bundling and funding the types of audiovisual culture that circulate through a multi-channel environment, and that get promotional attention and space for viewers to choose from. Made-for-TV movies and mini-series in the 1990s were strategic programming tools in this commercial process.

Programming networks focus branding campaigns around slogans such as 'It's Not TV, It's HBO', 'TBS, The TV Haven for the Regular Guy', 'TNT, the Greatest Movie Studio on Television' or 'Lifetime, Television for Women'. Programming networks rely on high-profile original movies and mini-series to promote and distinguish network identities. These more pricey original movies functioned less to win an event's rating period, as the sensational ripped-from-the-headlines movies did, but to add prestige to a programming network's brand image. TNT has produced long-format TV under the banner TNT Originals since 1990, with budgets that averaged $8 million in the 1999–2000 season, including *A Christmas Carol* (1999) starring Patrick Stewart, *Don Quixote* (2000) with John Lithgow, and the $24 million special-effects-heavy adaptation of *Animal Farm* (1999). Vice president of TNT Originals Robert DeBitetto said,

> These are such a part of our branding architecture, that if a movie gets Emmy nominations and critical raves and it gets us attention, then that's a home run for us. That's some of the programming that we talk about when we go to Madison Avenue, when we talk to the MSOs.

The marketing campaigns for these event originals have reached between $5 and $10 million, and often a large percentage of advertising time during an original's cablecast is devoted to promote future programming on the network, so rarely do advertising sales cover the expenses to produce and promote these events (Menichini, 1999; Schreiber, 1999).

A survey of the top ten-rated basic cable movies from 1996 to mid-1999 suggests a dramatic shift in the content and stories from the so-called 'disease-of-the-week' or 'women in distress' topics that dominated the genre a decade earlier. The USA Network's four-hour *Moby Dick* (1998) was rated first and second for each two-hour instalment, followed by five Westerns from TNT including *Last Stand at Saber River* (1997) and *Riders of the Purple Sage (1996)*. The Family Channel's *Night of the Twisters* (1996) ranked eighth, TNT's *Pirates of Silicon Valley* (1999) ninth, and Lifetime's *Fifteen and Pregnant* (1997) was tenth (Dempsey, 1999). The list demonstrates a marked shift away from women-centred stories and towards the male-skewed genres of action and the Western. Headline-driven movies such as Disney's *The Elian Gonzalez Story* (2000) still found a place on cable, but lacked the so-called 'evergreen' value for long-term repeat scheduling. Although these trends towards higher budgets, special effects and action suggest the gap between TV movies and Hollywood feature films is closing, the budgets for even the higher-profile made-for-cable movies average well below the $77 million budget for the average Hollywood feature in 1998 according to the Motion Picture Association of America (Menon, 2000). Original movies often find a place between Hollywood blockbusters and low-budget art-house productions. When TNT premiered its first original movie, *A Man for All Seasons*, in December 1988, two months after the channel launched, then TNT Executive Vice President Scott Sassa expressed an interest in filling this gap: 'They [Hollywood] have less expensive movies aimed at teens or major blockbusters. What they don't have is those nice, adult-oriented relationship movies done in the low-to-medium range.' In the 1990s, TNT originals were mostly Westerns, historical dramas and literary adaptations ('Made-for-Cable', 1989; Mills, 1990).

Other channels such as the Family Channel, A&E and Lifetime scheduled movies for more narrowly targeted audiences. For example, Jackie Byars and Eileen R. Meehan found in their study of Lifetime that the gendered scheduling dynamics of broadcast television – daytime programming for women, and family and male-skewed programming in prime time – no longer provided advertisers access to the sought-after and ever-increasing number of upscale working women in the 1980s. Lifetime provided this access, and in prime time scheduled original 'World Premiere Movies' that were mostly melodramatic stories centred on a 'strong, competent woman who overcame adversity'. For Byars and Meehan, a 'systemic challenge' to patriarchal and class structures in Lifetime originals was 'rare', and solutions were 'generally personal' (2000, pp. 149–56). The premium channels HBO and Showtime began making original movies in the early 1980s (Segrave, 1999, p. 166). HBO originals have attracted Hollywood stars to engaging material thought too controversial for theatrical or commercial broadcast release, and most are made for adult audiences. High-profile originals have included *The Josephine Baker Story* (1991), *Stalin* (1992), with Robert Duvall, and *If These Walls Could Talk* (1996) about women and abortion staring Demi Moore, Sissy Spacek and Cher (Katz, 1996; McConville, 1999; Weinraub, 1991).

The above survey of US cable networks revealed that within the multi-channel television environment of the 1990s, event made-for-TV movies and mini-series became central programming tools for gathering new viewers and distinguishing channel identities. Budgets for these long-format event programmes grew just as ratings continued to dilute as more cable and satellite-delivered channels vied for prominent space on cable systems. Programming networks showed willingness to forgo immediate profits from advertising sales during initial airings of these events because the wide exposure and prestige were thought to increase cable and satellite subscribers, and drive up viewership for a network's ongoing, regularly scheduled line-up of programming.

While event made-for-TV movies and mini-series in the 1990s became central to the gathering of new viewers and the distinguishing of channel identities, the domestic licence fees from programming networks fell far short of covering the inflating costs. If US television programmes have found international syndication revenues for decades, we now turn to the transnational restructuring of long-format production and distribution.

International conglomerates and long-format TV

The made-for-TV movie business has been dominated by independent producers since they emerged in the 1960s, but if US network broadcasters held considerable sway over the types of projects that were green-lighted, independent producers with ties to international partners have come to dominate the genre in the 1990s. Table 5.2 lists the major producers of TV movies and mini-series and their reported average annual output in 1998. Notice that the Hollywood studios and US network broadcasters produce a small percentage of the overall 298 telefilms reported in this study by *Video Age International*, while the top seven companies represent well over half of the total. These top producer/distributors all either began as independent producers for US and international syndication markets, or acquired companies that did so, carving out a niche in television programming made possible in part by the 1972 FCC rules that restricted network programming to three of the four prime-time hours, and prohibited networks from owning and syndicating programmes (Hilmes, 1990, p. 292). Many of these companies, including Saban, AAFI, WIN, Hamdon and Pearson built international distribution networks through syndicating programmes that Hollywood majors considered less profitable such as game shows, hour-long action series and children's animation. As these long-format producer/distributors formed partnerships with major commercial broadcasters around the world, non-US market interests increasingly informed production decision-making (Dempsey, 1998; Mahoney, 1989; Moran, 1998, pp. 25–71; Setlowe, 1997).

These international syndication markets expanded in the 1990s as regional commercial television broadcasting grew faster than local content-producing industries. These emerging terrestrial and cable/satellite channels typically relied on inexpensive imported programming, especially in the early years of operation. Europe was by far the largest market for US programme sales, and Germany, France and the UK each alone spent more on acquired programming than Australia, Canada and Japan combined. US television exports accounted for 55 per cent of total spending by European broadcasters

Table 5.2 TV movies and mini-series, producer/distributors at 1998

Production/distribution companies	Average annual output at 1998 (number of made-for-TV movies and mini-series)
Hallmark Entertainment	40
Alliance	28
Saban	25
All American Fremantle International (AAFI)	20
World International Network (WIN)	20
Pearson Television (acquired AAFI in 1997)	17
Hamdon Entertainment (renamed Carlton America in 1999)	13
Hearst	12
Paramount Television International	12
Columbia TriStar Television	11
Universal Television	11
NBC Studios	10
Kushner-Locke Company	8
MGM	8
Wilshire Court	7
Atlantis (merged with Alliance in 1999)	7
Jaffe/Braunstein Films	6
Van Zerneck-Sertner Films	5
Warner Bros. Television	5
The Wolper Organization	5
King World	4
Craig Anderson Productions	4
Storyline Entertainment	4
The Landsburg Company	3
Palone Company	3
Rosemont Productions International	3
Spelling Entertainment	3
Cates/Doty Productions	2
PolyGram	2
Total	298

Data compiled from *Video Age International*, vol. 6, no. 18 (October 1998), p. 1.

in 1996, and total spending on acquired programming in Europe overall rose by 55 per
cent between 1995 and 1999. Although US programming internationally has seen a shift
out of prime-time schedules as national broadcasters increase in-house and locally
commissioned production, the USA still dominated global television circulation in the
1996–7 season with approximately 70 per cent of all international programme exports
(*Screen Digest*, 2000, pp. 117–20; *Screen Digest*, 1997, pp. 81–2). The deregulation of
state monopoly television in the 1980s facilitated this rise of commercial broadcasting
in Europe, and a tripling of European advertising expenditures in that decade, mostly
for television, fuelled its rapid expansion (Barker, 1997, p. 155). Transnational consumer-product firms are the largest buyers of television advertising, and a select number
of companies with globally branded products, such as Proctor and Gamble, are the top
spenders in most of the largest national markets. The 1980s also saw a wave of mergers
among advertising agencies, and in the 1990s, the largest transnational firms consolidated their advertising expenditures into one of these mega-advertising agencies
(Herman and McChesney, 1997, pp. 58–9).

As the consolidation of consumer product firms and adverting agencies facilitated the
positioning of branded products in global markets, these advertisers and their agencies
formed partnerships with long-format producers/distributors to sponsor programming
for international markets. For example, World International Network (WIN) began in
1988 as a consortium of fourteen major broadcasters from around the world and the
international advertising agency NW Ayer, to produce original movies and mini-series
for its international partners. NW Ayer represented multinational conglomerates such as
AT&T, General Motors, Proctor and Gamble, Citicorp and Gillette, and the broadcasting partners included the following: Central Independent Television in the UK,
NDR/ARD in Germany, RAI in Italy, Rede Globo in Brazil, TF1 in France, the Seven
Network in Australia, Tohokushinsha Film Co. Ltd in Japan and Korea, Univisa/Protele
for Spanish-speaking Central and South America, and Transworld Television Corp. for
the Middle East, Southeast Asia and Africa. WIN founder Larry Gershman offered very
broad and crude guidelines for programming including statements such as, 'comedies
don't work', 'in Latin America family pictures tend to do better on free television than
do action/suspense thrillers, which work everywhere else in the world', 'touchy-feely
movies ... don't always work internationally' and 'in Europe and Asia, thrillers work better than soft dramas' ('Larry Gershman', 1999). Gershman seems to be suggesting that
the genre of original movies most prevalent in the late 1980s, those focused on women
protagonists and family relationships, were less marketable internationally. If WIN's
original movies tended towards action thrillers, dual titles for US and international
markets made use of different generic modifiers to position them as women-centred
dramas or thrillers. For example, *The Price She Paid* (1992), starring Loni Anderson
in the role of a rape victim, which aired on CBS in the US, was changed to *Plan of
Attack* for the international market. And the US title *A Woman Scorned: The Betty
Broderick Story* (1992) was changed to *Till Murder Do Us Part,* the former marketing
to headline-recognition in the US, and the latter to its generic status as a mystery
('World', 1992).

This question of marketability and international taste has implications for a genre that in the 1980s found mostly women viewers through offering strong female protagonists who confronted important social issues, and thus the perceptions of these gatekeepers of international distribution carry considerable weight in redefining the genre. International distributors often cite action-oriented programmes as having widespread popularity, but one might question this as more of a marketing imperative than a universal cultural bias. While top executives at these international distributors are overwhelmingly male, biases arising from decision-maker sensibilities are intertwined with economic imperatives to find alternatives to the vast amount of male-skewed sports programming that dominates international television schedules. One Canadian producer of long-format television put it this way: 'marketing research says that the only people who watch TV-movies are women from 18 to 49, and unless it's a sports program, there is nothing that men will actually make time to watch' (Setlowe, 1997). This demographic imperative informed a Hamdon Entertainment executive's perception that 'romantic, story-driven pieces' have international appeal, just the opposite of Gershman's perception above (Guider, 1999). Contradictions such as these reveal how gatekeeper perceptions construct vulgar accounts of gender difference in the service of marketing imperatives that demand universal guidelines for circulating transnational programmes.

The Canada-based film and television conglomerate Alliance, which merged with fellow Canadian media giant Atlantis, produced twenty-eight TV movies in 1998. The combined company produces and distributes motion pictures and owns broadcast and cable networks in Canada, but the majority of its revenues come from developing television series and long-format television for the international market. Just as US cable channels have increased their use of big-budget event programmes to draw attention and create prestige, these critically praised projects also provided marketing value for the production company. In referring to *Joan of Arc* (1999) and other event mini-series such as *Nuremberg* (2000), which sold to TNT and starred Alec Baldwin, Alliance/Atlantis Chairman and CEO Michael MacMillan said, 'Strategically it's that sort of locomotive property that will help us continue to attract the best and brightest talent and will also help us negotiate larger sales deals and package deals with customers throughout the world' (Schreiber, 1999, p. 58). International television licensing revenues comprise 80 per cent of the company's total revenues, and world-historical subjects such as *Nuremberg* and *Joan of Arc*, and international stars of European origin such as *Joan of Arc* co-stars Jacqueline Bisset and Peter O'Toole suggest textual strategies for creating mini-series that play to transatlantic audiences.

These transnational producer/distributors of long-format television have extended the spatial economies of production and distribution beyond national borders to include territorial market concerns in the Americas, the Asia Pacific, and especially in Western Europe. Event television movies and mini-series promote and extend these international industry alliances just as they aid programming networks build brand awareness. But the audience epistemologies that inform production decisions are quite crude. These globally produced event productions follow promotional imperatives and generic parameters of prestige rather than engage with the lived diversities across the different territories. These transnational alliances have not steered far from the American-accented English language that the large and fickle US market demands.

The relocation of labour

While the Canadian-based Alliance/Atlantis is dependent on the licence revenues of its southern neighbour, in the 1990s US producers of long-format television have increasingly migrated north where Canadian tax credits at the federal and provincial levels, growing production infrastructures, a soft currency and experienced crews have made Canada the leading runaway production location for US television and feature film production. A June 1999 report commissioned by the Directors Guild of America and Screen Actors Guild found that of the 308 made-for-TV movies and mini-series developed in the USA in 1998, 139 were economic runaways (compared to thirty in 1990), 90 per cent of which were shot in Canada. The Canadian tax credits offer rebates on labour costs of between 22 per cent and 46 per cent. This coupled with a depreciation of the Canadian dollar to 69 US cents in 1999 from 90 cents in the early 1990s saved US producers over 25 per cent of total production costs (Madigan, 1999). US broadcasters and cable networks alike scheduled made-for-TV movies shot in Canada, including *Cabin by the Lake* for USA Network, *The Spring* for NBC and *Up, Up and Away* for The Disney Channel, all filmed in British Columbia in 1999 (Shaw, 1999). In the five years upto 1999, Showtime purchased forty-eight TV movies from Toronto-based producer Dufferin Gates (Wright, 1999). Tax incentives required the use of below-the-line Canadian labour, which bolstered employment opportunities for hundreds of craft labourers, but the creative decision-makers and on-screen labourers such as the director, writer and lead actors were rarely Canadian (Vlessing, 1999).

Hallmark Entertainment producers Robert Halmi Sr and his son Robert Halmi Jr were the most prolific makers of made-for-TV movies in the 1990s. *Scarlett* marked a turning point in the types of long-format television the Halmis produced for the US and international market that called for fewer topical and headline-derived stories, and more elaborate event-productions from literary classics such as *Jason and the Argonauts* (2000), *Journey to the Center of the Earth* (1999), *Arabian Nights* (2000), *Don Quixote*, *A Christmas Carol*, and fantasy originals such as *The Magical Legend of the Leprechauns* (1999) and the mini-series *The Tenth Kingdom* (2000) (Fabrikant, 1997). The Halmis decreased TV movie production from eighty-six in 1996, to fifty-seven in 1997 and forty in 1998, while revenues and profits more than tripled in that period.

As the budgets of these fantasy originals continue to increase, least-cost production practices have sent almost all of Hallmark's productions overseas where favourable currency exchange, tax incentives, subsidies and wages undercut those in the USA. We have seen above that Canada is the most frequent location for long-format television runaways, but European studios have also attracted English-language television production in the 1990s. The Shepperton and Pinewood Studios in London have long housed Hollywood productions, but Thatcher-era union-busting has made labour costs there 35 per cent less than in the USA. Among the mini-series that Hallmark shot in London studios were *Gulliver's Travels*, *The Odyssey*, *Merlin* (1998) and *Cleopatra* (1999). The German studios outside Berlin where Fritz Lang filmed the classic *Metropolis* (1926) were revitalised when the East German government sold them to international private investors after unification. Though the eastern region cannot compete with Cologne and Munich in terms of film subsidies, a regional state bank has set up a production fund to attract foreign productions. With thirteen sound stages and a newly constructed special effects centre, Babelsberg Studios offer comparable facilities to London's at lower costs considering a depreciated mark and so-called 'flexible' labour arrangements. In 2001 Hallmark was shooting the mini-series *Hans Christian Andersen* there, and has co-produced a number of English-language projects with Babelsberg International Film Produktion including *Voyage of the Unicorn* (2001), *Arabian Nights* and *The Tenth Kingdom* (Hils, 1998; Kindred, 1999; Tagliabue, 1996).

No European studio has attracted more Hollywood productions in recent years than Prague's Barrandov Studios. Europe's second largest production facility, the formerly state-owned studios have lured six of the seven major Hollywood studios since 1999 with shooting costs that are two to six times less expensive than in London or Paris (Krosnar, 2001). Extras earn $100 per day in Los Angeles and under $16 per day in Prague. But as the Czech Republic prepares to join the European Union by 2004, many believe prices will move towards EU rates, rendering the studios vulnerable to Hollywood flight. Meanwhile, Czech film-makers have received little support from either the studios or from Parliament to bolster local productions (Hamm, 2001). Hallmark benefited from Prague's old-world architecture, surrounding forests and cheap labour in shooting the *Lost Empire* (2001) and *Mists of Avalon* (2001). For two mini-series that required scenes of a ship on the open seas, Hallmark built a special horizon tank on the southern coast of Victoria, Australia, to shoot *Moby Dick* and *Noah's Ark* (1999). While currency exchange and cheap labour made shooting in Australia 30 per cent cheaper than in the USA, *Moby Dick* also qualified for special subsidies and tax breaks under the Australia-UK co-production treaty. Widely recognised as the greatest American novel, the television adaptation qualified as 'Australian' and 'British' programming as most on- and off-screen labour were residents of either country. As the treaty was designed for non-US industries to pool financial and creative resources to bolster national cultural expression against a steady tide of US imports, the subsidised production met with controversy in Australia as the principle above-the-line creative positions (director, writer, lead actors) were either English or American (Fidgeon, 1997; Woods, 1998).

To further probe the transnational dynamics of long-format production and distribution, we now turn to the case of the Hallmark Network, an international channel for Hallmark TV movies and mini-series, and an example of the increasing trend of international network expansion.

International network branding

In 1994 Hallmark Cards Inc. purchased the Halmis' TV movie production company RHI for $365 million to form Hallmark Entertainment. Since 1951, the greeting-card maker has sponsored TV movies for CBS under the marque 'Hallmark Hall of Fame'. These prestigious events aided CBS in the audience-monitored sweeps months of February, May and November, and promoted card sales for Hallmark in the months preceding Valentine's Day, Mother's Day and Christmas. In the early 1990s Hallmark Cards made several failed attempts to enter the US cable television business, but with access to the Halmis' library of 'family-oriented' long-format programming, they launched the Hallmark Network in 1995 (Baron, 1991). Because the inventory of rights for Hallmark Entertainment programmes existed outside the USA and the largest television markets in Western Europe, Hallmark launched first in the Benelux countries in August 1995, and in Mexico, North Africa, Australia and New Zealand within a year. As of 1999, the Hallmark Network was available in over sixty countries with 20 million subscribers including most of Eastern and Western Europe (3.4 million), Latin America (7.8 million), and in East and South Asia (8.2 million) including Taiwan, Malaysia, India, Korea and China. Because many pay-services ban advertising, subscriptions comprised 87 per cent of total revenues, with only 6 per cent from advertising. The Hallmark Network launched in the USA in August 2001 after acquiring the Odyssey Network in 1998, a channel that was launched in 1988 by an interfaith coalition of seventy religious groups ('Prospectus' 2000, pp. 39, 45).

The genesis and expansion of Hallmark's international programming network exemplifies a particular path through the emerging global dynamics in cable/satellite television delivery. Hallmark is but one of many programming networks that have been expanding globally throughout the 1990s including the Discovery Channel, MTV, HBO, TNT, USA Network, the Sci-Fi Channel, the Cartoon Network and the Disney Channel. While these channels expanded internationally from base networks developed in the US market, the Hallmark Network is similar to the Warner Channel and MGM Gold which first launched movie channels in territories outside the USA. The costs of launching a satellite-delivered programming network are enormous, and only highly capitalised media companies can sustain the initial expenses. The Hallmark Entertainment Network worldwide lost $92 million dollars in 1998 and 1999, despite owning a large library of television programming (Goldsmith, 2000). These barriers of entry coupled with the strength of national-content industries determine distribution in many cases. This has meant that cable/satellite television has a disproportionate amount of programming from US-based media conglomerates compared to terrestrial television. Throughout Latin America, the above US channels receive the highest ratings on cable systems which are 90 per cent owned by US conglomerates, except in Argentina, which has a long history of locally originated cable networks and a 60 per cent cable penetration rate (Sell 2001; Sinclair, 1999, pp. 84–6, 165).

Hallmark's territorial expansion offers one example of how the global initiatives of international channel formation meet territorial market and cultural difference. This process finds centralising tendencies in strategic marketing, scheduling and operational management, and localising processes in territorial feed customisation, regional sales centres and tactical promotion. Marketing, programming, scheduling and broadcasting are orchestrated out of the Denver, Colorado office, where the channel broadcasts sixteen different feeds in twenty-three languages as of 2001. Each channel typically premiered thirteen to twenty TV movies per month, and 70–80 per cent of total programming came from the Hallmark library, with the balance consisting of locally acquired programmes. Each feed contains a single programming stream, with space for up to six different language subtitling tracks. Regional offices in London (Europe, Middle East, Africa), Miami (Latin America) and Hong Kong and Singapore (Asia) execute sales and marketing campaigns, and co-ordinate subtitling/dubbing (Flint, 1995; Kiesewetter, 1999; Parrish 2001; 'On Way', 1998; Paxman and Woods, 1995; Wayne, 1999).

Various cultural and economic factors determine the customisation of feeds, but market size, cable/satellite penetration and channel space prioritise expansion. Because dubbing is up to ten times more expensive than subtitling, the majority of feeds are in English with subtitling. Brazil and Italy are two exceptions. Audiovisual imports to much of Latin America have conventionally been subtitled, and according to Hallmark executives, cable/satellite television subscribers are largely upper-income professionals who desire to hear the English language track. In Latin America, the network began in Mexico on a Mexican satellite, then switched to pan-European satellite that reached the entire continent. Mexican accented Spanish was replaced by a Colombian 'neutral' Spanish which had acceptance from Argentina to Mexico. The single pan-Latin American feed carried little advertising because of restrictions in Mexico. A large and unrestricted advertising market in Argentina provided the economic incentive to later split the feed. Similar economic priorities guided the feeding and language strategies in the pan-Asian region. As of 2001, the network had a pan-regional feed, and separate feeds for India, Australia and New Zealand. The pan-regional feed focused on the Taiwan market, the most developed multi-channel market in Asia, with a 65 per cent cable penetration rate as of 1996. Because of this, all Mandarin subtitling is in a Taiwanese dialect. Subtitling in Thai and Korean is also offered. The Asia feeds typically offer more action and sci-fi programming than other regions, including series such as *Star Trek* and *Sliders*. An office in Hong Kong manages the regional feeds, though the network has not found coverage on Hong Kong cable networks as of 2001. Translations are done in each territory, but the Denver office conducts reviews, often with translators who travel between the USA and the export territory, and are more sensitive to vernacular changes (Buchanan, 2001; Parrish, 2001; 'Prospectus', 2000).

As national market size prioritises regional channel customisation, the network seeks to harmonise the channel's brand image across territories. The Denver-based marketing department hired Lubin Lawrence, a research firm in New York which specialises in developing international corporate brands, to conduct in-home focus groups with 500 potential viewers per country in Argentina, Poland, the United Kingdom, India and Taiwan. The psychographic-based research began with questions that search for the 'fundamental human values' of the participants. According to Andy Karofsky, Hallmark Vice President of marketing, the core values of 'wanting to feel connected to family and friends, wanting a feeling of having a place in society and being challenged' were found in the study to be 'similar throughout the world' (2001). The researchers then try to identify how these values are satisfied in a viewing experience, and how the network can promote itself in a way that promises to contribute to these values. Hallmark used the research to help define a 'global brand essence' throughout the network, which initially centred around the tag-line 'Celebrate Life', but was refined to 'Great Stories That Move You'. A promotional statement reads: 'Today's Hallmark Channel is a brighter, warmer place where viewers feel good watching and feel good about themselves.' 'Vivid colors' and 'bold and contemporary imagery' inform the promotional graphics intended to express 'energy' and 'optimism' ('Hallmark Channel', 2001). The network brand is shaped by the branding parameters of the parent card company, though Hallmark Cards does not have a presence in most of the channel's markets. None the less, the programming conforms to the dictates of the card company's image, as Hallmark marketing director Jodie McAfee explained:

> all of our movies at worst would be PG (Parental Guidance). No gratuitous violence, no gratuitous sex and no foul language. From a value standpoint, we try and uphold what the card company considers a very high standard of family values ... [with] wonderful stories which are content neutral.
>
> Jacobs, 1997

But these 'universal values' derive less from empirical evidence than from Hallmark's global initiatives to regulate the commodity value of the channel across territories. As Ien Ang has argued, audience epistemologies such as these do not represent the lived diversity of television viewers, but rather provide an 'objectified category' of a mythically coherent 'audience' which television industries can act upon and control (Ang, 1994). The research methodologies begin with a search for universal fundamental human values within a pool of existing cable/satellite subscribers, an élite of high-end consumers in most markets. Even within these class-specific groups, universal values serve different management and risk reduction initiatives rather than represent human essentialisms. Universals are thus 'found' and demonstrated through empirical evidence. This 'evidence' then validates and operationalises the branding campaigns that focalise certain aspects of the network's programming. These messages of global uplift aimed at middle-class pay-TV audiences and multi-channel distributors mirror consumer-product advertiser promises of the same. The so-called programme content neutrality guided by the Mid-Western Bible-belt values of Hallmark Cards evokes the spectre of cultural imperialism. But the received meaning of these content parameters are far from uniform, and can actually diversify programme schedules. Hallmark interviewed young mothers in five cities in India who said they found the overly suggestive content of existing television programmes, from Hindi film songs to western music channels, unfit for their children. Hallmark's non-gratuitous PG programming provided options for the these viewers, even as the western canonical adaptations recalled the colonial legacies there. While 180 Hallmark stores throughout the country promoted the network with displays and videos, Hallmark's literary status opened promotional campaigns into 250 schools where sample programmes were shipped (Chatterjee, 1999).

Conclusion

This essay followed the transformation of 'must see' long-format television through the rapid global reorganisation of the culture industries in the 1990s. As the multi-channel television era emerges we find the dynamics of ownership conglomeration and conduit fragmentation producing a new commodity form in the branded international programming network. Just as the television network moves from a space of transmission for collecting a national mass-audience to one focused on targeting more narrowly defined special-interest groups, the long-format programming that drives network branding campaigns is ever dependent on global audience reach. While these prestige-seeking productions have gravitated towards marketable genres, evergreen content, high production values, stars and other characteristics similar to the Hollywood feature film, these programmes, produced first and foremost for the US audience, come before us by way of new alliances among major commercial broadcasters around the world. Never straying from the English language, and often adapting works from the western literary canon, mini-series and TV movies none the less are ever dependent on the gatekeeper perceptions of their international producer/distributors. As this digital age of circuit proliferation promises a diversified and democratised audiovisual culture, we find instead a further distanciation between programme-makers and viewers. As programmes reach broader and more diversified international audiences, international marketing prerogatives necessitate decision-making drawn from ever vulgar audience epistemologies. US multi-channel television culture is intertwined in these post-national systems of global media production.

What are the implications, then, for multi-channel culture outside the USA? Most explicitly, the evocations from leading long-format producers that textual universalism resides in western canonical literature can only remind us of the colonial legacies that underpin the cultural imperialism critique. But beyond measures of textual value, we also find what Toby Miller has described as a 'New International Division of Cultural Labor', where currency devaluation and cheap labour attract temporary production and destabilise work forces (1998, pp. 171–3). Also, the pay-TV infrastructures that house international networks are far from universally accessible, which is of minimal concern to networks that programme for a global middle class, a small fraction of the total population in many regions. As per the centre/peripheral exchange throughout the early stages of network expansions, strategic decisions remain anchored in the USA, while tactical localisation occurs, but through priorities of market size and value. Lawrence Grossberg has argued that the 'particular codes of difference' as registered in textual *content* are less relevant to describing the range of diverse expression under capitalist representational systems than are the *forms* of productive processes through which representations circulate (1999, p. 28). As television enters a digital multi-channel television era the commodity form of the branded international programming network, and the long-format television programmes that promote them, have emerged as defining trends for our digital futures.

Acknowledgments

The author would like to thank the following for their valuable comments and support: Nitin Govil, Mark Jancovich, James Lyons, Anna McCarthy, Toby Miller and Shawn

Shimpach. Also, a special thank you to the following staff at Crown Media and Hallmark Entertainment for generously giving their time and expertise: Andrew Brilliant, Richard Buchanan, Andy Karofsky, Kim LeGate, Gene Parrish, Suzanne Sell, Todd Sokolov, Martha Strauss and Sarah Toynton.

Bibliography

'Hallmark Channel', Promotional CD-ROM, (2001).

'Larry Gershman: Pioneering Ad-Hoc Networks', *Video Age International*, vol. 6, no. 19 (1999), p. 40.

'Made-for-Cable: Reaching for Stars and Viewers', *Broadcasting*, vol. 7, no. 117 (14 August 1989), p. 51.

'On Way to 15 Million', *European Media Business and Finance*, vol. 8, no. 8 (20 April 1998).

'Prospectus', *Crown Media* (22 March 2000).

'World International Network (WIN) to Distribute the Producers Entertainment Group's First Television Movie Internationally Starring Loni Anderson and Anthony John Denison', *Business Wire* (26 March 1992).

Ang, Ien, 'Understanding Television Audiencehood', in Horace Newcomb (ed.), *Television: The Critical View* (New York: Oxford University Press, 1994), pp. 367–86.

Barker, Chris, *Global Television: An Introduction* (Oxford: Blackwell, 1997).

Baron, David, 'Hallmark Enters Cable Business', *Digital Business*, vol. 1, no. 6 (11 November 1991), p. 10.

Bowes, Elena, ' "Scarlett" Miniseries Readies for Global Debut', *Electronic Media* (14 February 1994), p. 28.

Bowser, Andrew, 'Cable Networks Score with Big-ticket Original Movies, Miniseries', *Broadcasting & Cable* (26 October 1998), p. 46.

Buchanan, Richard, Director, Programme Operations, Crown Media International, Inc. Interview, Denver, Colorado (24 July 2001).

Byars, Jackie and Meehan, Eileen R., 'Once in a Lifetime: Constructing "The Working Woman" through Cable Narrowcasting', in Horace Newcomb (ed.), *Television: The Critical View* (New York: Oxford University Press, 2000), pp. 144–69.

Carter, Bill, 'CBS is Betting on ' "Scarlett" to Get Back in Ratings Hunt', *New York Times* (14 November 1994), section D, p. 1.

Carugati, Anna, 'Eventful Television: Europe Sees Value in Big-Budget Miniseries', *Electronic Media* (14 February 1994), p. 22.

Chatterjee, Purvita, 'Kermit and Hallmark Channels to Indianise Programming', *Business Line* (8 July 1999).

Citron, Alan, 'Growing Trend in Hollywood Is to Bypass the Box Office for Pay TV', *Los Angeles Times* (28 July 1992), part D, p. 1.

Coe, Steve, 'Frankly, CBS and RHI Give a Damn', *Broadcasting* (11 November 1991), p. 28.

Curtin, Michael, 'On Edge: Culture Industries in the Neo-Network Era', in Richard Ohmann (ed.), *Making and Selling Culture* (Hanover: Wesleyan University Press, 1996), pp. 181–202.

Dempsey, John, 'Lifetime Pacts for Pearson Pix', *Daily Variety* (5 November 1998), p. 3.

Dempsey, John, 'Cable's Mad for Made-Fors', *Variety* (26 July–1 August 1999), p. 17.

Fabrikant, Geraldine, 'For TV Producers, What Plays in Peoria Does Not Play Abroad',
    New York Times (10 November 1997), section D, p. 1.

Fidgeon, Robert, 'Moby Dick's Epic Trauma', *Herald Sun* (24 December 1997), p. 8 (edition 2).

Flint, Joe, 'Hallmark on the Go', *Daily Variety* (6 July 1995), p. 3.

Gitlin, Todd, *Inside Prime Time* (New York: Pantheon Books, 1983).

Goldsmith, Jill, 'Crown Plans $288 Mil IPO', *Daily Variety*, (1 February 2000), p. 6.

Gripsrud, Jostein, *The Dynasty Years: Hollywood Television and Critical Media Studies*
    (London: Routledge, 1995).

Grossberg, Lawrence, 'Speculations and Articulations of Globalization', *Polygraph*, no. 11
    (1999), pp. 11–48.

Guider, Elizabeth, 'Hamdon Gets Its Hands on Telepix', *Variety*, (25–31 January 1999), p. 60.

Hamm, Jennifer, 'Could Prague's Film Boom Go Bust?', *The Prague Post* (22 August 2001).

Harmon, Amy, 'Exploration of World Wide Web Tilts from Eclectic to Mundane', *New York
    Times* (26 August 2001), section 1, p. 1.

Herman, Edward S. and McChesney, Robert W., *The Global Media: The New Missionaries of
    Corporate Capitalism* (London: Cassell, 1997).

Hilmes, Michele, 'Pay Television: Breaking the Broadcast Bottleneck', in Tino Balio (ed.),
    Hollywood in the Age of Television (Boston, MA: Unwin Hyman, 1990), pp. 297–318.

Hils, Miriam, 'Power of Babelsberg', *Variety* (23–9 March 1998), p. 18.

Jacobs, Jennifer, 'Hallmark Reaches Out to the Masses', *Business Times* (Malaysia)
    (22 December 1997), Companies, p. 6.

Karofsky, Andy, Vice President, Marketing, Crown Media International, Inc. Interview, Denver,
    Colorado (24 July 2001).

Katz, Michael, 'HBO, a Cable Original', *Broadcasting & Cable*, vol. 41, no. 126 (30 September
    1996), p. 66.

Kiesewetter, John, 'Tonight's "Night Ride Home" is Beloved Series' 200th Telecast in 49 Years:
    Hallmark's Hall of Fame Tradition' (7 February 1999), p. G1.

Kindred, Jack, 'German Special Effects Center Challenges Hollywood', *Deutsche Presse-Agentur*
    (30 March, 1999).

Krosnar, Katka, 'Take One: Prague', *Newsweek* (19 March 2001), p. 40.

Lafferty, William, 'Feature Films on Prime-Time Television', in Tino Balio (ed.), *Hollywood in the
    Age of Television* (Boston, MA: Unwin Hyman, 1990), pp. 235–56.

Liebes, Tamar and Katz, Elihu, *The Export of Meaning: Cross Cultural Readings of 'Dallas'*
    (Oxford: Oxford University Press, 1990).

Lohr, Steve and Holson, Laura M., 'Price of Joining Old and New Was Core Issue in AOL
    Deal', *New York Times* (16 January 2000), section 1, p. 1.

Lowry, Brian, ' "Scarlett" Eyes Turn to "Blue" ', *Daily Variety* (17 November 1994), p. 1.

Lowry, J. and Robinsbrian, Max, ' "Scarlett" Has Nets Maxed out on Minis', *Variety*
    (21–7 November 1994), p. 1.

Madigan, Nick, 'Canucks Pluck Biz Bucks', *Daily Variety* (25 June 1999), p. 1.

Mahoney, William, 'U.S. Syndicator Aims at Worldwide Market', *Electronic Media* (16 October
    1989), p. 41.

Mahoney, William, 'Viacom's Visionary', *Multichannel News*, vol. 5, no. 1 (January 1999), International Supplement, pp. 9–11.

McConville, Jim, 'Home Grown Flavor: Cable Networks Hope for Harvest from Original Fare', *Electronic Media* (20 September 1999), p. 1.

Menichini, Mike, 'Originals Drive Network's Brand', *Electronic Media* (19 July 1999), p. 16.

Menon, Vinay, 'X-Men Wizard to Abandon World of Special Effects', *Toronto Star* (19 August 2000), Business section.

Miller, Toby, *Technologies of Truth: Cultural Citizenship and the Popular Media* (Minneapolis: University of Minnesota Press, 1998).

Mills, Nancy, 'Shooting Their Own', *Los Angeles Times* (30 September 1990), Calendar, p. 7.

Moran, Albert, *Copycat Television: Globalisation, Program Formats and Cultural Identity* (Luton: University of Luton Press, 1998), pp. 25–71.

Nava, Mica, 'Framing Advertising: Cultural Analysis and the Incrimination of Visual Texts', in Mica Nava, Andrew Black, Iain MacRury and Barry Richards (eds), *Buy This Book: Studies in Advertising and Consumption* (London and New York: Routledge, 1997) pp. 34–50.

Parrish, Gene, Director, Programme Operations, Crown Media International, Inc. Interview, Denver, Colorado (24 July 2001).

Parsons, Patrick R. and Frieden, Robert M., *The Cable and Satellite Television Industries* (Boston, MA: Allyn and Bacon, 1998).

Paxman, Andrew and Woods, Mark, 'Hallmark Calling Card: Latin Web', *Variety* (6–12 November 1995), p. 52.

Puttnam, David, *Movies and Money* (New York: Vintage Books, 2000).

Rapping, Elayne, *The Movie of the Week: Private Stories, Public Events* (Minneapolis: University of Minnesota Press, 1992).

Schiller, Herbert, *Mass Communication and American Empire* (New York: A. M. Kelley, 1969).

Schneider, Michael, 'May Sweeps Deja View: Theatrical Repeats Will Run Amok in May Sweeps', *Electronic Media* (5 April 1999), p. 36.

Schreiber, Dominic, 'Building an Event', *Television Business International* (December 1999), pp. 24–5.

Schulze, Laurie, 'The Made-for-TV Movie: Industrial Practice, Cultural Form, Popular Reception', in Horace Newcomb (ed.), *Television: The Critical View* (Oxford: Oxford University Press, 1994), pp. 351–76.

Screen Digest, no. 306 (April 1997), pp. 81–2.

Screen Digest, no. 342 (April 2000), pp. 117–20.

Segrave, Kerry, *Movies at Home: How Hollywood Came to Television* (Jefferson, NC: McFarland, 1999).

Sell, Suzanne, Vice President, Research and Media Planning, Crown Media International, Inc. Interview, Denver, Colorado (25 July 2001).

Setlowe, Rick, 'MOW Growth Area O'Seas', *Variety* (22–8 September 1997), p. M19.

Shaw, Russell, 'Northern Locale Drives TV Costs South', *Electronic Media* (2 August 1999), p. 18.

Sinclair, John, *Latin American Television: A Global View* (Oxford: Oxford University Press, 1999).

Sinclair, John, Jacka, Elizabeth and Cunningham, Stuart, *New Patterns in Global Television: Peripheral Vision* (New York: Oxford University Press, 1996).

Streeter, Thomas, *Selling the Air: A Critique of the Policy of Commercial Broadcasting in the United States* (Chicago: University of Chicago Press, 1996).

Streeter, Thomas, 'Blue Skies and Strange Bedfellows: The Discourse of Cable Television', in Lynn Spigel and Michael Curtin (eds), *The Revolution Wasn't Televised: Sixties Television and Social Conflict* (New York: Routledge, 1997), pp. 221–42.

Tagliabue, John, 'Film Redux in Europe', *New York Times* (24 February 1996), section 1, p. 33.

Todreas, Timothy M., *Value Creation and Branding in Television's Digital Age* (Westport, CT: Quorum Books, 1999).

Tran, Mark, 'Who Gives a Damn?', *The Guardian* (London) (10 November 1994), p. T10.

Tunstall, Jeremy, *The Media Are American* (London: Constable, 1977).

Varis, Tapio, 'International Flow of Television Programs', *Journal of Communication*, no. 34 (1984), p. 1.

Vlessing, Etan, 'Profile: Canada', *Television Business International* (December 1999), p. 32.

Waterman, David and Weiss, Andrew A., *Vertical Integration in Cable Television* (Cambridge, MA: MIT Press, 1997).

Wayne, Hicks L., 'Changing the Channel', *Denver Business Journal*, vol. 29, no. 50 (12 March 1999), p. 1A.

Weinraub, Bernard, ' "Scarlett" Entices CBS Group into an $8 Million TV Accord', *New York Times* (4 November 1991), p. 1.

Wildman, Steven S., *International Trade in Films and TV Programs* (Cambridge, MA: Ballinger, 1988).

Woods, Mark, 'Aussie Coprods' Global Focus', *Variety* (19–25 January 1998), p. 82.

Wright, Emma, 'Flexible Packages', *Television Business International* (December 1999), pp. 30–3.

6

'Must See' Queer TV: History and Serial Form in *Ellen*

Anna McCarthy

In American network television, one manifestation of the 'must see TV' paradigm is a promotional strategy that characterises entertainment division products, particularly episodes of prime-time TV shows, as media events. *Media event* is a term we generally associate with spectacular, non-fiction TV forms. It includes coverage of external crises, in which interruptive news reporting takes over the schedule, and it encompasses broadcasts like the state funerals examined by Dayan and Katz (1992), 'high holidays' coded as collectivising national displays. But the media events of 'must see TV' are of a different sort. Highly scheduled and publicised, 'must see' media events are generated from within the institution of TV entertainment. Often, they are momentous occasions in the life spans of comedy and drama series, occurring at temporally significant moments in the annual broadcast schedule; end-of-season cliffhangers and series finales are two obvious examples of this phenomenon. 'Must see TV' events generally involve major plot shifts, such as marriages, and they may coincide with events in the economic institution of television, most notably 'sweeps week', when local television markets are measured in order to set advertising rates.

Interestingly, this kind of manufactured eventfulness is particularly evident in series that are nearing the end of their life cycle. Many shows, especially sitcoms, become messy and baroque when they start to lose steam. Plots undergo major developmental speedups, characters undergo sudden reversals and rapprochements with each other, and preachy 'issue shows' start to appear (the final seasons of *M*A*S*H* furnish instructive examples of all of the above). In this stage of a series' 'evolution', promotional discourse takes eventfulness and seriousness over the top, most obviously in the sermonising language through which announcers alert viewers of important upcoming episodes ('Friday, on a very special *Mr Belvedere*'). The recurrence of media event discourses around late-season sitcom episodes on American television is consistent and recognisable enough to have spawned 'jumptheshark.com' an entire website devoted to the phenomenon. (The title refers to a stunt pulled by the Fonz in a late episode of *Happy Days*, a series that underwent a very extended wind down.) Although risible, these 'must see' media events are worth noting, as they often represent moments when 'politics' are allowed to enter the world of prime-time light entertainment – usually

in the form of taboo subjects, like pregnancy or drug use, or through the introduction of racially or sexually 'minoritised' characters. Through such devices, producers
seek to inject a sense of relevance into the otherwise flabby plotlines of late-season
sitcoms.

The signifiers of the 'must see TV' event as a form of political display were certainly
evident in the case of the 'coming out' episode of the sitcom *Ellen*, which aired on 30
April 1997. The programme was defined as a media event in three distinct ways. It was
a political moment in national culture, one in which a celebrity's declaration of lesbian
identity and pride became a matter for extended news coverage.[1] It was a moment of
extreme narrative development for the lead character in the show, one that had been
anticipated for an entire season. And, interestingly, many commentators proclaimed this
moment of 'must see TV' as a *structural shift* in the sitcom form: it was an occasion we
were all supposed to remember as the moment when gay lives 'finally' became part of
mainstream TV. In this respect, the broadcast was understood by many as a 'first' in the
genre. In short, the event was a *formal* one, in both the textual and the ritualistic sense
of the word, within television as an institution. Gay fictions and characters could
now permanently and officially be allowed to shape the structure of American sitcom
narrative (as opposed to haunting its edges very conspicuously, as Tony Randall's Sidney
did in *Love Sidney*, or lasting only temporarily, as was the case with Billy Crystal's
character on *Soap*).[2]

The sense of firstness that enhanced the broadcast's status as a media event simultaneously helped secure the perception that the show was also *history*. The adjective
historic was extensively bandied about in the entertainment news coverage of
DeGeneres' plans to come out in her sitcom. Yet, in such coverage, the act of placing
the episode in history ran into complications. Commentators often followed up on
their descriptions of the show's lesbian character and star as something that had never
before occurred in television with the somewhat contradictory assertion that gay characters and stars had existed on the small screen for a very long time, offering long lists
of the queer people of all sorts who have appeared on television in decades past. Such
moments often led also into genealogical recitations of other 'first' milestones in the past
liberalisation of the sitcom's representational politics. A writer in the *Denver Post*, for
example, noted:

> In bringing her character out of the closet, DeGeneres joins the ranks of other TV 'firsts.'
> She'll be in the pop pantheon with the first black dramatic co-star in a regular series (Bill
> Cosby in 'I Spy,' 1965); the first black sitcom star (Diahann Carroll in 'Julia,' 1968); the first
> Hispanic sitcom (Norman Lear's 'A.K.A. Pablo,' which came and went in 1984, starring Paul
> Rodriguez); and the first unmarried woman allowed to have a sex life in prime time (career
> gal Mary Richards in 1970's 'The Mary Tyler Moore Show'). TV already has dozens of gay
> supporting characters; the numbers have increased steadily since Billy Crystal played TV's
> first openly gay character in 1977's 'Soap.' At the end of this month, TV will count a gay lead
> in a regular series, too.
>
> Ostrow, 1997, p. E-01

This litany of firsts is interesting in its errors (why no mention of *Beulah*, or Desi Arnaz?) and also because its very length diminishes the impact of *Ellen*'s first. But this only tells us how manufactured 'firsts' are. Indeed, no-one worked harder to produce a sense of firstness than DeGeneres herself, who repeatedly sought to align the episode with other pioneering moments in history. Most notably, in an interview with Diane Sawyer, she compared herself to Rosa Parks, the black woman whose 1955 refusal to move to the back of a Montgomery bus features prominently at the beginning of many popular narratives of the American Civil Rights movement.

This attempt to link Civil Rights activism and television representation tells us something about the historical logic behind DeGeneres' understanding of social change and her role within it. It is a logic based upon a sense of identity, and of historical progress, in which race- and sexuality-based oppressions are rendered commensurable or at the very least analogous to each other. The assumption that sexuality is 'like race' in some way or another is predominant on many different social levels, from the legislative arena to everyday political vernaculars, although its role in progressive social change is an ambivalent, contradictory and disjunctive one, to say the least (Halley, 2000). Although hard to accept, this model of historical change is certainly characteristic of the way sitcom history often gets told. Indeed, DeGeneres' self-fashioning as a gay Rosa Parks affirmed such visions of what might be called the liberal progressive narrative of TV history. A key element in popular and professional understandings of the history of the sitcom's 'evolution', this is the idea of the genre as a mirror of broader currents of social change. This narrative often consists of whiggish tales in which the sitcom form became more socially responsible. Certain names figure prominently in this process, most notably *All in the Family* producer Norman Lear. Lear, the story goes, not only re-tooled the demographic of the situation comedy, he also changed its cultural politics. Clearly, this history is a highly racialised one; many of its milestones have to do with non-white characters, or, in the case of one of the major ones, with the circulation of figures of white racism in the character of Archie Bunker. Given this situation, DeGeneres' Rosa Parks comparison does not seem all that surprising.

As a programme which articulated a project of lesbian visibility through the publicity discourse of 'must see TV', *Ellen* makes an instructive case study in the processes through which programming structures, narratives and conventions serve as arenas for the expression, and management, of cultural or identity politics in American network television. As this chapter details, the liberal narrative of TV history turns out to be crucial, and crucially inadequate, for such a task. From the moment when the coming out episode marked the show as 'must see TV' to the very different forms of historicisation that accompanied the series' subsequent period of apparent failure, ending in cancellation, the programme's producers relied on historical characterisations, both within the episodes and in their promotions, to argue for the show's political importance. But these forms of historical discourse were not, indeed could not be, coherent. Indeed, as I will detail in this essay, *Ellen*'s attempts to affirm the liberal narrative of televisual progressive politics and to secure a place within it often worked to expose the inadequacy of

this narrative. This occurred not only in the difficulties involved in rendering race and
sexual identity somehow commensurate, but also in the fact that the show could not
resolve its incompatible models of temporality and history. It was stuck between the
spectacular eventfulness of 'must see TV' on the one hand, the predictably structured
seriality of the sitcom form on the other.

Forms of tension and contradiction are of course characteristic of the historiographic
voice of American television as an institution. A sense of history is, as Mimi White notes,
hardly a scarce commodity in television's everyday speech:

> Across an array of genres and events of different orders, television invokes 'history' as a
> meaningful term. Yet it is obvious that the result of this process . . . is not homogeneous or
> unified, and indeed, hardly conforms to the most common uses of the term history.
>
> 1989, pp. 282–3; see also Caldwell, 1994, p. 167

This is particularly notable in non-fiction television, frequently characterised by a seemingly compulsive urge to narrate its 'live' perspective on external events as historical,
eventful and truthful. The unremarkable, ordinary flow of the regular television schedule is crucial for this process. As Mary Ann Doane notes, it is through the rupture of its
own routine that television appears to have 'access to the momentary, the discontinuous,
the real' (1991, p. 238).

The incoherences of *Ellen*'s sense of history stem from the way it sought to attach a
sense of identity politics both to the interruptive attention-getting mode of address
associated with spectacular 'must see TV' and to the ongoing routines of seriality that
define 'uneventful' television. The explanation of the show's failure offered by ABC's
then-President Robert Iger illustrates this dynamic concisely. Evincing a curiously
durational sense of identity, he explained that *Ellen* 'became a program about a character who was gay every single week, and . . . that was too much for people' (quoted
in Huff, 1998, p. 77). This discomfort on Iger's part explains why, despite the fact that
ABC claimed frequently that the show's ratings were suffering, the network stepped
back from intensively publicising the gay *Ellen* as 'must see TV' after the coming
out episode. But Iger's statement is noteworthy for another reason too – specifically, for
the way it opposes gayness and televisual seriality, as if the ongoing flow of situations
and character development that defines the contemporary sitcom form is unable to
accommodate a same-sex world of desires and identifications. Iger's fantasy of gay
identity as a thing that can be switched on for special occasions – for sweeps week, perhaps – voices something more than an institutional concern that the show would now
be 'about' the character's identity as a lesbian and her relation to queer culture. Its fear
of a quotidian, ongoing lesbian life on TV suggests that although the network could
support queer television as 'must see TV', it could not sanction a lesbian invasion of serial television's more modest form of history-making, its ongoing, regularly scheduled
place in televisual flow. In this respect, the institutional crises surrounding everyday
gayness in *Ellen* and in the sitcom form repeated queer crises in seriality that had previously occurred in melodramatic television genres. As Joy Fuqua notes, similar concerns

with the ongoing representation of homosexuality arose when gay characters first entered soap opera (1995, pp. 199–212). However, the narrative trajectory of Steven Carrington, the gay character in *Dynasty*, raises the possibility that the extremist plotting conventions of serial melodramas allow for a more elastic sense of character and sexuality. After the murder of his male lover Carrington found a female partner, switched briefly back to a male partner, then fell in love with a woman again – a sexual history which suggests that melodrama's conventions can be used to prevent same-sex desires and identifications from becoming ongoing aspects of a series' unfolding narrative. As I will suggest, the politics of *Ellen*'s final season should be understood in this context. In this period, the programme sought to transfer its political affinities from a notion of queer TV as 'must see TV' to one in which gay life is not particularly remarkable, becoming part of television's repertoire of ongoing ways of narrativising the everyday. The process, I think, revealed a great deal about the limits of the liberal narrative of progressive television history. In its final season and in its finale, the show articulated in the quasi-complicit, quasi-ironic voice of the 1990s auteur sitcom the institutional and textual paradoxes of liberal history-making on television.

Serial versus episodic homosexuality

One of the many curious aspects of the sitcom as a television genre is the fact that its historical consciousness is itself a historical development. The distinction between episodic and serial narrative that Iger referenced in his remarks on *Ellen* was a paradigm-shifting moment in the development of the genre in the 1970s. In this period, in contrast to the Paul Henning 'rural' sitcoms of the 1960s, sitcoms began to take on characteristics of serial narrative, as part of the overall serialisation of prime-time television that Jane Feuer has traced in these years. This transformation was popularly explained as a transformation in the sitcom's audience and in American society, although, as Feuer notes, this explanation obscured factors such as shifting patterns in markets, and in network relations with production companies, in favour of the liberal tale of progress in which the medium became more socially responsible (1992, pp. 151–2). This narrative of the sitcom's development and liberalisation is not as simple as it seems. It at once brings history, in the sense of historical struggles for social justice and in the sense of ongoing serial development, into the textual repertoire on-screen, while simultaneously erasing the institutional history and politics that shaped this process. The emergence of seriality and, with it, ongoing character and story arcs was thus overdetermined as a moment when history started to figure prominently in the sitcom form. But if seriality marked a transformation within the sitcom's relationship to history, it was a partial transformation at best. Gay and lesbian characters were certainly part of this supposed liberalisation of the sitcom in certain ways, as in a key later episode of *All in the Family* in which Edith discovers that her recently deceased cousin was a lesbian who left a precious family heirloom to her lover. However, they were not generally part of the formal shift from purely one-off, static reiterations of the basic comic setup to fully fledged seriality. Indeed, one could argue that narrative development in sitcom was something of a hetero privilege; it is telling that Feuer's primary example of this trend is the development of Sam and Diane's relationship in *Cheers*, as it foregrounds the extent to which sitcom seriality seems to revolve around romance plots and couples. In this respect, the developmental path of TV comedy, in which the form appears to 'grow into' seriality, mirrors normative developmental narratives of sexuality: queer desire gets left behind as the genre 'matures'.[3]

Thus, before *Ellen*, same-sexness was an interruptive, marginal force in the sitcom, its duration limited to one-off figures in 'very special' episodes and supporting characters. Indeed, one could argue that serialisation and the 'adult' re-tooling of the sitcom actually *limited* queer possibilities in the sitcom form. For this textual shift also involved the elimination of the fantastic as a sitcom subgenre. Patricia White identifies a firmly established role for queer visibility in the 1960s sitcom when she notes the 'gay subculture' of wizards and warlocks who thronged on the narrative margins of the show *Bewitched*; as she astutely points out, Agnes Moorehead's character Endora 'literally cast a dark shadow over heterosexual relations each week when her credit . . . appears on a black cloud of smoke blotting out 'Derwood' and Samantha's embrace' (2000, p. 192). With the rise of the serialised situation comedy, rooted in some sense of the everyday, queerness became increasingly a matter for narrative *management*. As Lynne Joyrich notes, *Roseanne* thematised this very state of affairs in a famous 1994 Halloween episode in which Dan, Fred and Jackie conspire to make Roseanne think Fred is gay. After she catches Dan and Fred in bed together, she produces a detonator and blows the house up. Queerness here destroys not only the narrative arc but also the very fabric of the domestic sitcom's diegetic universe. But not permanently: next week, home life will resume as usual (2001).

Ellen's coming out episode was momentous because it promised to make queer life something other than an interruptive force, something potentially assimilated into the repertoire of romantic and personal situations replayed weekly on the prime-time sitcom. But the logic through which this occurred was a heteronormative one. Although it may have inaugurated a queer developmental moment in the sitcom, the coming out episode did so via conventions particularly associated with shows based on romantic *heterosexual* tensions, for example the domestic help romance subgenre exemplified by *The Nanny* and *Who's the Boss*. In these shows, frequent hints, one-offs and missed connections abound from season to season. They set up a sense of romantic tension that can last several years, with the implicit promise that it will be resolved at the end of the series. Similarly, the revelation of the 'Puppy Episode' was anticipated via a series of ongoing hints, winks and 'almosts' which communicated the impending development. This technique was self-reflexive and ironic in its references to the publicity the show was getting, but it simultaneously structured the plot development in very conventional, 'hetero-identified' sitcom terms, of which it seemed to have no awareness.

In its embattled, post-coming out season, *Ellen* did not succeed in achieving serial homosexuality, with all the connotations of normativity and routine attached to it. Some episodes were quite forthrightly queer tales, whereas others were clearly pitched as allegories for the institutional battles being fought between the producers and the networks behind the scenes. In these latter broadcasts, the show reverted to its earlier, more episodic structure. These programmes primarily involved the regular cast of characters who predated the coming out episode; they did not feature Laurie, Ellen's new girlfriend, nor indeed any references to the narrative arc of Ellen's experiences as a first-time participant in a lesbian relationship. Many of these allegorical episodes attempted to call televisual norms and conventions into question through visually presented, semi-ironic comparisons between the acceptance of racial diversity and the acceptance of queerness. These comparisons tend to hint at the idea of a double standard, as in 'G.I. Ellen', where a Chinese-American Robert E. Lee scoffs at the idea of women playing soldiers. However, the racial analogies remain only partially articulated – visually coded rather than verbally stated. Because they communicate their polemic through implication, these moments seem offered up by the show's producers as tutelary examples of how to make sitcom history in a 'quiet' way – not by lecturing, but through parable. The Chinese-American Confederate General may communicate a spurious analogy, one which unravels when you ask how queerness on TV can be comparable to colour-blind casting, but the character nevertheless seems offered as a loose metaphor for the progress of the sitcom. The polemic he supports is the idea that the genre is on a pathway towards increasing liberalisation, one based on the widening of the pool of minoritarian subjects available as stock character types. However, the fact that this sense of progressive history is not stated directly but rather hinted at through comedy marks these allegorical episodes as convoluted, quasi-closeted political speech acts, ones that replicate the institutional and textual conundrum of queer representation within serial prime-time television more than they resolved it.

The episode called 'Ellen in Focus' rewards closer examination because of the way it advances the racial analogy through an insistent engagement with the criteria that determine whether TV shows 'succeed' or 'fail' – a pointed issue for the producers as the network started to distance itself from the lesbian content, citing ratings as evidence that the show was a failure. In this episode, Ellen and her friend Joe join a focus group to discuss a TV pilot written by Ellen's friend Paige. The pilot, a detective programme, features a short male lead because Paige wants to curry favour with her short male boss; Ellen's covert mission is to enter the focus group and swing people's opinions in favour of the show. The choice of this setting is significant. Staging the action within a key institutional scenario in the test marketing of television programmes is an obvious reference to the show's behind the scenes battle over ratings. What is interesting about it, however, is the way its allegorical political speech is uttered – via a discussion of the history of the situation comedy and of the political stakes involved in its representational codes. As in the Civil War re-enactment episode, the allegory is advanced on the level of character. One focus group member complains that a short cop character is not 'realistic'. Another adds that short actors are meant to be funny, not heroic, on television. Ellen and Joe try to convince them otherwise, but finally a group member called Emily, played by black actress Marcia White, gets frustrated and blurts out 'I just prefer characters that are normal.' In a parodic, lecturing tone,

Ellen responds,

> What is normal? I mean come on. If we put different characters on TV right now, in twenty
> years from now our kids won't think it's so weird to be different. I mean before The *Beverly*
> *Hillbillies*, people used to think it was weird to eat dinner off a pool table.

A long discussion of the history of sitcoms follows, using examples all drawn from the pre-serialisation history of the form (the group discusses, for example, the actual locations of Petticoat Junction, Mayberry, Hooterville and Mount Pilot).

Classic sitcom history thus becomes the means for delivering broader 'messages' about the role of queer people in television, affirming the liberal narrative of television history that positions programming as a pedagogical form that will raise better, more tolerant children. The fact that a black woman, Diahann Carroll, occupies a central position in this liberal tale suggests that the casting of a black woman as the prompt for Ellen's humorous lecture is a form of ironic commentary on the changing nature of norms in television. It is ironic in the sense that this black female character appears to have no historical knowledge; we are meant to note that she is unaware of the fact that characters 'like' her were once largely excluded from sitcom casts. This is presumably in order to communicate how far the genre's casting practices have come, and to caution viewers to be aware of the dangers of historical amnesia. We can read in this moment an echo of post-Civil Rights era activist anxieties, a concern that the present generation (viewed as complacent and, the implication is, fully enfranchised) is ignorant of the struggles of the past and, by extension, in danger of losing political consciousness in the future. As a rhetorical move, this casting strategy seems intended as a call for a (somewhat incoherent) coalitional politics of representation. It is as if the writers are trying to show black viewers that they should be invested in the idea of gay and lesbian characters on television because the situation of gay and lesbian viewers today is analogous to that of black viewers in decades past.

This analogical approach to identity politics in the sitcom, an approach which I am arguing structures a number of the episodes of the final season, has important consequences. It requires that the show's moments of activist speech must be confined to the representation of aspects of homophobia that are easily rendered analogous to race – like internalised homophobia, a topic treated in several episodes. What we see only rarely is the direct representation of difficult aspects of queer daily life, including the ongoing fact of having to negotiate oppressive straight behaviour. This happens really only in one episode, where we see Ellen and Laurie get 'the treatment' when they try and get a hotel room with a double bed. And interestingly, in this episode we see a more complex understanding of the relation between sexual politics and racial politics, as Ellen and Laurie end up bonding with an interracial couple who, like, them, are waiting endlessly for a table in a restaurant. But this episode is somewhat exceptional. In the context of a show's 'developmental' leap into queerness, striving towards serial homosexuality, the continuing need to find analogies for same-sex desire in other modes of social identity remind us of how difficult an issue – institutionally, formally, politically – the ongoing representation of queer everyday life on television can be. And it communicates forcefully the fact that making queer television history within the prime-time sitcom is inevitably an act of 'making do'. These closeted, allegorical episodes of *Ellen*'s final season were institutionally critical and self-aware, and very much in step with the intertextual and ironic strategies of the auteur sitcom of the 1990s. But they simultaneously failed to challenge the analogical models of identity and political change that structure 'official' histories of the sitcom form.

Making queer television history

In the final episode of the series, the producers returned to the interruptive structure of the media event with a much-hyped hour-long broadcast that sought, more explicitly than any of the past season's episodes, to simultaneously expose and enter the liberal narrative of TV history. The episode was a fictionalised documentary parodying star biography programmes, like *E! True Hollywood Story*, that make up a large amount of programming on cable television networks in the United States (other examples are *Biography* on the A&E network and *Behind the Music* on VH1). As a finale, this broadcast was curious, as it did not tie up any loose ends in the series. In fact, the season did not really crystallise in this episode in any sense at all. An unsentimental break with Ellen Morgan's life, it fully abandoned the narrative arc of her relationship to Laurie in order to explore the possibilities of non-narrative television as a site for queer TV historiography. In embracing a non-serial, non-narrative form as a final attempt to create queer 'must see TV', the episode fully exploited television's contradictory historiographic procedures, and called attention to the unassimilable forms of difference that, in resisting analogy, challenge both the progressivism and the coherence of these procedures.

The humour of the episode, which narrated Ellen's fictional lifetime in show biz, lay in the way it placed Ellen DeGeneres at the centre of the entire history of the sitcom form. She appears here as a shapeshifting historical subject similar to movie characters like Forrest Gump and Zelig who are miraculously present at key moments in the visually rendered national past. In this case, the past in question is the TV past, and its protean subject is a sitcom main character. We learn about fictional Ellen's life and the decades-running show via the conventions that have increasingly come to define American *cable* documentary: clips from (fictionalised) past eras of the show, recycled stock footage, celebrity interviews and promotional 'behind the scenes' entertainment news. In a clip parodying the popular 1950s panel show format, for example, we see DeGeneres as an urbane, cigarette-smoking host of a (*What's My Line*-like) show called *Spot the Commie*, cracking Groucho-style jokes. In another clip, presented as a segment of the original and 'unaired' pilot of her sitcom, she plays the witty, martini-drinking wife of a businessman played by Woody Harrelson. And in yet another 'fragment' from the 'classic' era of the show she is incarnated as a pregnant Lucille Ball type, grinding coffee beans with her feet in a giant vat – a tribute to a Lucy episode in which Lucy and Ethel stamp on grapes. Interwoven with the clips and celebrity testimonials is an on-the-set interview with Ellen and Linda Ellerbee.

'*Ellen*: A Hollywood Tribute' presented a queer view of the cable biography show's recycling of the television past and its modes of TV stardom, trading on popular knowledge of the history of sitcom programme forms on TV. It offered a rewriting of the liberal narrative of the sitcom's role in progressive television history, one in which – as I will discuss presently – racial analogies continued to play a problematic and, in some cases, undermining role. The episode's awareness of this liberal narrative is signalled in the humorous attribution of a number of 'firsts' the show achieved over the course of its fictional forty-year run. In one of the interviews with Linda Ellerbee, DeGeneres notes, 'We were the first show where characters got trapped in a meat locker. Where someone has two dates on the same night . . . Where someone learns a valuable lesson.' Over the course of the show her innovation is described, variously, as: the first appearance of a 'single woman' on TV, the first appearance of a 'pregnant woman' on TV, and also – following a replay of a climactic moment in the Puppy episode in which she agonises about being a thirty-five-year-old in the closet – 'the first time on television somebody was honest about their age'. Among the number of 'firsts' attributed to DeGeneres over the course of this episode, the lesbian plot of *Ellen* is strikingly absent. As a polemical strategy, this purposive elision both complies with the programming politics of the closet that would deny any specificity to queerness and asserts the problem that queerness poses for TV's representational politics: the *difficulty* of making same-sex desire uneventful, serial, everyday. Elsewhere, indeed, the episode's rhetoric seems to suggest that this is something that can only happen in a queer television future. When Ellerbee asks DeGeneres why she is not making a big deal out of the fact that she 'came out' on national TV, DeGeneres jokes that the 'gay thing' was 'just the spin the network put on it. They're gay crazy over there.' She then reiterates the official 'lesson' of this particular, final episode: comparing queerness to saying the word *pregnant* on TV, and echoing a line of dialogue from the allegorical episode 'Ellen in Focus', she says 'I mean, twenty years from now it's going to be one fat "so what".'

Instead of a racial analogy, this moment offers up an analogy based on similarities between the representation of reproductive status and the representation of same-sex desire. In fact, this pregnancy analogy serves as the dominant framework for the episode's understanding both of the formal transformations of the sitcom and the popular reassessments of the genre's politics that accompanied these changes. In the '*Lucy*' clip, which we see first, the dialogue calls attention to Ellen's pregnancy via euphemistic references like 'a bun in the oven' in order to underscore the absurdity of sitcom morals and to expose the structure of open secrets on which they are often based. This readily understood indictment of the network's ambivalent treatment of queerness on *Ellen* is supported by a clip from a 'later season' of the programme. This clip, which parodies Norman Lear-era sitcom codes, seems intended to remind us of the fact that certain shows, like *All in the Family*, have always generated controversy. In this clip, a discussion of Audrey's abortion and her 'right to choose' is followed by a scene in which Ellen delivers a shock to her grumpy, Archie Bunker-like father, introducing him to her large family of newly adopted children – a troupe of black kids in Afro wigs who deliver wisecracks over funky 1970s urban sitcom theme music.

This parody of 1970s sitcom realism exemplifies the way this final episode approached the act of historical rewriting, namely, via the familiar sitcom logic in which irony and sincerity comfortably coexist. In this scene, a discussion of women's reproductive rights is meant to foreground the centrist and pedagogical liberal politics of the sitcom's 'lessons' and, it would seem, to support them at the same time. It begins with Paige telling Audrey that she and Ellen have burned their bras. Audrey responds, 'Well sisters, while you were out burning symbols of the white, patriarchal establishment, *I* got an abortion'. As the laugh track echoes incongruously, Paige hastily adds in a serious, lecturing tone 'which I'm sure was a hard choice, but ultimately yours to make'. Audrey makes a peace sign and the scene ends. Affirming reproductive rights and at the same time parodying their gradual inclusion in the liberal political spectrum of (the fictional version of) *Ellen*, the clip offers one 'official' account of the way queerness might be allowed to enter the sitcom. According to this version, lesbian desire can be thought of as parallel to the historical narrative of female reproductive (hetero)sexuality – appearing first via innuendo and suggestion, then via the episodic 'issue-based' narrative structure of the Lear era.

However, alongside the official analogy between queerness and pregnancy, the episode cannot resist the identitarian power of the racial analogies on which the show based its sense of history and politics throughout its last season. The analogy resurfaces in covert ways via the generally parodic use of two hoary conventions of cable biography programmes. The first is the interpolation of celebrity testimonials, excised from interviews conducted in the minimal *mise en scène* of a dark, setless studio, between the historical 'clips' of *Ellen*'s past and DeGeneres' interview with Ellerbee. The second is the use of stock footage and still photographic inserts to break up interviews. In keeping with the spoof aesthetic, the episode introduces stock footage somewhat randomly into the interview segments. (When Ellen mentions having slept with the Kennedys, for example, we see a brief shot of JFK and RFK that seems meant as an ironic sendup of the decontextualising visual strategies of History Channel documentaries.) Both of these conventions are devices through which black people's images are made present within the episode, and in this respect they serve as potent reminders of the limits of identity analogies in activism and in historiography, undermining the liberal narrative of progressive television history that '*Ellen*: A Hollywood Tribute' seems to promote. This is because the episode, while it finds an analogy between pregnancy and queerness acceptable, also displays a marked inability to speak its racial analogies directly, resorting instead to an incoherent, visually conveyed language of hints. The hesitance with which it invokes racial analogies might signal a half-awareness of the problems such analogies pose, not only as ways of thinking about the politics of identity, but also as historical statements about television, given that segregationist programming strategies, casting standards and narrative situations continue to define the prime-time TV line up in the United States.

In the first instance, the rupture occurs through Diahann Carroll's presence among the celebrities major and minor who testify on the topic of Ellen DeGeneres's importance in TV history. The humour running throughout these testimonials derives from the fact that they are often unable to recall who Ellen is. This fits with the larger political goal of the show, namely, to allow gay lives to appear as banal and unremarkable as the lives of any other sitcom character, and thus to assert that the most groundbreaking queer television is television in which queerness doesn't seem groundbreaking at all. In her interview, Carroll gives a sincere and heartfelt speech of admiration which, when she finishes it, is clearly about Ella Fitzgerald. When the producer interrupts from off-screen and says, 'No, no, Ellen DeGeneres,' she looks blank. 'Who?' The use of Diahann Carroll to enjoin this idea that queer television should *not* be considered remarkable places her in a somewhat paradoxical speaking position. After all, she herself is a fragment of TV history, one often both forgotten and resurrected in the same rhetorical instance, as we saw in a journalistic passage quoted at the very beginning of this essay. Her appearance in this episode asserts the historicity that she is asked to deny verbally, namely that there are *limits* to the principle of equivalent identities on which official sitcom history advances. In what ways is Diahann Carroll 'like' Ellen DeGeneres? Furthermore, her presence encourages us to reflect on the *whiteness* of gay television as represented by *Ellen* and by the 'gay TV' craze of the 2000–1 season, in which, despite numerous shows with gay characters, only one is not white (Carter on *Spin City*).[4] This sense of television's continued representational homogeneity, despite the supposed progress made by decades of black visibility in the sitcom, can only halt optimistic historical narratives of the queer television future, or at least force them to incorporate a more complex view of identity.

We can discern an awareness of the limits of such narratives in the episode's use of the other convention of cable TV historiography – stock footage. Although this footage is often used parodically, this is not *always* the case, and the moments in which it is used differently are notable. In one particular instance, recognisably momentous historical footage appears in the episode as a seemingly more straightforward kind of 'truth-bearing' form of evidence. In the leadup to the fictional clip of the sitcom *Ellen* in its Lear-era incarnation, Ellerbee asks Ellen if she remembers that the 1960s was also a 'dark time' for America. She speaks over snippets of stock footage edited together in a manner immediately recognisable from televisual narratives of national history. As Ellerbee intones, 'this was a turbulent era. War, racism, unrest: difficult topics for humor,' we see images of Vietnam war demonstrations and of Civil Rights protesters being hit by hoses. The latter footage, blurry and degraded, appears to be lifted from a video copy of *Eyes on the Prize*, the 1987 Blackside Films' documentary of the Civil Rights movement. Its anachronistic usage alongside images of Vietnam war protests, only confirming damning views of television history as an amnesiac fiction, comes as a shock, and undermines in its indigestible realness the narrative of progressive sitcom politics it is invoked to support. Although the episode's ongoing comparison of pregnancy and queerness signals an acceptance of the idea that analogies for sexual identity are a form of political speech, this Civil Rights footage communicates the problems with analogies as ways of thinking about identity politics and social change.

Whether this footage is intended to be read this way is another matter. Given that its use is not only a decontextualisation but also a somewhat desecrating lack of engagement of the issues of representation that come with historical footage, it more likely reflects an unthinking desire to find a shorthand way of signalling awareness of the conventions of the cable documentary while borrowing the economical mode of

storytelling associated with it. The result is a view of political justice via civil rights and
the diversification of character types on television as equivalent forms of social change.
At the very least, the footage promotes the idea that representation on television is the
true test of whether equality has been achieved. At this moment in the episode, the final
season's clearly undecided relation to the politics of racial analogies opens up some
cracks in the official story of the sitcom.

Many in the industry would hold up the example of *Will & Grace*'s 2000 Emmy sweep
to argue that even though *Ellen* 'failed', it 'won' a place for everyday, serialised leading
gay characters at the sitcom table. What I have tried to do in the foregoing is shift the
fulcrum point of debates over the show's success and failure, debates which would seem
to insist that cultural representations always *either* open up *or* close down political possibilities – rather than rendering, or re-drawing, the relationships between different
political narratives. My argument has been that the show succeeded not so much in its
stated goal of broadening the representational horizons of the sitcom, but in another
way. It succeeded in exploring the terms of queer representation in prime-time serial TV,
and it did so through an interesting, if not entirely worked out or cognisant relationship
to the contradictory understandings of history and identity that define the dominant view
of political progress in the entertainment divisions of networks. As the culmination and
definitive statement of this search for a queer future in the TV past, the final episode
raised, without resolving, the conundrum of queer visibility on TV. It was not 'in control'
of its ability to reconfigure relations of continuity and interruption, of eventfulness and
uneventfulness, of commensurable and incommensurable identities, by any means.
Rather, *Ellen*'s final season seems to suggest these contradictions can be played out in
the narrative, and historiographic, voices of prime-time network television – in this case,
the modes of representation that characterise particular sitcoms once they have 'jumped
the shark'. If only because of its beleaguered, pre-cancellation status, *Ellen* achieved an
uncommon queer metadiscourse on TV programming forms – 'must see' and uneventful TV, the serial and the episodic – and their relation to history. And in so doing, the
show actually set an interesting agenda for queer Media Studies, one that goes beyond
matters of positive and negative images of gay characters, by challenging us to ask how
the figure of the queer subject intersects with, and challenges, television's institutional
structures of representation.

Acknowledgments

I am indebted to Victoria Johnson and Patricia White for generously sharing tapes and
thoughts at different moments in the course of the writing process, and to members of
the NYU Faculty Working Group in Queer Studies for their very helpful commentary.
These arguments are explored in more detail in '*Ellen*: Making Queer Television
History', *GLQ*, vol. 7, no. 4 (2001).

Notes

1. There were good reasons to be ambivalent about the politics of *Ellen* as a moment of
   mainstreaming within television as an institution. Eric Clarke notes in *Virtuous Vice* that

DeGeneres' media pronouncements around the coming out episode only enforced normative ideals of representative gay citizenship, most notoriously when she denounced 'Dykes on Bykes' as queer extremism in a *Time* magazine interview (Clarke, 2000, p. 7). Indeed, DeGeneres explicitly rejected any connection to defiantly queer forms of publicity. As comic Lea Delaria pointed out, celebrating the episode as a historic moment within lesbian and gay political circles was an assimilationist celebrity worship that devalued the work of entertainers like herself, 'butch dykes . . . drag queens, and nellie fags' who defy heteronormative conventions of stardom (Walsh, 2001).

2. It should be noted that this is a nationally specific phenomenon. Perhaps because of the legacy of the music hall, the queer possibilities of the situation comedy in Britain seem quite different. Ongoing queer characters in situation comedies like *Are You Being Served?* did not enter the realm of national controversy (Finnegan, 2000, p. 63; Woollacott, 1986).

3. My thanks to Ann Pellegrini for pointing this out to me.

4. I am grateful to perceptive audience members at the University of Texas, Austin, for bringing this example to my attention.

Bibliography

Caldwell, John, *Televisuality: Style, Crisis, and Authority in American Television* (New Brunswick, NJ: Rutgers University Press, 1994).

Clarke, Eric O., *Virtuous Vice: Homoeroticism and the Public Sphere* (Durham, NC: Duke University Press, 2000).

Dayan, Daniel and Katz, Elihu, *Media Events: The Live Broadcasting of History* (Cambridge, MA: Harvard University Press, 1992).

Doane, Mary Ann, 'Information, Crisis, Catastrophe', in Patricia Mellencamp (ed.), *Logics of Television* (Bloomington: Indiana University Press, 1991), pp. 222–39.

Finnegan, Brian, 'Nowt so Queer as Sitcoms', *Irish Times*, (29 July 2000), weekend section, p. 63.

Feuer, Jane, 'Genre Study and Television', in Robert C. Allen (ed.), *Channels of Discourse, Reassembled* (Chapel Hill: University of North Carolina Press, 1992), pp. 138–60.

Fuqua, Joy V., 'There's a Queer in my Soap!: the AIDS/Homophobia Storyline of *One Life to Live*', in Robert C. Allen (ed.), *To Be Continued: Soap Operas around the World* (New York: Routledge, 1995), pp. 199–212.

Halley, Janet, '"Like Race" Arguments', in Judith Butler, John Guillory and Kendall Thomas (eds), *What's Left of Theory? New Work on the Politics of Literary Theory* (New York: Routledge, 2000), pp. 40–74.

Huff, Richard, 'Who Killed "Ellen"? Exec Blames DeGeneres', *Daily News* (New York) (6 May 1998), p. 77.

Joyrich, Lynne, 'The Epistemology of the Console', *Critical Inquiry*, vol. 27, no. 3 (2001), pp. 439–67.

Ostrow, Joanne, 'Will "Ellen" the Show and Ellen the Star Outlast TV Buzz?', *Denver Post* (8 April 1997), p. E-01.

Walsh, Jeff, 'Butch Dyke Comic Delaria Boasts New Album, Roasts Ellen', *Oasis*, online gay youth magazine (April 1997) <www.oasismag.com/Issues/9704/cover.html> (accessed November 2001).

White, Mimi, 'Television: A Narrative – A History', *Cultural Studies*, vol. 3, no. 3 (October 1989), pp. 282–300.

White, Patricia, *UnInvited: Classical Hollywood Cinema and Lesbian Representability* (Bloomington: Indiana University Press, 2000).

Woollacott, Janet, 'Fictions and Ideologies: The Case of Situation Comedy', in Tony Bennett, Colin Mercer and Janet Woollacott (eds), *Popular Culture and Social Relations* (Milton Keynes: Open University Press, 1986), pp. 206–18.

7

'You're not going to see that on TV': *Star Trek: The Next Generation* in Film and Television

Roberta E. Pearson and Máire Messenger-Davies

The two-part *Star Trek: The Next Generation* episode 'The Best of Both Worlds' shows the first full-scale conflict between the United Federation of Planets and the implacable Borg, half-human, half-cyborg villains intent on assimilating all alien life forms. In a crucial scene in the first part, Captain Jean-Luc Picard of the *USS Enterprise* lies bound and helpless, and seemingly dehumanised, on the Borg ship as his captors finish his transformation into their spokesman, Locutus. The camera cuts from a high-angle shot of the captain, apparently permanently lost to his crew and to his viewers, to a tight close-up of his profile, marred by the Borg implants. In the corner of Picard's eye lies a single tear. A simple, standard televisual technique – a cut from a wide to close-up shot – is replete with narrative function, setting up the next episode – 'he's not really assimilated, how will he escape?' - and reassuring the viewer of the integrity of a beloved central character. Such are the economical techniques of classic television storytelling.

The eighth *Star Trek* feature film, *First Contact*, again deals with a Borg incursion into Federation space, but this time the progression is from close to wide. The film begins with an extreme close-up of Picard's eye, filling the entire screen. This time the camera zooms back, and back, and back, with no cutting, to reveal the vast inhuman space of a Borg ship, Picard's by now tiny figure occupying one small regeneration slot among thousands of others. Jonathan Frakes, Commander Riker in both *The Next Generation* (*TNG*) television series and feature films and director of *First Contact*, said of this shot:

> I think we have the longest pullback in movie history. The shot starts inside Picard's pupil, then pulls back through the black of his eye, the iris, the white, then hundreds of thousands of miles out into space and right into this incredible Borg hive. It's breathtaking. You're not going to see that on TV.
>
> <www.tvgen.com/tv/magazine/961118/ftr2c.sml>

Despite differences of scale, which are also differences of narrative style, specific to the two media, the two sequences function similarly with regard to their narrative content. The television scene reveals to the viewers, if not the *Enterprise* crew, that the now half-Borg Picard may be rescued, since he retains enough humanity to mourn the stripping of his humanity. The film follows the spectacular pullback with several shots showing Picard's transformation by the Borg, then with Picard's false awakening from this night-mare recollection, then with his real awakening. The sequence gives *Trek* non-initiates crucial backstory while letting *Trek* initiates know that Picard still suffers from Borg-induced trauma. Both sequences provide the audience with crucial information about the narrative and the character: first, on television, that Picard can still cry and may be saved and second, on film, that Picard was captured by the Borg and his unresolved feel-ings will probably play a large part in the following story.

There are differences of response in the representation of character, which are also medium-specific. In the television episode, Picard lies silent and unmoving as the probes enter, the tear his only visible response to assimilation. In the film, assimilation clearly hurts, Picard flinching and gasping as the probes enter him in the Borg ship dream sequence and screaming in fear and pain as an implant erupts through his cheek in the false awakening dream sequence. His more overt reactions in the film match the larger space of the fictional Borg hive and the real cinema screen. Actor Patrick Stewart, who plays Picard, commented about his character's journey from television to cinema:

> I felt that we should find more intensity, more action, more of those classic elements that an action hero ought to have. . . . His feelings are much more on the surface, he gets angry quicker, he gets excited quicker, we just turned up the volume.
>
> Green, n.d.

In transferring a highly successful television series from the small screen to the large, the producers of the *Star Trek* films adhere to the prime directive of giving audiences what they're 'not going to see on television'. The producers lure audiences into the cinema with promises of zooms that travel hundreds of miles into space; massive Borg hives; the entire Federation fleet attacking a Borg cube. Intensive spectacle, axiomatic for any would-be blockbuster sci-fi film, is taken by some academics as the defining character-istic of the genre. Says Annette Kuhn,

> If science-fiction cinema possesses any distinctive generic traits, these . . . have to do in large measure with cinematographic technologies and with the ways in which these figure in the construction of diegetic and spectatorial spaces: while science-fiction films may certainly tell stories, narrative content and structure *per se* are rarely their most significant features.
>
> 1999, p. 11

Spectacle may overwhelm narrative in films such as *Jurassic Park* or *Independence Day* but not in the *Star Trek* films, which come complete with pre-established characters and pre-established audiences who know and love them. *Trek* producers must not only provide spectacle, they must match this spectacle by 'turning up the volume' on the characters, while at the same time maintaining consistency with the characters' previously estab-lished traits and backstory. *Star Trek* film producers balance delicately between spectacle and narrative in a manner required neither of producers of one-off sci-fi films nor of producers of other cult television programmes. This article explores this delicate balance to illuminate the historically specific characteristics of both media formats, the big-screen sci-fi blockbuster and the small-screen continuing-series television drama.

Star Trek film and television

Star Trek has been on American television and cinema screens almost constantly since 1966, when the first *Star Trek* series, the one with Kirk and Spock, premiered. Years of syndication and a growing fan base followed the series' 1969 cancellation, resulting first in the *Trek* feature films, beginning with *Star Trek: The Motion Picture* (1979), with Kirk and Spock, and then in *TNG*, which premiered in 1987 and was cancelled in 1994 to allow the cast to take over the *Trek* cinema franchise. The seventh feature film *Star Trek: Generations* (1994) constituted the formal handing over from the old crew to the new, as Captains Kirk and Picard finally had the historic confrontation the fans had been longing for. *First Contact* (1996), the next in the series, not only was the first *Trek* feature to star just the new crew, it was made by members of the same production crew who had worked on the television programme: executive producer Rick Berman; director Jonathan Frakes (who had previously directed several episodes of the series); writers Brannon Braga and Ron Moore together with scenic designers, makeup artists and others. As social scientists would say, the continuity of the production team keeps several variables constant, rendering the comparison between television and film more valid. But the same crew also produced both *Generations* and the ninth *Trek* film *Insurrection*, so why choose *First Contact* for the comparison?

First, this film performed most strongly of the three at the box office and was most favourably received by both critics and fans.[1] Second, and more importantly, the film depends heavily on backstory from the television series. The villainous Borg first appeared in the second season episode 'Q Who', in which the omnipotent entity Q hurled the *Enterprise* far off course and into the path of a Borg cube. The two-part cliffhanger, 'The Best of Both Worlds' ('BOBW'), that ended season three and began season four, had a Borg invasion penetrating all the way to Sector 001 (Earth) and the Borg assimilating Captain Picard. The immediately following season four episode 'Family' dealt with Picard's recovery from his Borg-induced trauma and thus counts as part of the Borg metanarrative. Three subsequent *TNG* episodes, the season five 'I, Borg' and the two-parter 'Descent' that ended season six and opened season seven, also featured the Borg, although these episodes did not centre as much upon Picard. It is the focus on Captain Picard in 'BOBW', 'Family' and *First Contact* that makes these the ideal texts for a comparison between television *Trek* and cinema *Trek* which will render the differences between the two media formats in high relief. These differences stem not from inherent characteristics of television and film, but from historically specific conditions of production and reception that result in a higher degree of spectacle in *Trek* cinema than television and require a concomitant adjustment in narrative structure, particularly with regard to the construction of character. These historically specific conditions of production and reception relate to the nature of the audiences, production circumstances, narrative structures and image capacities of the two media.

Amid the pre-release publicity barrage for *First Contact*, Patrick Stewart was quoted as saying: 'I think that audiences should know that they don't have to be Trekkies to get a lot from the movie' (<*roughcut.features/gas/patrick—stewart*>). The *Trek* series' appeal to choice demographic categories ensures profitability from advertising revenues even without the huge audiences enjoyed by more highly rated programmes. But since *Trek*'s regular viewers alone cannot guarantee a film blockbuster status, the producers had to attract non-*Trek* viewers into the cinema as well. As scriptwriter Ron Moore said about the first *TNG* film *Generations*, 'It has to appeal to a different audience. . . . We wanted to do something that was broader and had more action and adventure' (Gross, 1995, p. 137) *Starburst Magazine* judged that *First Contact* had successfully broken 'out of the Trekker fan base and appealed to a broader audience than usual. The film grossed $92 million in the United States, second only in domestic box office take to *Star Trek IV: The Voyage Home* which took $110 million' (Anon., 1998, p. 14). More action and adventure, of course, imply more spectacle, the *sine qua non* of most megahits in the New Hollywood – *Titanic*, *Jurassic Park*, *Star Wars* and the like. Action, adventure and spectacle also travel across national boundaries more easily than character and dialogue, ensuring that films perform well in the lucrative foreign markets that provide an increasingly large percentage of the box-office gross.[2]

But breaking out of the Trekker fan base does not mean abandoning the it; the film offers competent viewers additional pleasure by referencing aspects of the *Trek* metaverse, especially the backstories of well-loved characters. For example, in several *TNG* episodes Picard had escaped to the holodeck to re-enact the adventures of the twentieth-century pulp detective hero, Dixon Hill. In the movie *First Contact*, Picard lures two Borg drones into his Dixon Hill holodeck programme and kills them with holographic machine-gun bullets. In the first season episode 'The Naked Now' Data had sex with security chief Tasha Yar. In *First Contact*, Data, counting back to his encounter with Tasha, tells the Borg queen that it has been eight years, seven months, seven days and three hours since he has had sex. Action, adventure and spectacle attract non-fans. *Trek* intertextuality, often character-based, appeals to the fans – or at least some fans, for not all engage with the text in the same way, each devotee seeking his or her own pleasures. As Camille Bacon-Smith and Henry Jenkins have shown, *Trek* fandom splits roughly along gender lines, with males more concerned with the technological and military aspects of the programme and females fascinated by the characters, as illustrated by the fact that the vast majority of fan fiction writers are women (Bacon-Smith, 1992; Jenkins, 1992). *Babylon 5* fans similarly exhibit a range of textual engagements, some appreciating the complexities of the series' five year-long narrative arc and others the superior computer-generated graphics (Kuppers, forthcoming). It is unlikely, however, that such pleasures are mutually exclusive, at least within television fandom. Some sci-fi cinema fans, by contrast, might single-mindedly focus only on the spectacular aspects of the text. In his study of the UK reception of *Judge Dredd*, Martin Barker found that some respondents derived their pleasure solely from a visceral response to the action sequences, caring not a whit for the narrative which, to them, simply seemed to get in the way of the spectacle (Barker and Brooks, 1998).

Cinema's longer production schedules and larger budgets also encourage the inclusion of greater spectacle than in television. Television programmes usually shoot about eight to ten pages of script per day versus a film's two to three pages. Jonathan Frakes, who has directed in both media, commented, 'You don't have the time [for extended action sequences]. The [scriptwriters] write the scope but you don't have time to shoot it' (Reeves-Stevens and Reeves-Stevens, 1996, p. 262). Each *TNG* episode had a budget of around $1.2 million while *First Contact* had a budget of around $40 million. All involved in the transition of the *TNG* crew from the small screen to the large anticipated changes resulting from the more generous shooting schedules and budgets. Ron Moore, *TNG* scripter and co-writer with Brannon Braga of *Generations*, said that he and Braga watched all the previous *Trek* films before beginning their script. We

> wanted to get a feel for how *Star Trek* transferred to the big screen and what the action sequences were like. We got very, very used to writing tightly controlled space battles on the series where there were only two exterior shots when a phaser hits and you shake the camera a lot.
>
> Gross, 1995, p. 137

'Best of Both Worlds', with its confrontations between the *Enterprise* and the Borg cube, together with several sequences set inside the latter, ranks as one of the more effects-intensive of the *TNG* episodes, perhaps accounting for its popularity among a certain segment of fandom.

The effects of restricted versus generous budgets and shooting schedules are apparent in the Federation/Borg battles of 'BOBW' and *First Contact*. In the former a Starfleet admiral describes the action via subspace transmission; the *Enterprise* arrives only at battle's end, navigating amid the ruined hulks of Federation starships drifting in space. In the latter, the bridge crew listens to subspace transmissions from Sector 001, but Captain Picard orders them into the action; the *Enterprise* joins other starships in attacking the Borg cube. Space battles were not the only beneficiaries of the move to cinema. Executive producer Rick Berman commented that on the television programme 'We never had the time for the R&D necessary to make the Borg what we always wanted them to be like. Nor did we ever have the money' (Reeves-Stevens and Reeves-Stevens, 1996, pp. 250–1). More time and money resulted in a meaner, tougher Borg complete with mottled, decaying skin and more realistic body armour as well as in one of *First Contact*'s most impressive special effects, the head and shoulders of the Borg queen descending from a great height to meld with a waiting body.

Time and money also determine narrative structure. As Jostein Gripsrud argues, the commercial basis of American television crucially determines textual form and content.

> Programmes last for either one hour or a half-hour . . . and must be constructed so as to allow for commercial breaks at certain intervals. All of this obviously imposes very definite premises for temporal features of programme forms, such as length and rhythm, and thus also limits and influences the dramaturgy, the forms of narration and characterisation that may be employed.
>
> 1995, p. 51

TNG, like all other 'hour'-long shows on American television, actually runs for forty-five minutes, the other fifteen minutes being devoted to advertisements. Four commercial breaks dictate the programme's rhythm with advertisements inserted after the credit sequence and at three other points before the end, resulting in the classic five-act structure of western drama. But while theatre audiences usually watch the whole play, fickle television audiences may desert to another programme during the commercials. Producers counter this tendency with mini cliff-hangers at the end of the first four acts, putting the characters into peril, having them face unexpected revelations and the like. The final act, of course, restores the opening equilibrium, although in the ultra-humanist *Trek*, the characters have often learned a salutary lesson from the episode's events. The intensity of the narrative progression and the shortness of the acts (approximately nine minutes apiece, although the pre-credit 'hook' tends to run shorter and the other acts a bit longer) leaves room for little that does not directly advance the story. No textual time is available for extended space battles, even were the production time and money available to shoot them. This is not to say that *TNG* was devoid of spectacle: it featured the 'tightly controlled space battles on the series where there were only two exterior shots when a phaser hits and you shake the camera a lot' that Ron Moore spoke of, as well as transporter beams, tractor beams and other special effects sequences.

But the uninterrupted, 120 or so minutes of the *Star Trek* films can accommodate lengthier and more intensive special effects sequences than the forty-five minutes of the five-act television programmes. *First Contact* is exemplary in this regard. CNN's Dennis Michael claimed that it had 'more action than all the previous films put together' and was 'designed to stimulate the adrenal glands as well as the brain' (1996). One might infer from Michael's comments that film critics don't expect *Trek* films to be as spectacular as others in the sci-fi genre, leading one to ask whether spectacle functions differently in these films than in other sci-fi blockbusters. In recent considerations of the place of spectacle in the sci-fi film, academics have returned to some longstanding debates in film studies concerning the tension between narrative, the forward progression of a story, and spectacle, the provision of visual pleasure. Drawing on the work of Tom Gunning on the 'cinema of attractions' and of Laura Mulvey on the function of the female form in the classical Hollywood cinema, some have argued that the big budget, blockbuster sci-fi films of the 'post'- or New Hollywood deliberately eschew narrative and character in favour of visual pleasure (Gunning, 1990; Mulvey, 1975).[3]

> Popular science-fiction movies like *The Terminator* (1984) and *Predator* (1987), offering almost continuous spectacular action, seem to have succumbed almost entirely to the siren call of the sensuous spectacle.
>
> Grant, 1999, p. 28

> Positive reception of the films of mainstream digital cinema depends as much on a *fascinated spectator*, immersed in dazzling and 'spellbinding' imagery, as on identification with character and the machinations of plot and theme.
>
> Darley, 2000, p. 103

> Spectacular special effects function as a spectacle that interrupts or even disrupts
> the narrative: the special effect may simply be so striking as to constitute a kind of
> showstopper.
>
> Landon, 1999, p. 38

As critics of both Gunning and Mulvey have pointed out, predicating a theory upon a
clear distinction between narrative and spectacle poses definitional difficulties, since the
same shot may be seen by some as pure spectacle and by others as having a narrative
function. Lacking the space to engage in this argument, I must merely assert that the
majority of effects-intensive scenes in the *Trek* films serve to advance the narrative too.[4]
Even the spectacular opening pullback in *First Contact* occurs in a sequence which provides crucial backstory on the Picard character. The initial battle with the Borg sets up
the time-travel plot, as the Borg sphere ejects from the Borg cube and hurtles back to
the twenty-first century to conquer the defenceless Earth. The space-walking sequence
on the surface of the *Enterprise*'s massive hull, with its allusions to *2001*, shows the heroes
preventing the Borg from contacting the collective.

Of course, all this spectacle looks very different when viewing *First Contact* on video.
Technological advances have greatly improved the resolution of the television image but
it still remains smaller than the cinema image – a domestic scale. Says John Corner

> In the late 1990s, television images are often of very high definition, with excellent colour
> and stability. The comparability with cinema is therefore strong (a point to which the
> extensive home video market is testimony). Yet screen size persists as an important
> distinction between cinematic and televisual image projection. . . . Even allowing for the new
> range of large screen systems, most television is watched on screens which are many times
> smaller than those of the local cinemas and this has important consequences for the
> aesthetics of the television image.
>
> 1999, pp. 25–6

The members of the *Trek* production team involved in the feature films got to
play with a bigger screen as well as with more time and more money. David Carson,
who directed several *TNG* episodes as well as the first feature film, *Generations*,
explained that

> Laser things and beam-ins and beam-outs, have to be treated differently on the largescreen
> because you can see it all so much more clearly. Similarly in terms of color schemes, like
> exactly how dark the bridge is, and the fact that you can't light it flatly . . . When youput it
> upon the big screen, I think you're going to need more contrasts, more light and shade.
>
> Gross, 1995, p. 141[5]

Borg cubes, as well as their occupants, also had to be redesigned for the cinema.
Production designer Herman Zimmerman, who worked on both the series and
the films, said,

The Borg ship is basically the same cube that was seen on the television series but with considerably more detail. . . . When you blow up something made for television to the size of a cinemascope screen in a theater, you need a great deal more detail.

Reeves-Stevens and Reeves-Stevens, 1996, p. 252

Screen size still determines the aesthetics of television, the smaller, flatter and less detailed image both militating against long-shot spectacle, and encouraging close and medium close shots of characters, which in turn encourage certain kinds of genres and narratives.

To quote Corner again, 'In popular television series drama, the extensive use of close-up and medium close-up provides for the special kinds of character familiarity, proximity, and everydayness which these fictions seek to generate in exploring dimensions of the domestic and the social' (1999, p. 31). *TNG* does resemble other television dramas in its use of close-up and medium close-up: the act climaxing mini cliff-hanger sequences, for example, frequently close with a tight shot of Captain Picard, or, in his absence, of another central character. These shots provide for character familiarity, proximity and the exploration of the social, but, given the kinds of narratives in which these characters act, they do not always connote either everydayness or the domestic. As Corner himself observes, 'A lack of adequate differentiation between narrative types has . . . been a deficiency in much criticism and research' (1999, p. 59). A close-up of Jean-Luc Picard can be, but is not necessarily or even predominantly, the equivalent of a close-up of Phil or Grant Mitchell in *Eastenders*, since character construction differs greatly between the sci-fi and soap opera genres.

Captain Jean-Luc Picard in film and television

To summarise the argument so far; first, historically specific conditions of production and reception result in more spectacle in *Trek* cinema than in *Trek* television and second, narrative and character remain important in *Trek* cinema but function in a different way to that in *Trek* television. The remainder of this essay looks at the character of Captain Jean-Luc Picard in the *TNG* episodes 'BOBW' and 'Family' and in the film *First Contact* to ascertain more precisely how and why narrative and character function differently in the two media. What precisely did 'turning up the volume' on Picard entail?

Answering this question requires defining what is meant by a character, and here we run into difficulties, for surprisingly little has been written about the subject since the days of humanist literary critics such as A. C. Bradley, who tended to consider characters primarily in terms of their psychological motivations. Structuralist literary theory offers little help, for as Jonathan Culler said several years ago, 'Character is the major aspect of the novel to which structuralism has paid the least attention and been the least successful in treating' (1975, p. 230). When structuralists such as A. J. Greimas or Vladimir Propp did consider characters, they tended to reduce them to a function of the narrative. Comparing Picard's narrative functions to those of the hero of a Russian folk-tale will not, I suspect, much advance our understanding of the differences between *Trek* film and television. Post-structuralism, with its insistence on the dissolution of meaning, has concerned itself hardly at all with characters, who are replete with meaning. Film and television theory has almost nothing to say on the subject, with the important exception of David Bordwell's investigations of cinematic narrative.[6] In *The Classical Hollywood Cinema* Bordwell defines a character as a bundle of qualities, or traits (1985, pp. 13–14). He goes on to say that characters are individualised with particular traits, tics or tags.

> Their traits must be affirmed in speech and physical behaviour, the observable projections of
> personality. . . . Even a simple physical reaction – a gesture, an expression, a widening of the
> eyes, constructs character psychology in accordance with other information. . . . Hollywood
> cinema reinforces the individuality and consistency of each character by means of recurrent
> motifs. A character will be tagged with a detail of speech or behaviour that defines a
> major trait.
>
> 1985, p. 15

Here are the qualities and traits that constitute the character of Jean-Luc Picard over 178 episodes of *TNG*.

1. **Embodiment** The character is played by actor Patrick Stewart and is therefore physically co-terminous with Patrick Stewart: Picard must look and sound like Stewart.[7] For American audiences, one of Picard's defining characteristics is Stewart's English accent.

2. **Dialogue** Picard has a rather more elevated, formal pattern of speech than the other characters, together with a pattern of wry humour and understatement. He has certain tag phrases (engage; make it so; indeed; so it would seem) and is given to delivering eloquent speeches.

3. **Gestures** Stewart gives Picard a standard repertoire of gestures: a downward movement of the hand to accompany the command 'Engage'; a tugging down of the uniform tunic that fans have affectionately dubbed the Picard manoeuvre; the steepling of the fingers or the rubbing of the lower lip in thought.

4. **Recurrent motifs** Repeated behaviour serves to construct Picard as the consummate cultivated and intellectual European. Picard drinks Earl Grey tea; quotes Shakespeare and other classical authors; listens to and plays classical music; reads (including Homer in the original ancient Greek); knows about history and archaeology; fences and horserides. But Picard's fondness for Dixon Hill, like other hard-boiled detectives a hybrid figure of intellect, action and sexuality, reveals another side of his character, one that perhaps chafes at the restraints of his command position.[8]

5. **Traits** As shown in his speech and actions, Picard is a man of intelligence, courage, integrity, compassion, courtesy, reason and rigid self-control. He is also a man of peace who, when possible, opts for the diplomatic rather than the military solution.

Embodiment, dialogue, gestures and recurrent motifs remain fairly constant between 'BOBW' and *First Contact*. In the film, Picard looks, sounds, moves and to some extent behaves like Picard: he listens to classical music (Berlioz); quotes a classical author (Herman Melville); demonstrates detailed knowledge of Federation history; and runs the Dixon Hill holodeck programme. But his traits, the essence of his character, seem to have undergone a rather radical transformation, for the television Picard had been a cerebral hero and the cinema Picard is an action hero. In 'BOBW' Picard resists the Borg with eloquent language and will power. When first captured, before his transformation into Locutus, Picard speaks with the Borg collective.

Borg: You speak for your people.

Picard: I have nothing to say to you. And I will resist you with the last ounce of my strength.

Borg: Strength is irrelevant. Resistance is futile. We wish to improve ourselves. We will add your biological and technological distinctiveness to our own. You will adapt to service us.

Picard: Impossible. My culture is based on freedom and self-determination.

Borg: Freedom is irrelevant. Self-determination is irrelevant. You must comply.

Picard: We would rather die.

Borg: Death is irrelevant.

Picard's resistance is not futile, but takes a rather passive form. The *Enterprise* crew succeed in rescuing Picard from the Borg cube and the android Data attempts to use the captain's mental link with the collective to order the Borg to break off their attack. Unfortunately, the Borg's primary systems cannot be accessed, but Picard mutters 'Sleep, Data, sleep,' suggesting that the android order the Borg to regenerate. Data does so, the Borg sleep and the cube explodes. The Federation wins the day, not with a fleet of mighty starships but because of one man's will power, Picard having fought through his Borg programming to make the crucial connection with Data. Cerebral heroism at its best. In contrast, in *First Contact*, Picard gets up close and personal with the villains, resisting the Borg not with inspiring speeches about freedom and self-determination or subtle suggestions about programming but rather with big phaser rifles, holographic machine-guns and newly developed musculature. From the moment Picard suspects that the Borg have invaded the *Enterprise* he takes charge of the situation, striding through the corridors at the head of his security forces, brandishing a phaser rifle and shooting at any Borg that moves. He also figures prominently in the three extended special-effects-intensive action sequences not centred on space battles. In the Dixon Hill holodeck sequence mentioned above, Picard does an Al Capone, machine-gunning two Borg drones. On the Enterprise's exterior hull, a space-suited Picard floats from one side of the huge saucer section to the other and then engages in hand-to-hand combat with Borg drones. In the film's climactic sequence in the Engineering section, Picard imitates the behaviour of a Sly or Arnie: stripped down to his vest and showing off his new muscles, he climbs a dangling cable to escape the deadly plasma that engulfs the Borg queen and her drones. Action heroism at its most quintessential.

The historical conditions of production and reception delineated above determine that the television Picard be a cerebral hero and the cinema Picard an action hero. It's cheaper and less time-consuming to have your hero send the villains to sleep than to best them either in a space battle or in effects-intensive hand-to-hand combat. But if, for the reasons already specified, cinema *Trek* has to add spectacle but retain a focus on familiar characters, then your hero must figure prominently in the spectacular sequences. The *Trek* producers tried to make Picard more action-oriented in the first *TNG* feature film, *Generations*, but apparently felt that they didn't get it quite right. Executive producer Rick Berman said of *First Contact*,

> Let's do a story where Jean-Luc Picard can stop brooding and can start being more of an action hero. . . . The character tends to be a little more introspective than others. It was time to have our captain actively involved in a very heroic as well as a very fun adventure.

Yet Berman reassured fans that Picard would remain as complex a character as he had been in television. 'There are elements of this film where Picard's emotional core is challenged. It's not as if he's become a two-dimensional figure at all' (Reeves-Stevens and Reeves-Stevens, 1996, pp. 258–9).

The scriptwriters made Picard an action hero without reducing him to two dimensions, but did they maintain consistency with the character traits established over 178 episodes of *TNG* ? As director Jonathan Frakes put it, 'There was great concern that Picard – due to his hatred of the Borg – would come off like a deranged, obsessed, revenge-filled madman. Patrick Stewart had to work very hard to avoid that' (www.tvgen.com/tv/magazine/961118/ftr2c.sml). At least one fan opined that Stewart hadn't succeeded.

> Did you NOT see *First Contact*, with Jean-Luc brooding in his cabin, giving orders left and right, with nary a concern for his crew's well-being? It finally took a 21st(?) century technician to bitch his ass out good for him to come around. Prior to that he was bordering on frothing at the mouth loony!
>
> alt.tv.star-trek.voyager, 1998

In the process of bitching Jean-Luc's ass out good, the twenty-first century technician, Lily (played by guest star Alfre Woodard), calls him Captain Ahab, the script deliberately paralleling our hero to literature's greatest deranged, obsessed, revenge-filled madman.[9] Picard's behaviour up to this point in the film bears out Lily's accusation. A man noted for self-control howls with rage as he machine-guns Borg drones, then prepares to smash their faces to pulp with the gun butt. A man noted for compassion digs through the Borgified body of a crewmate in search of a Borg co-processor without a shudder. A man noted for his courtesy accuses his trusted comrade, the Klingon Worf, of cowardice. A man noted for his reason and intelligence ignores all suggestions from his crew

and orders them to fight to the death. A man noted for putting personal concerns second to the high humanist ideals of the Federation swears that he will make the Borg pay
for what they did to him. How and why does *First Contact* take a character established
over 178 *TNG* episodes as an exemplary figure of western humanism and turn him into
Captain Ahab? Or, we might rather ask, is it possible to maintain character consistency
between *Trek* television and cinema?

Patrick Stewart doesn't think so.

> The series . . . by its very nature, because people were watching us every week, was often
> much more relaxed. When we were elevated to film status, we knew we had to leave a lot of
> that behind. The canvas was bigger, the risks were greater, the immediate audience was much
> wider, and the need to have something more intense was there.
>
> scifi.com, 1998

The historical conditions of production and reception that Stewart refers to – the bigger
canvas, the greater risks, the wider audience – all account for Picard's transformation from
cerebral to action hero. But it may be the difference between the relaxed nature of people
watching every week and the intense nature of people watching every two or three years,
or in other words, the difference between the narrative structures of series television and
the feature film, that accounts for Captain Picard's becoming Captain Ahab.

With occasional exceptions, such as James Bond or Jean-Luc Picard, cinema characters usually appear only in one film. Characters in long-running American television
series can appear in a hundred or more texts – 178 in the case of *TNG*.

The one-off feature film has to rapidly establish a character's defining traits. Television
can accumulate defining traits in a more leisurely way across episodes, but must also
maintain character consistency over a much longer narrative arc. When television characters transfer to the screen, however, they become more of a one-off affair, not only for
that portion of the audience with no prior knowledge of them, but in another sense as
well. David Gerrold, a sci-fi writer associated with *Star Trek* since its earliest days,
explains that the need to maintain a character over tens of episodes means that the average episode of a television series does not deal with the most important events in a
character's life. 'These characters are going to be back next week – so you know that
what you're seeing this week isn't all that important,' cause next week's gonna be a whole
new adventure' (1996, p. 47). By contrast, films often centre precisely on the most
important events, meaning that the scriptwriters can push characters further, have them
behave in a more extreme fashion. As scriptwriter Brannon Braga said, 'Because it's a
movie you can take big risks with the characters and do more event kind of plotting techniques, because you're not obligated to do an episode the following week' (Gross, 1995,
p. 139). Not only will you not see the longest pullback in movie history on TV, you won't
see Jean-Luc Picard 'frothing at the mouth loony' either.

You can however see him weeping in the mud, for the events in 'Best of Both Worlds'
were so central to the character's life, so traumatic for Picard, that the scriptwriters
felt the need to provide him with some catharsis – an indication of how the long-running

TV series, with its relative stability of production teams, can permit established writers to innovate and experiment, even in quite avant-garde ways (see the Riker-directed episode from Series 5, 'Cause and Effect') once the series and its characters are established in the public mind. In the episode following 'BOBW', 'Family', the deeply shaken captain, having been forced by the Borg to aid in the destruction of thirty-nine starships and the deaths of 11,000 members of Starfleet, returns to his family home in France, where his long-estranged brother, Robert, helps him to come to terms with his dreadful experience. As in *First Contact*, Picard exhibits uncharacteristic behaviour: he contemplates leaving Starfleet, indulges in solitary drinking and punches his brother. It's this punch that precipitates the climactic fight with Robert that leaves Jean-Luc weeping in the mud, lamenting the fact that he wasn't good enough or strong enough to stop the Borg. Brannon Braga was asked whether *First Contact* was a 'redux of "Family" in which Picard returns home to try to recover from the ordeal he faced in the now classic Borg story, "The Best of Both Worlds"? That's *really* where the catharsis took place.' Braga replied:

> Yeah, there's some concern there, but I think it's different. I think that in 'Family', he was basically a rape victim. He was dealing with anger, remorse and violation, but he was dealing with it in a more passive way. This movie is more of a *Moby Dick* kind of story. He's vengeful. This is a Picard that is bent on destroying the Borg once and for all, no matter what the cost, even if it means destroying his ship and his crew. It has a different flavour to it, so I'm not too worried.
>
> Anders, 1997, p. 17

Not only a different flavour, but a different purpose. In 'Family', Picard's 'more passive way' of dealing with his anger, remorse and violation re-integrated him not only into Starfleet but into the episodic narrative structure of series television. Next week's episode found him back on the bridge, as urbane an exemplar of western civilisation as ever. *First Contact*'s more active, vengeful Picard better suits the role of the one-off feature film hero. We may be tempted to wonder how Picard and his superiors dealt with the aftermath of yet another traumatic encounter with the Borg: did Starfleet commend him, court-martial him or confine him to a mental hospital? But since we wouldn't see him again for another two years, it doesn't really matter. And when we did see Picard again, in *Star Trek: Insurrection*, he was involved in an entirely different adventure, although still playing action man. And when we see Picard in *Star Trek X*, which internet rumours have dubbed *Nemesis*, he will undoubtedly be more inclined to action than to intellect, for that is the nature of cinematic *Star Trek*.

Notes

1. *First Contact* grossed $91.8 million domestically and $54 million internationally; *Generations*, $75.6 million and $42.4 million and *Insurrection*, $70.2 million and $47.7 million <www.boxofficeguru.com>.
2. Among recent blockbusters, *Pearl Harbor* made 51.2 per cent of its profits internationally and *Hannibal* 52.7 per cent. The percentage of the foreign gross for the *TNG* films has been

steadily increasing: *Generations*, 35.9 per cent; *First Contact*, 37 per cent and *Insurrection*, 40.5 per cent <www.boxofficeguru.com>.

3. It is worth remembering that the big-budget, effects-intensive sci-fi film dates from the late 1970s, the success of such films as *Star Wars* and *Superman* establishing the genre of the sci-fi blockbuster. Prior to that, science-fiction had been largely confined to serials and the bottom half of the double bill, A-films such as *Forbidden Planet* (1956) a rare exception.

4. With the possible exception of *Star Trek: The Motion Picture*, which some fans, including myself, disliked precisely because our beloved Kirk, Spock and McCoy took a back seat to the spectacle.

5. Of course, other American television programmes are more visually innovative than *TNG*. *The X Files*, for example, is famous for its chiaroscuro scenes-lit-by-flashlight. But given the equally famous obscurity of *The X Files* plots, I wonder whether there is a connection between narrative clarity and visual clarity, as was the case with film noir.

6. In fairness, I should mention Murray Smith's *Engaging Characters* (1995) but it deals more with spectators' cognitive responses to characters than it does with the ways in which narratives construct characters.

7. *Star Trek* being science-fiction however this rule is not inviolable. In one episode, a transporter accident transforms Picard into a twelve-year-old, and we are meant to accept a twelve-year-old actor as Picard.

8. We are indebted to Mark Jancovich for this point.

9. It is perhaps reductive to characterise Herman Melville's complex character, developed over several hundred pages in such fashion. Nevertheless, these would be the character's primary connotations for those who have not read the novel. It should be noted that a previous *Trek* film, *Star Trek II: The Wrath of Khan* also invoked Ahab, but constructed a parallel between him and the villain not the *Enterprise* captain.

Bibliography

<alt.tv.star-trek.voyager>, wyldekarde@email.msn.com (20 October 1998).

Anders, Lou, 'Brannon Braga: Writing From Scratch', *Star Trek: First Contact Official Movie Souvenir Magazine*, Titan Magazines (1997).

Anon., 'Star Trek: Insurrection', *Starburst* (October 1998).

Bacon-Smith, Camille, *Enterprising Women: Television Fandom and the Creation of Popular Myth* (Philadelphia: University of Pennsylvania Press, 1992).

Barker, Martin and Brooks, Kate, *Knowing Audiences: Judge Dredd, Its Friends, Fans and Foes* (Luton: University of Luton Press, 1998).

Bordwell, David, *The Classical Hollywood Cinema* (London: Routledge, 1985).

Corner, John, *Critical Ideas in Television Studies* (Oxford: Clarendon Press, 1999), pp. 25–6.

Culler, Jonathan, *Structuralist Poetics* (Ithaca: Cornell University Press, 1975).

Darley, Andrew, *Visual Digital Culture: Surface, Play and Spectacle in New Media Genres* (London: Routledge, 2000).

Gerrold, David, *The Trouble with Tribbles: The Full Story of the Classic* Star Trek *Show* (London: Virgin, 1996).

Grant, Barry Keith, 'Reason and the Visible in the Science-Fiction Film', in Annette Kuhn (ed.), *Alien Zone II* (London: Verso, 1999).

Green, Ray, 'Patrick Stewart's Re-generation', Box Office Online Cover Stories (n.d.), <www.boxoff.com/covernov96.html>.

Gripsrud, Jostein, *The Dynasty Years: Hollywood Television and Critical Media Studies* (London: Routledge, 1995).

Gross, Edward, *The Making of the Trek Films* (London: Boxtree, 1995).

Gunning, Tom, 'The Cinema of Attractions: Early Film, Its Spectator and the Avant-Garde', in Thomas Elsaesser (ed.), *Early Cinema: Space, Frame Narrative* (London: BFI, 1990).

Jenkins, Henry, *Textual Poachers* (New York: Routledge, 1992).

Kuhn, Annette, 'Introduction to Part One', in Annette Kuhn (ed.), *Alien Zone II* (London: Verso, 1999).

Kuppers, Petra, 'Quality Science Fiction: *Babylon 5*'s Metatextual Universe', in Sara Gwenllian-Jones and Roberta E. Pearson (eds), *Worlds Apart: Essays on Cult Television* (Minneapolis: University of Minnesota Press, forthcoming).

Landon, Brooks, 'Diegetic or Digital? The Convergence of Science-Fiction Literature and Science-Fiction Film in Hypermedia', in Annette Kuhn (ed.), *Alien Zone II* (London: Verso, 1999).

Michael, Dennis, 'New Star Trek film aims for the gut, not just the head' (23 November 1996), <www.cnn.com>.

Mulvey, Laura, 'Visual Pleasure and Narrative Cinema', *Screen*, vol. 16, no. 3 (1975), pp. 6–18.

Reeves-Stevens, Judith and Reeves-Stevens, Garfield, 'A First Look at *Star Trek: First Contact*', in J. M. Dillard (ed.), *Star Trek: First Contact* (New York: Pocket Books, 1996).

scifi.com, 'Inside *Star Trek: Insurrection*' (1998), <www.scifi.com/insurrection>.

Smith, Murray, *Engaging Characters: Fiction, Emotion and the Cinema* (Oxford: Clarendon Press, 1995).

8

Brave New *Buffy* : Rethinking 'TV Violence'

Lisa Parks

The day after the murders at Columbine High School in Littleton, Colorado, I received a phone call from my father who told me that one of the boys responsible for the shootings – Eric Harris – was a relative of mine, a second cousin whom I had never met. Stunned, I continued to watch news of Eric and Dylan's intricately orchestrated attack. Like others I scrutinised Harris's picture in newspapers, read his diary entries and wondered what his parents were like. I also witnessed the brutal cultural backlash that followed the shootings. I'm referring to the witch hunts of Goth youth, the scapegoating of TV, computer games and music, and the general refusal to recognise violence as an ideological and institutional problem. I was frustrated to find once again that media effects specialists and moral conservatives were setting the terms upon which we discuss and analyse media violence. With the exception of Henry Jenkins who testified at a Congressional hearing after the Columbine incident, TV and Cultural Studies scholars were largely silent in these public debates.

One of the ways I've tried to process my own strange connection to these events has been to try and imagine a critical discourse on TV violence that would complicate existing paradigms and contribute to ongoing public debates. Armed with hundreds of quantitative studies, media effects researchers have convinced regulators, the public and even industry executives that TV violence leads inevitably to aggressive behaviour, desensitisation and a fear of victimisation (Anon. 1996). Rather than trying to debunk media effects research, I want to use the popular TV series *Buffy the Vampire Slayer* as a site from which to reframe the question of TV violence, to try and develop ways of discussing these issues from a Television and Cultural Studies perspective.[1]

Buffy is a perfect site for this kind of reframing for several reasons. First, the show regularly represents what are classified as 'violent incidents', and the TV industry recognises this by imposing a cache of ratings and parental advisories on the screen during each episode. Most *Buffy* episodes are classified as TV 14, which strongly cautions parents that material may be unsuitable for people under the age of fourteen, and are labelled with DSLV warnings, which stand for 'intensely suggestive dialogue', 'intense sexual situations', 'strong coarse language' and 'intense violence'.[2] Second, *Buffy* was one of many sites of popular culture to be scapegoated after the Columbine shootings, which was somewhat ironic given that Eric Harris wrote in his diary 'You know what I

hate? The WB network!!!! Oh Jesus, Mary Mother of God Almighty, I hate that channel with all my heart and soul' (Cullen, 1999). Third, *Buffy* challenges assumptions about
violence that are organised around sexual difference, offering a space to reconceptualise
the relationship between gender, power and aggression. Finally, despite being tagged an
'SLV' show, *Buffy* has helped to build an audience base for the WB Network. In 1999
alone the series increased the WB's viewership by 41 per cent, and its spinoff *Angel* which
premiered that season, further expanded the network's audience share. The show serves
as a fascinating case study for exploring how 'TV violence' might be recoded as 'must
see TV'.

Ironically, with its cache of parental warning labels, *Buffy* is exactly the kind of TV
violence that teens and parents need to see. The show's spectacular displays of physical
aggression often function as a means of exposing and de-naturalising invisible and institutionalised forms of violence that affect youth especially. In this paper, I use *Buffy the
Vampire Slayer* to complicate the meanings of 'TV violence', and I explore how its generic hybridity, gendered physical aggression, racial/ethnic representations and discourses
on social alienation provide new paradigms for thinking about TV violence. Despite
efforts by the press to pigeonhole *Buffy* as fluffy 'youth television', WB and the show's
creators insist that they strive for a 'multi-generational appeal'.[3] Rather than encouraging violent behaviour, *Buffy* has become an important pedagogical tool, providing
opportunities for adult and teen viewers alike to unravel and discuss the complex meanings of violence. As such this series 'must be seen' not only by viewers and fans, but
it provides crucial opportunities for humanities scholars to begin intervening in and
re-directing public debates on TV violence.

Complicating 'TV violence'

In 1994 researchers at American universities – including: the University of California,
Santa Barbara; the University of Wisconsin, Madison; the University of Texas, Austin;
and the University of North Carolina, Chapel Hill – began the largest study of television
violence ever undertaken. The project known as the National Television Violence Study
(NTVS), funded by the National Cable Television Association, assesses the amount,
nature and context of violence in entertainment programming over three years and
across twenty-three channels. The study also examines the effectiveness of ratings,
parental advisories and public service announcements about TV violence. The NTVS
has become the definitive study on TV violence in the United States not only because
of its comprehensive scope, but also because of the timeliness of its completion. The
results of the study were released at the very moment when high school shootings seemed
to become a national epidemic. As a result summaries of the study have circulated widely
among school teachers and administrators, parents groups, network executives and television writers, and it has come to dominate public discussions of youth, television and
violence in the post-Columbine era. The NTVS defines violence as 'any overt depiction
of the use of physical force – or credible threat of physical force – intended to physically
harm an animate being or group of beings'.[4] It warns parents about certain high-risk
factors suggesting, for instance, that attractive perpetrators are especially problematic

because viewers may identify with them. Other concerns include the representation of violence as being justified, going unpunished or having minimal consequences to the victim.[5]

By this definition *Buffy* certainly qualifies as 'violent TV', especially since each episode culminates in fight sequences during which Buffy, an attractive young woman, exerts physical force on groups of animate beings – namely, vampires and demons – and is valorised as a heroine as a result. Although neither *Buffy* nor WB were included in the NTVS, family values groups and educators have warned parents about the series. Familyeducation.com, for instance, recently published an article called 'Buffy Slays Parental Authority' cautioning readers that

> a TV show like *Buffy*, which mixes Goth fantasy themes with the real-life escapades of teenagers, is especially difficult for children to make meaning of. The real danger of ... Buffy ... is not that most children will return to school in September armed with cross-bows, but that they will become accepting of violence as part of school life
>
> Abel, 1999

An editorial writer for the *National Catholic Reporter* claims that the series represents teens 'as dangerous, explosive, always bringing trouble in their wake' (Allen, 1999, p. 17). He continues, 'So many people have been disemboweled in Sunnydale that instead of streets they ought to install steel grates so the blood and gore can just sluice right through' (ibid.). In September 1999, the Center for Media and Public Affairs in Washington, DC, released a study entitled 'Marketing Mayhem: Violence and Popular Culture', which ranked *Buffy* the seventh most violent show on TV with an average of fifty-nine violent acts per episode (compared to number one, *Walker Texas Ranger*, which had 112).[6]

The media scapegoating after the Columbine murders generated a moral panic that led some network executives to more carefully evaluate programme content. A month after the Columbine high school murders Warner Bros. CEO Jamie Kellner decided to pull two *Buffy* episodes from its 1998–9 schedule as a gesture 'of sympathy for the people in those (Colorado and Georgia) communities' (America Online, 1999). Kellner cancelled 'Graduation Day II' and 'Earshot' in May 1999 because they both contained scenes that in one way or another resembled the traumatic experiences that unfolded in American schools during the spring of 1999. 'Earshot' was almost prophetic, featuring an alienated high school boy who threatens to kill fellow classmates and then turn the gun on himself. 'Graduation Day II' was the season finale and although its violent battle between vampires and high school seniors was designed to be fantastic not realistic, the scene was none-the-less staged at a high school graduation ceremony and thus was felt to be 'inappropriate' given recent events (ibid.). Kellner's decision outraged *Buffy* fans, who believed the show was unjustly associated with the Columbine shootings because of its Goth sensibilities. *Buffy* fans quickly formed a coalition called 'Stand Up for *Buffy*' and raised enough money to purchase a full-page ad in *Variety* condemning WB's actions (*Variety*, 1999). The cancellations also perturbed *Buffy*'s creative team and prompted star Sarah Michelle Gellar to release a public statement in which she declared, 'There is probably no greater societal question we face than how to stop violence among our youth. By canceling intelligent programming like *Buffy*, corporate entertainment is not addressing the problem' (see Springer, 1999, p. 10). When asked if he felt any responsibility for the Columbine shootings, creator Joss Whedon shrewdly responded, 'No. I feel a responsibility because I wake up in the morning' (Whedon, 1999).

Many parents adopted knee-jerk responses to popular culture after the Columbine murders. Embracing the media effects studies which now dominate public discussions of media violence, they assumed that computer games like *Doom*, songs by Marilyn Manson and TV shows like *Buffy* were the culprits of violence in American high schools. Teens complained that the Columbine massacre triggered parental paranoia. Adults interrogated their kids, ransacked their rooms and began monitoring their activities more closely, especially since Klebold's and Harris's parents had been charged as liable for their sons' murderous acts. (Interestingly, a *Buffy* episode entitled 'Gingerbread' had critiqued this kind of parental panic months before the events in Littleton. The episode features parents who engage in a witch hunt for teens suspected of harbouring Goth sensibilities and wreaking havoc in the community.)

Some parents reacted differently, however, arguing that airing 'Earshot' and 'Graduation Day II' may have actually helped teens work through the trauma of recent high school violence. As one parent proclaimed during an AOL chat,

> I am a parent of a teenager. We watch *Buffy* together on Tuesday nights, one of the few times we actually spend 'quality time' together, enjoying the episodes and commenting upon them. I would have loved to be able to watch the post-Columbine 'violent' eps. with him in order to foster dialogue about these issues, but was denied that opportunity by the WB Big Brother policy. I am sure I am not the only parent who missed out on a potentially valuable experience with their children because of this.
>
> America Online Listserv, 1999

For some, *Buffy*'s representations of violence became a crucial means through which parents discussed important issues with their teenagers. First Amendment scholar Jon Katz claimed WB's cancellation did considerable harm because 'It ratified the notion that TV – not easy access to lethal weapons, poor parenting, uninspired and oppressive education, or mental illness – is responsible for the recent spate of high school murders in recent years' (1999).

The censorship of a media product often has the effect of attracting more attention to it and *Buffy* was no exception. The postponed episodes aired in Canada in May 1999 as scheduled and were bootlegged and distributed illegally on the internet that same week. Two months after his decision to postpone the episodes, Kellner was asked what he thought about the bootlegging. He replied, 'It's against the law, but it's fantastic. That people feel that passionately about this program makes me feel great' (America Online, 1999). With great fanfare, then, WB aired 'Graduation Day II' on 13 July 1999 and 'Earshot' two weeks before the season premiere on 21 September 1999. The episodes were re-run again during the 1999–2000 season, and the hype surrounding them no doubt drew new viewers to the series.

This situation raises important questions about the socioeconomic conditions that underpin the discourse of TV violence. Ultimately, 'Earshot' and 'Graduation Day II' were cancelled because of their acute social relevance. Decades of television entertainment have shown us just how financially lucrative socially relevant programming can be (see, for example, D'Acci, 1994; Feuer, 1995; Feuer, Kerr and Vahimagi, 1984; Gitlin, 2000; Taylor, 1991). Here the discourse of TV violence was determined as much by practices of network censorship and economic strategising as by the acts of physical aggression contained in these two episodes. We need a theory of TV violence that takes into account the ways in which TV networks work to regulate the meanings of TV violence for maximum financial gain. In this case, the WB Network became a temporary apologist for button-pushing content and then raced to capitalise upon it once Columbine faded from news headlines. The nineteenth-century words of a Goth-inspired Karl Marx seem all too perfect here: 'Capital is dead labour which, vampire-like, lives only by sucking living labour and lives the more, the more labour it sucks' (see Cubitt, 1996, p. 242). WB is at the centre of the Hellmouth and is precisely the kind of vampire that Buffy symbolically slays.

In his book *The Case For TV Violence* Jib Fowles claims that media effects research such as the NTVS has 'crowd[ed] out alternative viewpoints and produce[d] in some a numb-minded acquiescence' (Fowles, 1999, p. 49). I want to examine specific 'violent incidents' in *Buffy* in order to destabilise consensus thinking around the concept of TV violence and to call for new definitions of the term and other modes of analysis. I invoke the term TV violence to point to the broader socioeconomic inequalities and injustices that Television and Cultural Studies scholars have always been concerned with, and to highlight ideological and institutionalised forms of violence that are often invisible on the screen, but that have serious psychic and material effects. We need ways of discussing and debating these issues with media effects researchers in the public sphere so I have decided to use their unit of analysis – the violent incident – but I use it to demonstrate the ways in which generic hybridity, gendered aggression, racial/ethnic oppression and social alienation complicate existing definitions of TV violence. (For recent anthologies that develop different ways of studying and analysing media violence, see Prince, 2000; Sharratt, 1999.)

Generic hybridity

In *Buffy* violence is fickle. This is related in part to the generic hybridity of the series: its 'spasms of viciousness' are punctuated by the conventions of the soap opera, horror, comedy, music video, action and sci-fi genres (for further discussion see Hills, forthcoming). In the age of cable and satellite television, genres have been increasingly recombined to attract niche markets and coalitional audiences. Jane Feuer suggests that since the 1980s the typical viewing experience has been characterised as 'a rapid flow from one genre to another'.[7] Jim Collins argues that such generic hybridity creates what he refers to as 'tonal variation'. He explains,

At one moment, the conventions of a genre are taken 'seriously,' in another scene, they might be subjected to [a] . . . sort of ambivalent parody . . . These generic and tonal variations occur within scenes as well as across scenes, sometimes oscillating on a line by line basis, or across episodes.

1992, p. 345

Television writers are keenly aware of their use of different generic elements in story and character construction. Two of *Buffy*'s writers (Joss Whedon and Jane Espenson) worked on sitcoms (*Roseanne* and *Ellen* respectively) before *Buffy* and these experiences refined their ability to write between genres and to craft ironic shifts in dialogue, character and setting now known as 'Buffyspeak' (Parks, 1999).

Buffy's generic hybridity and tonal variation make it all the more difficult to isolate 'violent incidents' in the show. Consider, for instance, a scene from 'The I in Team', a fourth-season episode that explores Buffy's relationship to the Initiative (a state military effort to capture, study and re-create demons, vampires and monsters). In one sequence an Initiative mission to 'zap and trap' a demon is crosscut with a scene of Buffy and Riley's first lovemaking. In it the conventions of soap opera, action, science-fiction and music video are activated and woven together. Buffy jabs the demon in one shot and Riley removes her leather boot in the next. Buffy knocks the demon to the ground in one shot and kisses Riley's washboard stomach in the next. Throughout the sequence Karma's moody song 'Window to Your Soul' plays in the background as viewers are bounced from the battle to the bed. This alternation is symptomatic of the series' mul- tivalent discourse on violence as the meanings of physical aggression are contested and renegotiated with an exchange of desiring looks, rhythmic music and the tenderness of sexual touching. This crosscutting not only draws attention to major shifts in Buffy's character (as she becomes an agent for the Initiative, and the lover of Riley), but also poses an interesting conundrum for analysts of TV violence. How would one code this 'violent incident'? Is this an act of aggression or an act of passion? Who's being aggress- ive here, Buffy or Riley? Demons or the state? The point I'm trying to make here is that acts of physical aggression take on different meanings as the conventions of different genres are activated. We need to be insisting that studies of TV violence take these kinds of shifts into account, especially since television is a medium of re-combined formulas and in the age of narrowcasting and niche marketing genre mixing has become an important marketing strategy (Anon., 1996, p. ix).[8]

Gendering violence

Sometimes TV violence involves acts of self-defence. No episode reveals this point bet- ter than a second-season episode called 'Ted'. In this episode Buffy's mother, Joyce, falls in love with a hotshot salesman named Ted (played by John Ritter). While Joyce finds Ted to be a great companion and an even better chef, Buffy remains skeptical. Ted seems all too eager to step in as the family patriarch scrutinising her every move. During the episode's climax Buffy climbs through her bedroom window after a slow night of slay- ing only to find Ted lurking in the dark waiting to scold her. After an argument, he threatens to leave the room with her diary and they end up in a scuffle. Buffy kicks Ted down the stairs and he dies (temporarily, that is). It turns out that Ted is a serial killer robot, programmed to seduce and destroy women and then store them as trophies in his bachelor-pad basement.

Here the 'violent incident' operates as self-defence when a man manoeuvres his way into Buffy's bedroom and threatens her both emotionally and physically. We need to introduce into discussions of TV violence the issue of self-defensive behaviour, particularly since it can be a feminist practice. Symbolically, this sequence positions Buffy as defending the single working mother family and adolescent feminine mobility and privacy against a technocratic father figure. Here the violent incident operates as a fantasy of feminine control: this episode stages a rare instance in which a working family is protected by a physically powerful girl as opposed to the rationality of the patriarch or the brute strength of the state. As anthropologist David Graeber puts it Buffy is 'engaged in a struggle to save humanity from its authoritarian monsters' (1998, p. 29).

Most media effects researchers do not differentiate between offensive and defensive aggression. In *Real Knockouts*, Martha McCaughey argues that women's involvement in self-defence is key to feminist struggles because it 'disrupts the gender ideology that makes men's violence against women seem inevitable' (1997, p. ix). She explains, 'in embracing the pleasures of combat, women undermine the exclusive association between masculinity and physical aggression' (ibid., p. 178). Self-defence 'expands the possibilities for women's legitimate use of aggression against men's' and helps women to 'disembody a social order of female subordination' (ibid., pp. ix, 178). The violence in *Buffy*, then, may have less to do with the visible blood and gore of slaying and more to do with the show's rearticulation of the gendered social order. What is violent – that is, what truly assaults dominant logic – is a woman (well, not really a woman, a girl) who occupies a place in the field of vision with physical strength and has narrative agency and who is allowed to be weak/abject as well. Rather than entertain the notion that *Buffy* encourages inappropriate forms of physical aggression, we ought to identify this act of physical aggression – or this instance of TV violence – as a symptom of women's history, as the publicisation of a feminist discourse of self-defence.

To extend this discussion further, we could also consider how *Buffy* treats the issue of women in combat, an issue that is ultimately about who the state authorises to act violently. In another scene in 'The I in Team' Buffy sticks out like a sore thumb seated amongst a battalion of male soldiers receiving an assignment from Dr Walsh. She asks too many questions during the briefing, refuses to wear a military uniform (opting instead for an orange halter top), and talks about relationships while on the hunt. The episode conflates femininity with frivolity and positions 'woman' as a security risk that the military simply cannot afford. Of course, the best irony is that Buffy is more competent in combat than all of them combined. (She proves this both in the zap and trap mission and in the final act when she outmanoeuvres two demons assigned to kill her.)

Since this episode is about Buffy's reluctance to embrace military discipline and become part of the Initiative, its narrative constantly works to differentiate her from her male cohorts. In the battle scenes Buffy's physical aggression is marked as physical rather than technological, intuitive rather than rational, and spontaneous rather than planned. Buffy's acts of physical aggression are significant precisely because they do not comport with military practice and they expose the dominant social order's inability to recognise legitimate forms of female aggression. What I am proposing here is that the analysis of the 'violent incident' should not be limited to spectacular displays of physical aggression alone. We should consider these displays as an entry point for analysing institutionalised (and ideological) forms of violence that are often invisible. We might recode TV violence here, then, as the military's historical exclusion of women, or the construction of state-sanctioned aggression as a masculine necessity, or the captivity of biological specimens whose bodies are used to reinforce scientific and state authority and to perfect techniques of aggression (i.e., in the form of the character, Adam).

Whiteness as violence

One of the frequent remarks made by liberal and leftist viewers who watch *Buffy* is 'Yeah it's a great show, but it focuses only on white middle-class kids'. If Columbine has taught us anything, it's that disaffected white suburban kids are the ticking time-bombs in the USA despite attempts over the past decade by political leaders, moral conservatives and news media to label African-American men as such. More than ever, we live in an era of contestable white power. In *Buffy* whiteness functions as a centralised void that constantly works to (re)establish its primacy in relation to an array of ethnicised Others. *Buffy* thematises racial/ethnic difference in a variety of ways, but I want to focus on two episodes that utilise tropes of colonisation and ethnographic spectacle. Both 'Inca Mummy Girl' and 'Pangs' are 'return of the repressed' narratives which feature ethnic characters who return to Sunnydale to redress traumatic historical events. The first features an Incan princess Impata who was killed centuries ago at the age of sixteen and denied the experiences of a 'normal girl'. Tired of being nothing but a frozen artifact in a travelling museum exhibit, the mummy revivifies herself and reclaims her stolen adolescence by possessing the body of a Columbian foreign exchange student. Throughout the episode Impata graphically sucks the life out of several high school students in order to survive and she seduces Xander. When Impata and Buffy meet for a climactic fight atop the dusty vaults of the museum, she battles for her life, but eventually transforms into dust and falls through her lover Xander's fingertips.

'Pangs' features a Chumash Indian spirit named Hus who returns to Sunnydale during the week of Thanksgiving, just as the high school unveils its new Multicultural Center, to seek revenge on white settlers who stole his people's lands. He and other tomahawk- and bow and arrow-toting Indians go to battle with Buffy before she and her friends sit down for Thanksgiving dinner. This ironically played struggle between Chumash Indian spirits and white suburban teens ends up haunting the settler tradition of the Thanksgiving feast, challenging characters and viewers alike to digest the violence of white colonisation along with roast turkey and pumpkin pie. The interesting aspect of this episode is that it presents the viewer with an unresolvable dilemma: how can a pack of compassionate demon-fighting white suburban teens reconcile their fight against evil in the present with their society's colonial and racist past?

While these representations arguably reinforce the ethnic stereotypes of the sensual but volatile Latina and the fierce Native American, they also index historical and contemporary forms of violence directed against people of colour in the American southwest. In both of these episodes, acts of physical aggression are motivated by western appropriation of ethnographic artifacts (and the ongoing commodification of ethnicity) and by the historical trauma of colonisation. As Native American critic Gerald Vizenor suggests, 'This [white] obsession with the tribal past is not an innocent collection of arrowheads, not a crude map of public camp sites in sacred places, but rather a statement of [white] power and control over tribal images' (1992, p. 413).

While Impata and Hus are figured as ethnographic spectacles, they are used to bring forms of white violence (such as genocide and forced assimilation) into relief. As Fatimah Tobing Romy explains, ethnographic spectacle is a long-established tradition 'in which indigenous peoples are exhibited and dissected – both visually and literally'. Despite this, ethnographic spectacles can be used as possible sites of resistance as well. Some poets and artists, Romy writes, disrupt the ethnographic gaze 'by imagining (or perhaps listening to) the silenced displayed person, by destroying the shell of the ethnographic simulacrum which encases the historical person' (1996, p. 190). Both Impata and Hus function as ethnographic spectacles that managed to wrestle out of the museum case, so to speak. They return to the world as speaking and acting agents and threaten to wreak havoc on contemporary suburban life as a way of redressing colonisation. Commenting on his own re-enactment of ethnographic caricatures, performance artist Guillermo Gomez-Pena explains

> We want to bring back the ghosts and unleash the demons of history, but we want to do it in a way that the demons don't scare the Anglo-European others, but force them to begin a negotiation with these ghosts and demons that will lead to a pact of co-existence. The ghosts we are trying to unleash are extremely whimsical, irreverent, and grotesque, extremely crazy and picaresque.
>
> See Romy, 1996, p. 191

Impata and Hus are also irreverent ghosts who initiate pacts of coexistence only to be conquered by white suburban teenagers. Still, the 'violent incidents' in these episodes are significant for they not only articulate the trauma of colonisation, but at the same time expose white power's compulsion to re-establish its centrality by ultimately conquering the repressed figures who return to negotiate. Both Impata and Hus are placed back into their dusty graves, but the 'violent incidents' in these episodes have publicised the ongoing struggles of Hispanic and Native American peoples for cultural survival and autonomy, and called attention to television drama's inevitable resolution of conflict in favour of whiteness.

What is interesting about *Buffy* is that many episodes suggest the white teen characters' desire for racial/ethnic integration (or at least they construct teens with liberal pluralist values), but that the WB Network itself is simply unwilling to embrace such a policy. Characters of different ethnic backgrounds are always killed off at WB.

What about the violence of that? Within the context of the series, then, TV violence gives limited expression to ethnic peoples who have historically been subjected to various forms of white power, and it also serves as a reminder of the TV industry's own ongoing exclusion of people of colour. We need to insist that discussions of TV violence address the politics of ethnic/racial representation and the ongoing exclusion of people of colour from prime-time television. The 'blackouts' and 'brownouts' by African, Asian and Native Americans during the 1999–2000 season went a long way in drawing public attention to these issues. Although these programme boycotts did not result in widespread institutional reform, they did generate some 'colour adjustments' – more minority characters were created in select series and the networks committed to long-term efforts towards racial/ethnic integration.

Social alienation

A final form of violence that is not recognised within the parameters of media effects research is that of social alienation. Recent studies of media violence have focused attention upon alienated youth, but few have acknowledged that alienation itself often operates as a form of violence. Since social alienation is often used as narrative motivation for acts of physical aggression, I want to consider it as another form of TV violence. An episode called 'Invisible Girl', for instance, explores the world through the eyes of Marci Ross, a high school girl who becomes invisible literally after being ignored and overlooked for so long by her peers and teachers. A series of flashbacks dramatise Marci's feelings of insignificance. (We see her trying to talk to popular girls in the bathroom but being utterly ignored, raising her hand in class and never being called on. In her yearbook everyone has written the same thing: 'Have a nice summer.') Marci disappears for six months and no one notices until one day the invisible girl begins to attack schoolmates and teachers. In the climax, Marci kidnaps and tortures two girls with social visibility – Cordelia – who has just been crowned May Queen only because of her pretty face, and Buffy – the chosen one, the slayer. Marci holds Cordelia and Buffy captive in the Bronze and threatens to rearrange Cordelia's face with a scalpel that floats in midair. After slashing Cordelia's cheek, Marci explains that she'll use Cordy's pretty face to teach the world a lesson. Eventually, Buffy breaks free and just as she wrestles Marci to the ground, two FBI agents storm through the door to apprehend and 'rehabilitate' Marci. They take her to an FBI classroom where, they tell her, 'she'll be sure to fit in'. The final scene shows invisible Marci entering a classroom filled with other invisible students who are told to turn to a chapter in their textbook called 'Assimilation and Infiltration'.

The episode establishes continuities between Marci's social invisibility and her aggression. As Giles explains, 'she's been isolated for six months and loneliness has caused her to go mad'. Some might argue that this sequence legitimates aggression as a way of becoming visible (getting attention) or as a kind of teen vigilantism (out to correct the gap between the popular and the nerd), but this scene is designed as a lesson about alienation not aggression. On the stage curtain in the Bronze, Marci has written in gold glittery letters 'LEARN'. She chooses the Bronze – a local hangout – because this lesson is obviously not taught in school. Instead, the school reinforces alienation by rewarding those with pretty faces the title of queen. Marci uses the instruments of plastic surgery ironically, threatening to rearrange Cordelia's face and use it as a medium to broadcast what it means to feel unnoticed and ignored in a culture that values only the surface of pretty skin. (This act shares something in common with the way young girls often manipulate and disfigure Barbies, which can be read both as an adolescent critique of beauty norms and a fantasy of self-sculpting.) The episode's final scene critiques state violence as it schemes to assemble the alienated and transform them into its agents of social control. The state relies upon the marginalised to advance its own interests, to lurk, to spy, to be invisible to act in its interests. Here TV violence crystallises into a critique of feminine beauty norms, social alienation and state authority.

Social alienation was also a key theme in 'Earshot', which became the subject of public controversy in May 1999. As discussed, WB decided to pull this episode because the story involved a planned high school shooting and thus it shared an eerie resemblance with events in Littleton, Colorado. In 'Earshot' Buffy develops the ability to hear everyone's thoughts, absorbing the collective unconscious of Sunnydale. Sitting in the high school cafeteria one day, she overhears someone mutter 'This time tomorrow, I'll kill you all.' Since Buffy only caught an 'earshot' of the statement, she is unsure who exactly is plotting to kill her schoolmates. She assumes it is Jonathan (a short, geeky fellow who Buffy had earlier overheard saying 'You don't even look at me') and the episode culminates in a dialogue sequence between rifle-toting Jonathan and word-savvy Buffy in the school's bell tower.

Jonathan: 'Stop doing that!'

Buffy: 'Doing what?'

Jonathan: (frustrated and almost in tears) 'Stop saying my name like we're friends. We're not friends. You all think I'm an idiot. A short idiot.'

Buffy: 'I don't. I don't really think about you much at all. Nobody here really does. Bugs you doesn't it? You have all this pain and all these feelings and nobody's really paying attention.'

Jonathan: 'You think I just want attention?'

Buffy: 'No I think you're up here in the clock tower with a high-powered rifle because you want to blend in.' (more sympathetically) 'Believe it or not Jonathan I understand about the pain.'

Jonathan: 'Oh right. Because the burden of being beautiful and athletic. That's a crippler.'

Buffy: 'You know what I was wrong. You are an idiot. My life happens to on occasion suck beyond the telling of it. Sometimes more than I can handle. But it's not just mine. Every single person down there is ignoring your pain because they're too busy with their own.'

Buffy moves slowly towards the window of the clocktower, taking in the view below. It's filled with unsuspecting students. The same ones whose thoughts she'd been hearing not a day ago.

Buffy: 'The beautiful ones, the popular ones, the guys who pick on you. Everyone. If you could hear what they were thinking – the loneliness, the confusion. It looks quiet down there, but it's not. It's deafening.'

Buffy's lines exploit the motif of the episode – of overhearing others' thoughts – becoming Jonathan's superego and turning his own thoughts back at him, forcing him to hear himself and to rethink his motivations for what turns out to be his suicide attempt, an act which is often about being noticed. (This theme is made even more explicit in a later episode called 'Superstar', in which Jonathan becomes everyone's idol.)[9] The person who actually issues the threat is a disgruntled school lunch lady who devises a food poisoning scheme that is thwarted by Buffy and Xander. The 'violent incidents' in 'Earshot' ultimately become a way of recognising and working through anxieties of alienation that stimulate fantasies of physical aggression whether they are directed at the self or the social body. Towards the end of the sequence, Buffy encourages Jonathan, on the verge of his suicide, to look down at other students and to understand his pain as social pain. It doesn't affect him alone. *Buffy*'s writers constructed a world in which Jonathan set his gun down, but Eric Harris and Dylan Klebold unfortunately turned guns on others and then on themselves.

Obviously the theme of social alienation is not unique to *Buffy the Vampire Slayer*. In his book *Rational Fears*, Mark Jancovich suggests that early teen-targeted horror films

directly focused on the feeling of being alien, on the problems of 'fitting in' or 'adjusting' to the demands of the social world; and they often gave a far more agonised, pessimistic and critical portrayal of these problems than the more respectable productions of the bigger studios.

1996, pp. 199–200

Buffy certainly continues this tradition, but just as the 1950s culture of conformity was blind to the incisive social commentaries embedded within many B-movies, the 1990s has generated a culture of moral panic that is unable to recognise that youth-oriented television might actually confront the issue of violence rather than encourage it.[10]

Since media effects researchers focus on spectacular forms of physical aggression, they overlook ideologies of normality, which can be just as brutal. Social alienation functions in this series to complicate the very meanings of 'TV violence', challenging us to formulate analytical models that account for forms of violence that are institutionalised as part of a broader set of social relations. Media effects researchers insist that such violent incidents legitimate aggression as a way of getting attention, but we ought to instead ask why alienated youth see aggression as their only recourse? What is it about our social structure that leaves the alienated with so few ways to feel visible and significant? 'Invisible Girl' and 'Earshot' are both about the desire to be seen and heard and the violence of not seeing and listening. One of the most frequent questions asked about the Columbine killings is, how is it that Eric Harris was publicising his deathly fantasies on a website, documenting them with a video camera, writing about them in his diary – that is, using all the communication technologies at his disposal – and still not being seen or heard?[11] In a culture that so values visibility and spectacle, being invisible carries certain social costs. For it's the feeling of not having a place, not having a voice, not having presence, being invisible in the world today that motivates physical aggression.

If we as Television and Cultural Studies scholars can learn anything from the vicious rampage of Harris and Klebold, perhaps it is a lesson about what's at stake in not being heard. We need to be more vocal in public discussions and debates about TV violence. We need to complicate the 'violent incident', to use it as a way of turning public eyes upon ideological and institutionalised forms of aggression. Why shouldn't the category of TV violence also refer to representations of social alienation, state-sanctioned aggression, or self-defence? Why shouldn't TV violence refer to the historical exclusion of people of colour from prime-time drama? Or surgical strike TV images of US attacks on Iraq and Afghanistan? Or the violation of individuals' Fourth Amendment rights in reality-based programmes like *Cops* ? We need to extend the discursive terrain of TV violence to include other such issues. It's little coincidence that during the Columbine killings, the USA was pummelling Kosovo with smart bombs.[12] Some saw these as two non-related media events, but the militarisation of the state has everything to do with a high school culture of violence. *Buffy the Vampire Slayer* jabs us with this point week after week. The show has prowled on the fringes of network television while media researchers have conducted the NTVS, as alienated youths have sprayed their schools with bullets and as TV news replays images of the Columbine massacre. But more than any other public discourse *Buffy* speaks to the core of recent social crisis. Since we care about social power and television, we ought to defend the medium when it gets it right.

Acknowledgments

I would like to thank Garrett Krnich, T. Q. Gaskins, Stacey Mitchell and Amy Pocha for research assistance and taping, and those who attended my UCSB Women's Studies Colloquium for their helpful comments. An earlier version of this paper was presented at the Console-ing Passions Conference in 2000. My thanks go to Henry Jenkins, Jane Feuer, Moya Luckett and Laura Marks for their encouraging remarks. This paper is dedicated to my distant family members whom I have never met who are still trying to make sense of the traumatic events that unfolded in Columbine High School.

Notes

1. *Buffy* provides an opportunity to explore the relationship between the academic discipline of Television Studies and the practice of television writing. In our scholarship and teaching we focus on critical writing rather than creative writing. But if we're concerned about the politics of representation, we might do well to shift some of our attention towards the process of shaping not just critiquing televisual representation. There are not enough opportunities for our students to assimilate knowledge of textual criticism and then apply it

in a creative context. Because of its formulaic structure, those who work within this field must arguably be more resourceful and clever about generating aesthetic innovation and social commentary within such a rigid system of representation. We still know very little about the history of television narrative and part of this is due to the lack of theorisation of the relationship of critical writing and television writing. In some cases, television series such as *The Simpsons, South Park, Freaks and Geeks, The X Files* and *Buffy* to name a few, produce social critiques that are just as biting and insightful as those made by the scholars in the field of Television and Cultural Studies.

2. The Parental Guidelines for TV 14 indicate 'Parents Strongly Cautioned. *This program contains some material that many parents would find unsuitable for children under 14 years of age.* Parents are strongly urged to exercise greater care in monitoring this program and are cautioned against letting children under the age of 14 watch unattended. This program contains one or more of the following: intense violence (V), intense sexual situations (S), strong coarse language (L), or intensely suggestive dialogue (D)' (Anon., 2001).

3. WB executives and series creator Joss Whedon have indicated they do not consider *Buffy*'s viewers to be a primarily teen audience (Whedon 1999; America Online, 1999).

4. The *National Television Violence Study* includes programming between 1994 and 1997 from twenty-three broadcast, cable and premium television channels between 6am and 11pm.

5. The authors of the *National Television Violence Study* claim to analyse the context of violence by considering such variables as the nature of the perpetrator, nature of the target, reason for the violence, presence of weapons, extent and explicitness of violence, degree of realism of violence, whether violence is rewarded or punished, consequences of violence and whether humour is involved in violence (see p. 13). But this analysis doesn't take into account televisual elements such as characterisation, narrative, cinematography, sound, editing and *mise en scène*. We need a way of analysing TV violence that takes the medium as seriously as the method.

6. What set this study apart was its analysis of violence in different entertainment formats. The researchers analysed 573 separate popular culture products representing four distinct entertainment genres – prime-time television series, television movies, feature films and popular music. The study included episodes from *Buffy*'s 1998–9 season. Others on the 'Most Violent TV Series' list included *VIP, Xena, Oz, Mortal Combat, Viper* and *Crow* (Lichter, Lichter and Amundson, 1999).

7. Jane Feuer uses the series *Hill Street Blues, St Elsewhere, Moonlighting* and *LA Law* as examples of genre hybridity in the 1980s (Feuer, 1992).

8. Television programmes ranging from *Ally McBeal* to World Wrestling Federation showdowns now mobilise a variety of generic conventions (including that of the legal drama, comedy, the media event and music video) in their promotions as part of an effort to attract eclectic niche markets and form coalitional audiences.

9. In 'Superstar' Jonathan has become a debonair Bond figure who is adored by all and put at the centre of everyone's attention. As a secret agent, pop singer, author, slayer, lover, Jonathan lives out his fantasy of being adored by everyone and being good at everything. He goes from being insignificant nerd to a hypervisible pop icon. Here, acts of violence are motivated by a nerd's fantasy of social acceptance and public recognition.

10. Indeed, there is a tad bit of *The Donna Reed Show* in *Buffy*, which is interesting given that Whedon's uncle worked as a writer on the hit series. For a thorough examination of the 1950s culture of conformity, see Nadel, 1995.

11. Harris and Klebold made five videos before their attack with the hope that they would one day be shown around the world (see Gibbs and Roche, 1999).

12. For an interesting perspective on this, see Julia Meltzer's webart piece 'Kosovo, Colorado' at <www.immaterial.net/webart/kosovo-colorado>, which contrasts the war in the Balkans with the Columbine high school shooting.

Bibliography

Abel, Katy, 'Buffy Slays Parental Sensibilities', *FamilyEducation.com* (1999), <familyeducation.com/article/0,1120,1-7884,00.html> (accessed on 8 October 1999).

Allen, John, 'In Teen Gothic Genre, The Kids Aren't Alright', *National Catholic Reporter* (2 March 1999), p. 17.

America Online, 'Interview of Jamie Kellner', <www.aol.com> (13 July 1999) (accessed on 29 September 1999).

America Online Listserv, 'Parents Reactions to the Buffy Pulled Episodes' (1999), <www.aol.com> (accessed on 11 June 1999).

Anon., *National Television Violence Study* (Studio City: Mediascope, Inc., 1996).

Anon., *National Television Violence Study*, Executive Summary (Studio City: Mediascope, Inc., 1999).

Anon., TV Parental Guidelines Monitoring Group, 'TV Parental Guidelines' (2001), <www.tvguidelines.org> (accessed on 1 October 2001).

Collins, Jim, 'Television and Postmodernism', in Robert. Allen (ed.), *Channels of Discourse, Reassembled* (Chapel Hill: University of North Carolina Press, 1992), pp. 327–53.

Cubitt, Sean, 'Supernatural Futures: Theses on Digital Aesthetics', in George Robertson, Tickner, Lisa and Bird, Jon (eds), *Futurenatural: Nature/Culture/Science* (London: Routledge, 1996), pp. 237–55.

Cullen, Dave, 'Kill mankind. No one Should Survive', *Salon.com* (23 September 1999), <www.salon.com/news/feature/1999/09/23/journal> (accessed on 8 October 1999).

D'Acci, Julie, *Defining Women: The Case of* Cagney and Lacey (Chapel Hill: University of North Carolina Press, 1994).

Feuer, Jane, 'Genre Study and Television', in Robert Allen (ed.), *Channels of Discourse, Reassembled* (Chapel Hill: University of North Carolina Press, 1992), pp. 138–60.

Feuer, Jane, *Seeing Through the 80s: Television and Reaganism* (Durham: Duke University Press, 1995).

Feuer, Jane, Kerr, Paul and Vahimagi, Tise, *MTM: 'Quality Television'* (London: BFI, 1984).

Fowles, Jib, *The Case for Television Violence* (Thousand Oaks, CA: Sage Publications, 1999).

Gibbs, Nancy and Roche, Timothy, 'The Columbine Tapes', *Time* (20 December 1999), <www.time.com/time/magazine> (accessed on 9 May 2000).

Gitlin, Todd, *Inside Prime Time TV* (Berkeley: University of California Press, 2000).

Graeber, David, 'Rebel Without a God: *Buffy the Vampire Slayer* is Gleefully Anti-Authoritarian and Popular', *In These Times* (27 December 1998), pp. 29–30.

Hills, Matt, 'Reading Formation Theory and the Rising Stakes of Generic Hybridity', in Lisa Parks and Elana Levine (eds), *Red Noise:* Buffy the Vampire Slayer *and Television Studies* (working title) (Durham: Duke University Press, forthcoming).

Jancovich, Mark, *Rational Fears: American Horror in the 1950s* (Manchester: Manchester University Press, 1996).

Katz, John, 'Bootlegging Buffy: Era of Information Control is Over', (8 June 1999), <www.freedomforum.org/templates/document.asp?documentID=11579> (accessed on 29 January 2003).

Lichter, S. Robert, Lichter, Linda S. and Amundson, Dan, 'Merchandizing Mayhem: Violence in Popular Culture', Center for Media and Public Affairs, Washington, DC (1999), <128.241.132.235/archive/viol98.htm> (accessed on 3 September 2000).

McCaughey, Martha, *Real Knockouts: The Physical Feminism of Women's Self-Defense* (New York: New York University Press, 1997).

Nadel, Alan, *Containment Culture: American Narrative, Postmodernism, and the Atomic Age* (Durham: Duke University Press, 1995).

Parks, Lisa, 'Personal Interview of Jane Espenson, *Buffy* writer and co-producer', Mutant Enemy Studios, Santa Monica, California (8 December 1999).

Parks, Lisa and Levine, Elana (eds), *Red Noise:* Buffy the Vampire Slayer *and Television Studies* (working title) (Durham: Duke University Press, forthcoming).

Prince, Stephen (ed.), *Screening Violence* (New Brunswick: Rutgers University Press, 2000).

Romy, Fatimah Tobing, *The Third Eye: Race, Cinema and Ethnographic Spectacle* (Durham: Duke University Press, 1996).

Sharrett, Christopher (ed.), *Mythologies of Violence in Postmodern Media* (Detroit: Wayne State University Press, 1999).

Springer, Matt, 'Eye of the Storm', *Buffy the Vampire Slayer*, vol. 5 (Autumn 1999).

Taylor, Ella, *Prime Time Families* (Berkeley: University of California Press, 1991).

Variety, 'Ad', *Variety* (18 June 1999).

Vizenor, Gerald, 'The Striptease', in Russell Ferguson and Martha Gever (eds), *Out There: Marginalization and Contemporary Culture* (Cambridge: MIT Press, 1992).

Whedon, Joss, 'Seminar on Youth Television', Museum of Radio and Television (November 1999).

PART THREE

Commodity Audiences: Cults, Fans and Dedicated Audiences

9

Martial Law and the Changing Face of Martial Arts on US Television

Andrew Willis

Martial Law first aired on CBS on 26 September 1998 with the episode 'Shanghai Express'. It was an American television series starring Hong Kong martial arts superstar Sammo Hung, and ran for two seasons, producing a total of forty-four episodes. This chapter will examine the ways in which a clear sense of fan expectation, here of martial arts action, informed the design and creation of the show. While networks had often been dismissive of fan audiences in the past, the pursuit of an already existing fan base has become a vital part of industry strategies. By developing a show with an eye on pre-existing fans, this small but dedicated audience may be enough to see a new programme through its potentially troublesome early broadcasts and so help it to avoid cancellation. However, while martial arts fans, for example, might be attracted to a programme that showcased one of the greatest martial arts stars, if producers start to tinker with it in an attempt to open it up to a more mainstream audience, there is always the danger that the resulting product will fail to appeal to either the fans who had established the show or the mainstream audiences for which the show had been redesigned. This was the case with *Martial Law*. The result marginalised the very groups originally targeted by the show and led to falling viewing figures and eventual cancellation. However, *Martial Law* remains significant in a number of ways. It demonstrates the increasing influence of Hong Kong action cinema on US television audiences and productions and in so doing marks a number of significant shifts in the production of martial arts-based television in the USA. It was also the first series produced by a major network starring an Asian-American or Asian lead performer to be commissioned for a second season.

In her book on the impact of communication technologies, Patrice Flichy argues that technological developments have led to a breakdown in the traditional family unit's consumption of the media. She states, when discussing this in relation to music, that,

> When they were launched, the transistor and long-playing record benefited not only from a new form of music (rock) but also from a profound change in private life. The family did not disappear but it was transformed; the home was maintained but as a place in which individual practices were juxtaposed. Music was particularly well adapted to this new 'juxtaposed home'. Family members could all listen to the music they wanted in their rooms.

1995, p. 164

The television industry in the USA, and indeed across the globe, has gone through a similar period of audience fragmentation. Families now have a number of television sets around the house and family members consume programmes from an array of sources, from the traditional networks to speciality satellite and cable stations. This has resulted in significantly smaller viewing figures for top-rated, popular shows, and while this does not mean that the major networks have given up on family oriented shows, other factors have come into play.

Most particularly, it is these changes that have forced the industry to both acknowledge, and actively target, once marginal audience groups such as fans in order to provide a foundation for a mainstream television show. Perhaps the best example of this is science-fiction fans who are sought by the networks for shows such as the *Star Trek* spinoffs and *The X Files*. It is the loyalty and commitment of fans to genres, such as science-fiction, that has led networks to embrace them as central rather than marginal audiences. Furthermore, once one genre-based fan group has proved its worth, others come into the equation and, as a result, fans of martial arts-based action have become an identifiable audience group. They have been brought in from the margins of US cultural consumption and placed much more centrally as an audience group that has potentially similar generic loyalties to those of sci-fi fans.

There have been important factors in this change of attitude. The success of shows such as *Hercules: The Legendary Journeys* and *Xena: Warrior Princess*, which are influenced by Hong Kong action cinema and incorporate elements of martial arts fighting, have been significant, as has the continued popularity of comically violent programmes such as professional wrestling. As a result, while the violence associated with martial arts movies was previously seen as problematic material for television, these attitudes are changing. Programme-makers have accepted that violence based in comedy is now acceptable to audiences, thus paving one way for martial arts television to find a niche in the US networks' programming. Other factors that have also come into play will be discussed, but first I want to provide a history of the relationship between television, martial arts and its fans.

Martial arts on US television

One of the major figures in the field of martial arts cinema is Bruce Lee. Even though he died in 1973, he has had an enormous influence on people's conception of martial arts and martial artists. He came to prominence in the television series *The Green Hornet*, first broadcast on US TV between 1966 and 1967, which was made by ABC, who had been responsible for the earlier adventure series *Hong Kong*. In *The Green Hornet* Lee played the sidekick of the eponymous hero, and each week his character, Kato, would dispose of the bad guys through the use of his amazing martial arts skills. However, this part was not a breakthrough for Lee and did not lead to a deluge of other roles. Indeed, his experience after the success of *The Green Hornet* is very telling in relation to the images of martial arts that appeared on US TV.

Lee had hoped that he would be able to follow the success of *The Green Hornet* with another series in which he would feature in the central role rather than as a supporting player. With this in mind he assisted in the development of a project that he hoped would deliver such a role: *The Warrior*. This project became, perhaps, the best known of all the incarnations of martial arts on American television, *Kung Fu*, a show which ran successfully from 1972–5 on ABC. Originally the concept, a Shaolin monk wandering the old west, was developed in the late 1960s but there was no green light for the project from Warner Bros. and ABC, and Lee was only able to pick up small parts in TV series such as *Longstreet* (1971, Paramount TV). As a result, Lee left the USA to make films in Hong Kong, where he made two very successful pictures, *The Big Boss* (1971) and *Fist of Fury* (1971). While working in Hong Kong, he still hoped that *The Warrior* would be picked up back in the US, and that his popularity as Kato would land him the lead role. However, the producers were unsure whether a mainstream audience would accept an Asian actor in the lead role of a prime-time show, and Lee slowly realised that the executives' resistance would limit his chances. Indeed, in an interview with Pierre Berton, he indicated that he was well aware of this issue. In response to a question about the potential problems of a Chinese lead in an American series he said,

> Well, the question has been raised. In fact, it is being discussed, and that is why *The Warrior* is probably not going to be on . . . They think, business-wise, it's a risk. And I don't blame them . . . If I were the man with the money, I would probably have my own worry whether or not the acceptance would be there.
>
> Thomas, 1994, p. 144

As a result, on 7 December 1971, Lee received a telegram that stated: 'due to pressures from the network regarding casting', he had been dropped from the project (ibid.). In 1972 the pilot was aired under the new title *Kung Fu*.

Opting for what they thought was safety, the producers cast David Carradine as the lead in *Kung Fu*, a decision that left Lee feeling that he had been the victim of racism. A wider look at the Asian characters in circulation on US TV at this period does not do anything to disprove this view. Often Asian performers appeared as servants or assistants, as Lee himself had done in *The Green Hornet* (see, for example, Sammee Tong in *Bachelor Father* [1957–62], Victor Sen Yung in *Bonanza* [1959–72] and Miyoshi Umeki in *The Courtship of Eddie's Father* [1969–72]). In these programmes and others, as Wilson and Gutierrez note, the images perpetrate, 'the subservient, humble Asian image' (1995, p. 103). Certainly, many programmes featured martial arts after *Kung Fu* but these also maintained the policy of casting white actors in the lead roles. Like many American-produced martial arts films, television also chose to place martial arts within the context of already established genres. For example, after its initial setting in the Shaolin monastery, *Kung Fu* utilised the codes and conventions of the television Western rather than the historically set martial arts films popular in the Hong Kong cinema of the 1970s.

As a result, *Kung Fu* was clearly a response to the international success of Bruce Lee and the martial arts film, even if the executives were afraid to cast him in the lead. In much the same way, the next wave of martial arts movies to achieve box-office success also elicited a response from US television executives. A number of low-budget martial arts films focusing on the mysterious Japanese assassins, the Ninja, and their deadly martial arts skills, Ninjitsu, were box-office hits in the 1980s, the best known being probably *Enter the Ninja* (1982). These films had a tendency to cast American or European actors in the lead roles, such as in the case of *American Ninja* (1986) which starred Michael Dudikoff. NBC felt that this preoccupation would translate to television screens and developed a project to exploit this potential. *The Master* was first aired in 1984 but, unluckily, it only lasted for thirteen episodes. Casting was probably the root of the series' problems as it starred the veteran star of popular European Westerns, Lee Van Cleef, as 'the only westerner fully trained as a Ninja'. This was essentially the same premise as *Enter the Ninja* but, mainly due to his age, during the all important fight sequences, Van Cleef was often poorly doubled by a stuntman in a bald wig. As a result, and despite the obvious skills of Sho Kosugi as the heroes' nemesis, in a role that closely resembled his part in *Enter the Ninja*, the series was doomed. An excellent opportunity to bring martial arts to a mainstream US television audience had been missed. While martial arts skills became part of the makeup of many mainstream cops and detectives, it wasn't until the 1990s that martial arts television once again proved itself successful.

The syndicated series, *Renegade*, produced by TV veteran Stephen J. Cannell, began in 1992 and ran for 110 episodes. Once again the series appears at a time when martial arts were popular at the cinema box office, this time via Jean-Claude Van Damme (for example, *Bloodsport* [1988], *Kickboxer* [1989] and *Hard Target* [1993]) and Steven Seagal (*Nico* [1988] and *Under Siege* [1992]). Starring former soap star Lorenzo Lamas as Reno Raines, *Renegade* highlights martial arts in the credit sequence but actually contains very little hand-to-hand combat in the actual episodes. Indeed, it is possible to see the martial arts skills of central character, Reno Raines, as largely symbolic of his outsider status. He rides a motorcycle; he has long hair; and he can high kick. In this context, martial arts skills become little more than a fashion accessory. The programme, in which a framed cop, Raines, sought to prove his innocence, was fairly standard television fare, but it was a minor hit in syndication, proving that, even if only a peripheral element, martial arts were becoming more bankable. By April 1993, CBS weighed in with a heavyweight martial arts performer, former world karate champion and long-time action B-movie star Chuck Norris, as Cordell Walker in *Walker, Texas Ranger*.

Walker, Texas Ranger

With the success of their Chuck Norris vehicle, CBS found that there was definitely an audience for martial arts-based action television, and the series re-established the bankability of action/martial arts programmes. Norris had enjoyed some level of success in the post-Bruce Lee era of martial arts films, establishing a persona that clearly drew on the success of stoic stars such as Clint Eastwood while showcasing his karate skills. Norris's persona was immersed in films that clearly operated within established popular Hollywood genres, for example, the cop film, *An Eye for an Eye* (1981), the Vietnam war film, *Missing in Action* (1984), even Indiana Jones-style action/adventure, *Firewalker* (1986). His box-office appeal began to wane in the 1990s and coincided with the demise of Cannon Films who had backed many of his later star vehicles. With the end of

Cannon, the opportunities for Norris to star in theatrical releases diminished and television seemed a logical move for the fading star. It also proved his saviour. The Norris fan base, the size of which should not be underestimated, was ready to accept him in this new medium. *Missing in Action* had been a top earner when it was first released, causing *Halliwell's Film Guide 2000* to comment, with characteristic understatement, that it had 'caused quite a lot of box-office business around the world' (1999, p. 552): it was even more successful in the arena of home video. Certainly, the popularity of Norris at the box office and on video and his potential drawing power on television was not lost on CBS. While Norris's films may have been critically dismissed, he appealed to a sizeable and dedicated audience, many of whom were martial arts movie fans who remembered his iconic appearance alongside Bruce Lee in *Way of the Dragon* (1973) as well as his own movies.

CBS consciously drew on Norris's existing star image in the creation of *Walker, Texas Ranger*. The opening credits, for example, reference moments from his previous career: in one of his most successful films, *Lone Wolf McQuade* (1984), he had already played a Texas ranger and in *Good Guys Wear Black* (1977) he had famously performed a stunt in which he kicked in the window of a moving car, which was reproduced for the opening credit sequence of *Walker, Texas Ranger*. The references to these earlier performances suggest that the show was, at least in part, directed at an audience that was familiar with these moments and knew Norris as a star. This star status was also evoked through these other intertextual moments that drew on his screen persona. The success of *Walker, Texas Ranger* encouraged CBS to look for other stars who would also tap into the potential martial arts audience, and this search would lead to the development of *Martial Law*. However, before looking at this show in some detail, I want to explore some aspects of its background.

Martial Law: the background

Another key context for the production of *Martial Law* was the commercial success of Jackie Chan's *Rumble in the Bronx* (1995). For years, Jackie Chan had been one of the biggest stars in eastern markets, but it was not until *Rumble in the Bronx* that he finally made his breakthrough into the US mainstream. The film reached number one at the US box office and also ended the year as the most successful film in Hong Kong (Stokes and Hoover, 1999, p. 129). Chan also consolidated his popularity in the US with the release of another Hong Kong-produced film that was re-edited for an American audience, *First Strike* (1996). This film, like *Rumble in the Bronx*, was directed by Stanley Tong, who would be a key creative force behind *Martial Law*, but, despite its success, Tong was disappointed by the handling of the film by its US distributors New Line. It is therefore likely that one of the attractions of *Martial Law* was that it gave him more input into, and control over, the final product.

The success of these re-edited Hong Kong films was followed by Chan's first fully fledged Hollywood movie, *Rush Hour* (1998), a fairly conventional tale of mismatched cops solving their case – a Chinese diplomat's daughter is kidnapped – in an unorthodox manner. The success of Chan in the USA meant that CBS could now see the potential for an Asian performer to appeal to a crossover audience. Furthermore, Chan and other Hong Kong practitioners, such as directors John Woo, Kirk Wong and Ronny Yu, were not only proving that they could work successfully within the American industry, but also that they could bring projects in on time and in this budget. These factors all contributed to CBS's decision to offer Stanley Tong the opportunity to develop a project for them, a project that would become *Martial Law*. Tong argues that, from the outset, he was aware that he would need to attract a lead performer who could handle the action sequences that he envisaged as being at the centre of the programme. As he put it: 'If you want to do an action show, you really have to have an action star, like Sammo Hung. To do *Martial Law*, I had to have someone like Sammo to execute the choreography' (ibid., p. 316). However, the problem that faced him was that many people in the USA would ask the question: 'Who is Sammo Hung?'

Who is Sammo Hung?

While he may have been unknown to television executives and the mainstream US TV audience, Sammo Hung was a major star within the field of martial arts cinema. Sammo also brought something to the project with which no American performer could compete: he was 'the real deal'. Jackie Chan's star persona was very heavily founded on his 'authenticity': his films were marketed on the basis that he did all his own stunts, and the end credit sequences of his films often featured footage of them going wrong. Sammo could bring much of the same aura to television. He too had a reputation for performing his own dangerous stunts despite his heavy physical appearance and, without Sammo Hung's stunts, action choreography and performance skills, *Martial Law* would not have been the same show. It is therefore useful to outline how he gained such a reputation among martial arts film fans, a reputation that, I would argue, contributed greatly to *Martial Law*'s status within the world of US television.

As should already be clear, Sammo Hung is very much linked in the popular imagination with Jackie Chan. They attended the same Chinese Opera school and appeared together as part of the touring troupe *The Seven Little Fortunes*, before going on to make a series of enormously popular Hong Kong films. However, within the world of martial arts movies, Sammo Hung is very much a star in his own right. Born in 1952, he had become a significant presence within the Hong Kong martial arts film industry by the early 1970s. He was employed by the Golden Harvest Studio as a fight choreographer in 1970, and had worked in that capacity and as a bit part player until he was given leading roles in the mid-1970s. As a fight choreographer, Sammo Hung helped many Hong Kong stars look good in their action sequences, particularly Angela Mao, Jimmy Wang Yu and even Bruce Lee. He also worked with major, internationally acclaimed directors such as John Woo and King Hu. This foundation in Hong Kong martial arts and action cinema meant that, when the opportunity arrived to move into direction and to take lead roles, Sammo Hung was well placed to snap them up. In 1978, he directed *The Iron-Fisted Monk* and, from that point on, he developed a career as a director, lead actor and action choreographer, a career that, given his unmistakable figure, enabled him to establish himself as an instantly recognisable star.

Occasionally, he would team up with his former school pal Jackie Chan, making such Hong Kong hits as *Winners and Sinners* (1983), *Wheels on Meals* (1984) and *Twinkle, Twinkle Lucky Stars* (1986), but Sammo also directed a string of action-packed martial arts films, that were innovative in Hong Kong cinema through the development of new stunt and camera techniques. His films often featured comedy, and he even introduced supernatural elements in his influential *Encounters of the Spooky Kind* (1981). Sammo was therefore at the heart of the re-invention of Hong Kong martial arts cinema in the late 1980s and early 90s (see Hunt, 1999).

From the outset, *Martial Law* was also a significant departure for US martial arts-based television. As I have already suggested, previous martial arts programmes had been rather serious and dour. These shows drew on action movies of the 1980s and early 90s that starred Sylvester Stallone and Arnold Schwarzenegger or the more martial arts-focused variants that starred Jean-Claude Van Damme and Steven Seagal. While these films had moments of dry humour, usually delivered through dialogue, they did not have the physical comedy associated with elements of Hong Kong martial arts cinema. For example, much has been made of Jackie Chan's relation to silent film comedians such as Buster Keaton and Harold Lloyd, but this relation can also be established with the fight choreography and stunt work of Sammo Hung. It was this physical humour that distinguished *Martial Law* as an example of an US action television.

Martial Law was developed by André Morgan and Stanley Tong. Morgan was an American who had worked in the Hong Kong film industry, and he has claimed:

> The first film I worked on was *Enter the Dragon* with Bruce Lee. I was a translator and a set PA. Then, I worked on a film called *Hapkido* with Sammo Hung…between 1972 and 1978 I produced between 15 and 20 Chinese pictures. (Adventures in Television, 1998)

Certainly this allowed Morgan to make a number of contacts and, more importantly, to understand the working methods of Hong Kong film production personnel. Morgan and Tong wanted to create a contemporary martial arts television show for the 1990s and, according to Morgan, the development moved very quickly. Part of the reason for this were Morgan's connections within the industry. He had also been part of the team responsible for CBS's *Walker, Texas Ranger*, and was able to convince the network that *Martial Law* would be a perfect lead-in show. As a result, Les Moonves, president of CBS Television at the time, was committed to the show and pushed things forward to ensure the key players were in place. Morgan's knowledge and experience of Hong Kong cinema also explains the speed of development. He was confident in Sammo Hung and in his ability to carry the key central role of Sammo Law. As Morgan argued: 'the truth is, there aren't many martial artists who can do the kind of action that Stanley choreographs'. Undoubtedly Sammo was one of the few.

'Shanghai Express': Introducing Sammo Law

In the premiere episode of the series, 'Shanghai Express', many intertextual elements are used to underline the fact that *Martial Law* will deliver what martial arts film fans expect of its star. The pre-credit sequence involves Sammo's character in China uncovering a stolen car ring. He enters a warehouse and takes on a number of 'heavies'. The sequence is marked by the physical humour so typical of Hong Kong action cinema. Certainly, as noted, this would appeal to the fans of Hong Kong cinema who would be drawn to the pilot of *Martial Law* by the presence of Sammo Hung. The opening sequence makes good use of Sammo's size, which would certainly surprise those audience members not familiar with his heavyweight presence and amazing physical agility. He jumps from car roofs, high kicks and displays amazingly fast hand speed. While clearly using 'effects', this sequence seems designed to mark *Martial Law* out as different: it gives the Hong Kong cinema fans what they expect, but have not been given before on US television; and it shows viewers of action television that are not familiar with Sammo that the series offers something new. It is the skilful hitting of both these targets that explains the success of the series' first episode.

However, at the centre of the programme's success is Sammo. While Stanley Tong helped to develop the programme and acted as co-stunt co-ordinator as well as director on 'Shanghai Express' and other episodes, it is probably safe to assume that Sammo Hung, himself an experienced director and action director, had a hand in the fight co-ordination. CBS seemed aware of the fan base available for a Hong Kong performer. As noted earlier, this had been confirmed by the success of Jackie Chan, and CBS allowed the creative personnel to create a series that would deliver what that audience wanted, and indeed expected, and would also move their action television in the direction that action cinema, more generally, was moving.

The premiere episode of *Martial Law* draws on the codes and conventions of martial arts films in a number of explicit ways. A key factor in many martial arts films is underestimation, usually that of the hero by the villains or an opponent. This often provides a rich source of humour, particularly in Hong Kong films, when the root of the underestimation is often the racist attitudes of white criminals. Whatever the reason, it usually results in the hero 'kicking ass'. In the case of Sammo, he is underestimated because of his size. 'Shanghai Express' uses this key component of martial arts films and turns it on its head. Near the opening, Sammo Law arrives at Los Angeles airport in pursuit of the gang of car criminals and hoping to find his beautiful assistant (played by Kelly Hu) who has gone undercover. As he stands outside the terminal, he is persuaded to take an illegal taxi to the city centre. Instead of the city centre, however, he is taken to a remote area and robbed by a waiting gang. Throughout this sequence, those familiar with the star and his martial arts ability, as well as the generic conventions being evoked by the sequence, are invited to smile knowingly. The audience is invited to 'know' what is going to happen. The pre-credit sequence has already shown Sammo's fighting skills so we are in the privileged position of knowing more than the characters who are robbing him. The sequence is shot in such a way as to draw us into this position, suggesting that Sammo is about to explode. As the men surround him, he is placed in the centre of the frame, in the foreground and background the men stand within range of his deadly hands and feet. A head and shoulders shot shows Sammo looking around and judging distance, the camera then moves in closer so his face fills the shot. Then suddenly it cuts to a wide shot as the men get into their cars, drive off and leave Sammo standing alone. This sequence of shots reveals the high level of sophistication in operation within the premiere episode. Rather than simply giving the audience what they expect, it suggests that *Martial Law* will do even more; for example, a level of self-consciousness that will distinguish it from the show that it was designed to lead into, *Walker, Texas Ranger*, a series that takes itself very seriously. As a premiere episode, it is essential that 'Shanghai Express' captures the feel of the series and shows what it will deliver to martial arts fans who might not normally watch a lot of network television.

The ways in which 'Shanghai Express' engaged with audience knowledge and expectations operate differently for different sections of its potential audience. Certainly, the programme's use of intertextual knowledge offers various pleasures to different audience groups. For mainstream television fans, the premiere episode neatly produces a popular programme that celebrates their taste. Sammo is persuaded to attend a recording of the popular show, *The Price Is Right*, by one of his new American partners, Louis (Louis Mandylor). He is shown being selected to be a contestant and goes on to win the major prize. Sammo's enjoyment of American popular culture contrasts sharply with the attitude of his other partner, Dana Doyle (Tammy Lauren), who is shown as aloof and unable to relax. This is made clear by her attitude to *The Price Is Right*, which she dismisses but Sammo embraces. This sequence is carefully included to help define Sammo as a likeable character for mainstream television viewers. It also suggests that *Martial Law*, while offering something new, will not be critical of mainstream viewers or alienate them, but will give them something to enjoy. However, the programme also offers martial arts fans their own moments of intertextual pleasure.

Underestimation, as I have already discussed, is central to two of the premiere's funniest scenes. In one sequence, a tough detective mouths off at Sammo in a racist manner, and challenges him to beat him using any object he chooses. Sammo chooses a chalk eraser and duly covers the detective with chalk marks before finally leaving the eraser in his mouth. Here the audience is invited to laugh as soon as the challenge is issued and enjoy the loud-mouth's comeuppance. This sequence also introduces a key element within the series: Sammo Law can make anything a deadly weapon, so great are his martial arts skills. This is also central to the first martial arts set piece after Sammo's arrival in the USA. Sammo, Louis and Dana go to a suspect's house to question him but, at the suggestion of the American cops who are still unsure of his usefulness, Sammo goes and relaxes in the garden. While he is there, a suspicious pair of Asian gardeners arrive. They are wearing shoes whose soles are covered in large spikes that are designed to aerate lawns, and the pair attack Sammo. Once again, Sammo reacts with physical and mental agility, and the audience get to see a range of his martial arts moves. In a clear reference to his screen persona, he uses a small bench, something he is associated with from Hong Kong films such as *The Magnificent Butcher* (1979). The choreography and editing of the sequence are used to maximise the sense of speed and agility of Sammo's performance and crucially to incorporate comedy into the series. This sequence clearly illustrates the way in which *Martial Law* utilises a style of comedy kung fu normally associated with Hong Kong cinema and particularly with the films of Jackie Chan. The premiere episode of *Martial Law* is therefore carefully designed to appeal to those viewers who might be 'looking in' to see if it is like a Jackie Chan movie. Furthermore, following this set piece, as the suspect is taken out of his house, he turns to Sammo and says, 'That was cool all that Bruce Lee stuff'. He also asks, 'Where did you learn to do all that?', to which Sammo replies, 'Peking opera school'. Martial arts movie fans will know that Sammo Hung trained at the same opera school as Jackie Chan, and can laugh knowingly at this line, but it also indicates that his martial arts are designed for entertainment and moments such as this therefore reflect the extent to which 'Shanghai Express' wants to draw new viewers into the world of the show.

The initial response to *Martial Law* was positive. Sammo's physical appearance was commented upon by critics who were taken by the agility of a man of his size. Michele Greppi for the *New York Post* noted that

> the premiere episode is best when Sammo's dough-boy body is moving faster than seems possible. The fight sequences are often genuinely funny ... we applaud any action show that closes with proof it doesn't take itself seriously and only wants to leave us laughing.
>
> 1998, p. 49

Of course, Greppi is talking about the out-takes which accompanied the end credits of every episode, a tradition taken from Jackie Chan's films, and certainly something designed to show any unbelievers watching that it really is Sammo performing the acrobatic scenes they had just witnessed. It is the Hong Kong elements within *Martial Law* that may explain why it appealed to young males who normally did not watch that time slot. Ed Bark notes in the *Dallas Morning News* that, '*Martial Law* has been a steady Saturday night performer for CBS, winning its time period most weeks and attracting at least a smattering of young male viewers who otherwise ignore the network's older appeal line up.'

However, halfway through the first season of *Martial Law* the producers changed the show as a new direction was sought. Arsenio Hall was introduced as Tyrell Parker in the ninth episode, 'How Sammo Got his Groove Back', and became a regular cast member. At this point the show became more clearly a copy of Chan's successful movie *Rush Hour*. However, by the second season the changes became greater as new producers Lee Goldberg and William Rabkin wielded more influence. This highlights the power of producers in the US television industry. It is worth remembering that Newcomb and Alley (1983) argue that it is producers who are the driving force in television, and they have the overwhelming ability to make changes. Goldberg and Rabkin's changes included dropping regular actors Tom Wright, Tammy Lauren and Louis Mandylor. The effect was to make the show more like other American cop shows. The influence of Hong Kong action began to wane and the high levels of physical comedy, so fresh in the early episodes became less and less central. The cancellation of the show after the second season marks another lost opportunity for US martial arts TV. However, the early episodes of *Martial Law* tantalise us with what might have been.

Bibliography

Adventures in Television, 'Interviews with Stanley Tong and Andre Morgan from CBS Website' (Fall 1998), <www.lgoldberg.com/Martial%20Law%20Pages/interviews_with_stanley_tong_and_andre_morgan.htm (accessed 3 February 2003).

Bark, Ed, 'Martial Law Star Sammo Hung Is Refreshingly Open', *Dallas Morning News* (28 January 1999).

Bordwell, David, *Planet Hong Kong: Popular Cinema and the Art of Entertainment* (Cambridge: Harvard University Press, 2000).

Dannen, Fredric and Long, Barry, *Hong Kong Babylon* (London: Faber, 1997).

Filchy, Patrice, *Dynamics of Modern Communication: The Shaping and Impact of New Communication Technologies* (London: Sage, 1995).

Greppi, Michele, ' "Law" Man Sammo's CBS Ammo', *New York* Post (26 September 1998), p. 49.

Hunt, Leon, 'Once Upon a Time in China: Kung Fu from Bruce Lee to Jet Li', *Framework*, vol. 40 (1999), pp. 85–100.

Logan, Bey, *Hong Kong Action Cinema* (London: Titan, 1995).

Newcomb, Horace and Alley, Robert S., *The Producers Medium* (Oxford: Oxford University Press, 1983).

Stokes, Lisa Odham and Hoover, Michael, *City on Fire: Hong Kong Cinema* (London: Verso, 1999).

Teo, Stephen, *Hong Kong Cinema: The Extra Dimensions* (London: BFI, 1997).

Thomas, Bruce, *Bruce Lee: Fighting Spirit* (Berkeley: Frog Books, 1994).

Walker, John (ed.), *Halliwell's Film and Video Guide 2000* (London: HarperCollins, 1999).

Willis, Andy, 'Consumption and Change: Cynthia Rothrock, Jackie Chan and Martial Arts Movies in the West', in Julia Hallam and Nickianne Moody (eds), *Consuming for Pleasure: Selected Essays in Popular Fiction* (Liverpool: John Moores University, 2000).

Wilson, Clint C. and Gutierrez, Felix, *Race, Multiculturalism and the Media* (London: Sage, 1995).

10

Superman on the Set: The Market, Nostalgia and Television Audiences

Ian Gordon

> All the pain turned into elation. It was like somewhere none of us had ever been before. We feel like Superman.
>
> Luka Grubor, crew member of the gold medal British men's eight
> (Buckle, 2000).

> One of the odd paradoxes about Superman . . . is that while he is a hero of nostalgia, the constant changes in his character keep destroying the qualities that make him an object of nostalgia.
>
> Friedrich, 1988, p. 74

On 12 September 1993 *Lois & Clark* (*The New Adventures of Superman*) debuted on the American Broadcasting Corporation (ABC) Network. In its initial showings in the Sunday night eight o'clock timeslot it garnered third place behind CBS's *Murder, She Wrote* and NBC's *SeaQuest DSV*. Despite this slow start the show garnered solid ratings and more importantly for the ABC Network, a saleable audience of young adults (Cerone, 1994, p. H1; Sharkey, 1994, p. S2-1; Storm, 1994, p. Z2). By contrast when *Lois & Clark* debuted on 25 May 1994 in Australia it immediately entered the top ten shows and for the next two years was a major rating triumph for the Seven Network. The show was such a success that it posed a threat to the rival Nine Network's dominance of the ratings and as a consequence after two seasons Nine poached the series from the Seven Network (Oliver, 1994a, p. 7; 1994b, p. 23; 1995a, p. 7; 1995b, p. 4; 1995c, p. 7). The show's popularity in the two countries can be attributed to advertising and marketing and the resonance Superman struck with the audiences.

The market
The press often judges television series in the USA as successes or failures depending on their ratings. But behind the ratings lay an even more important determination for the television networks. The audience segment a series is directed to and its ability to attract strong ratings from that segment is more crucial than raw ratings. Indeed

Lois & Clark is an exemplary case in point of the importance of audience segmentation in the USA. In its Sunday-night timeslot *Lois & Clark* faced strong opposition from *Murder, She Wrote*, a series in its tenth year, but still consistently in the top ten-rated shows. *Murder, She Wrote* though was susceptible to a challenge from a show aimed at a younger audience since its high ratings were largely due to its total dominance in the ratings of the over-fifties audience. But at the same time as *Lois & Clark* took on *Murder, She Wrote* so too did a Steven Spielberg produced television drama *SeaQuest DSV*. Both *SeaQuest DSV* and *Lois & Clark* were aimed at an audience between eighteen and forty-nine years and the particularly lucrative eighteen to thirty-four market that is the prime target for advertisers. Betsy Sharkey in an August 1994 *New York Times* article put it succinctly: 'since advertising pays the bills in television, network executives listen' to advertising needs. *Lois & Clark*'s fight to become a 'must see' television show then was actually directed at a particular audience segment that it could deliver through the networks to the advertisers. With audience segment as the major target the struggle was not against *Murder, She Wrote*, but against *SeaQuest DSV*. In the 1993 season this struggle attracted press attention and much was made of the contest. At season's end *Lois & Clark* finished sixty-fourth in overall rankings and *SeaQuest DSV* eighty-second. *Murder, She Wrote* ranked ninth. In the 1994–5 season the rankings were fifty-seventh and sixty-fifth respectively with *Murder, She Wrote* again ninth. The bottom line of these ratings was that ABC could charge advertisers $132,000 for a thirty-second spot on *Lois & Clark* whereas CBS could only charge $116,000 for the same time on *Murder, She Wrote*. Much press coverage was devoted to this three-way contest but of the some 5,000 major print media mentions of *Lois & Clark* between 1993 and 1996 fewer than 1 per cent made mention of the commercial bottom line concentrating instead on the appeal of the respective shows (Cerone 1994, p. H1; Graham, 1995, p. D1; Sharkey, 1994, p. S2-1; Storm, 1994, p. Z2; Weinstein, 1995, p. H1).[1]

Such was the situation in *Lois & Clark*'s first two seasons. In its third season the landscape of Sunday-night television had undergone significant change. Most importantly CBS moved *Murder, She Wrote* from Sunday night to Thursday night. In part this change was brought on by CBS's attempts to attract a younger audience, which would entail higher profits through sale of advertising time, and by other external pressures. In 1994 CBS had lost the rights to telecast American football on Sunday afternoon to the Fox Network. This loss meant that the network lost a feed-in audience to its Sunday-night prime-time line-up. In the 1995 season CBS's dominance of Sunday night came under further threat when NBC decided to move its high-rating comedy series *Mad about You* to the 8pm slot in an effort to lift its ratings on that night. CBS responded by shifting *Murder, She Wrote* and scheduling a successful comedy of its own, *Cybill* in the timeslot. The repercussions for *Lois & Clark* were that the show then faced two successful shows that had been established in other timeslots and that appealed to the same audience demographic. Although *Lois & Clark* held its own in the rankings for most of the season and peaked as nineteenth-rated show on 11 and 18 February for wedding episodes, its ratings began to dip immediately following probably because the wedding in fact was between Clark and a clone of Lois. By the time the couple were married on 6 October

1996, in an episode entitled, 'Swear To God, This Time We're Not Kidding', fewer and fewer people were watching and the show reached only 7.5 million households as opposed to the 12 million plus it had reached in February (Associated Press Wire Service, 1996; Bark, 1995, p. Q14; Jensen, 1994; Mifflin, 1995, p. 13; Moore, 1995, p. 38; Sharkey, 1994, p. S2–1; Storm, 1994, p. Z2; Weinstein, 1995, p. H1).

The series then was not an outstanding ratings success but a solid performer that attracted enough of the right kind of audience to be renewed for four seasons. One problem the show had was deciding just how to attract its target audience. Originally Warner Television conceived *Lois & Clark* as a light romance, along the lines of an earlier series, *Moonlighting*. The object was to develop a suitable vehicle to feature a Time Warner property, Superman. In its first season Deborah Joy LeVine produced the series and she had to make some adjustments when its timeslot was changed to the Sunday-night prime family viewing slot. Instead of appealing primarily to women the series had to attract a much broader audience. In the second season Warner replaced LeVine with a man and the series took on a more action approach. The ratings for the new season dropped. Warner executives consulted fans of the show through internet discussion boards and realised that *Lois & Clark*'s appeal lay in the romance. With the show losing viewers at a rapid rate, Hatcher and other actors from the series made guest appearances on AOL and other internet chat forums in late 1994 to reassure fans that the romance would return. When the show eventually did return to romance on 12 February 1995 it jumped twenty-five spots in ranking from the previous episode. Although the difficulties over the show's focus caused problems for the producers it was also a potentially advantageous situation since the premise of the show neatly fitted the ratings-driven thematic needs: a show centred on the relationship between Superman/Clark Kent and Lois Lane by its very nature should have been able to mix romance and action. It may well be that the producers did get the mix of romance and action right for its target audience. The series' failure to win a greater audience share in the USA might have been because of the intense competition it faced. The immediate success of the series in Australia suggests that this interpretation has some validity (Cerone, 1994, p. H1; Graham, 1995, p. D1; Grahnke, 1995, p. 43; Holloway, 1995, p. 7; Miller, 1995, p. Z1; Zoomway, 1997a).[2]

The press coverage leading up to the Australian debut painted a multi-various depiction of *Lois & Clark*. A report in a Sydney paper noted that the series contained 'plenty of sexual tension' and starred Hatcher whose role in a *Seinfeld* episode had made her breasts famous. Around the same time the *Melbourne Age* represented the show as family fare (Lawrence, 1994, p. 3; Thomas, 1994, p. 140). One explanation for the series success in Australia was offered by journalist Jon Casimir who described it as part of a broader return to romance, but a romance in which the women have been recast as feisty professionals, whereas the characters of the men remain much the same. Another journalist, Philippa Hawker, regarded the show as 'cheerfully timeless, futuristic and nostalgic in the same frame' (Casimir, 1994, p. 11; Hawker, 1995, p. 15). Detailed ratings for the show suggest that both Casimir and Hawker were correct in their judgments because the audience stretched across all age groups and the gender divide. For instance, twice as many men than women between the age of sixteen and twenty-four watched the show. On the other hand some 20 per cent more women than men between the age of twenty-five and thirty-nine watched the show. The show also ranked number one with children between the age of five and ten ahead of *Winnie the Pooh* and *The Simpsons*. For teenagers between thirteen and seventeen the show was ranked fourth behind *The Simpsons* at number one (Warneke, 1995, p. 10). *Lois & Clark* then was an important show for advertisers since it let them target a wide audience spectrum including the lucrative thirteen to seventeen market that represented 10 per cent of the Australian population and had disposable income of some $4 billion (Dale, 1995, p. 24). It was this market more than any other that prompted the Nine Network to poach the series from Seven through a deal with Warners (Hornery, 1995, p. 34; Oliver, 1995a, p. 7; 1995b, p. 4; 1995c, p. 7).

Teenage girls reportedly found Cain attractive and evidence suggests that teenage boys found Hatcher likewise desirable. *Lois & Clark*'s producers made every effort to mix romance and sex appeal. Warner Television, which had an agreement with one of the largest internet service providers, America Online (AOL) promoted Terri Hatcher, who played Lois Lane, as a pin-up. Indeed the synergies between the series, AOL and Time Warner could be seen as early as December 1994 when *People* magazine (a Time Warner publication) reported that a pin-up of Hatcher had set a record for internet downloads. For the next two years Hatcher was frequently reported as the Queen of the Internet and took her place in a Parthenon of pin-ups alongside Betty Grable, Marilyn Monroe and more current favourites such as Elle MacPherson, Pamela Lee and Madonna. Warner also promoted Dean Cain, who played Superman/Clark Kent, as the thinking woman's crumpet. *People* magazine noted that he was a former star footballer who had dated Brooke Shields during their Princeton college years. Promotion of the physical attributes of the stars was matched by accounts of their intelligence. Hatcher reportedly had left college almost by accident after unintentionally winning an acting spot while accompanying a friend to an audition. When both Cain and Hatcher wrote scripts for the show it was duly reported in the press (Beck, 1994, p. D16; *Business Wire*, 1995; Elberg, 1994, p. E1; Gable, 1994, p. D3; Huff, 1995, p. 7; Marshall, 1996; *People Weekly*, 1994, p. 123; *People Weekly*, 1996, p. 188; Reed, 1994, p. 35; Roush, 1994a, p. D3; Roush, 1994b, p. D3; Roush, 1996, p. D3; Russell, 1995, p. 98).

It is probably fair to say, as does comic-book historian Les Daniels (1998, p. 173), that a great part of the show's appeal lay in two good-looking people getting it on. But *Lois & Clark*'s appeal extended beyond an audience looking for a romance novel with pictures, or the sweaty palm brigade intent on closer observation of Terri Hatcher. The show appealed to audiences for whom Superman in his many guises, and indeed Lois, were familiar figures. The timelessness that Hawker (1995) noted would seem to have been deliberately created by the series producers to provoke memories of earlier versions of Superman and indeed to draw those without memories of earlier versions into a realisation that they existed. That is to say a large dose of nostalgia was involved in the popularity of the show. But the nostalgia on display in *Lois & Clark* is of a different order to that displayed in other television shows.

Nostalgic television shows

It is not uncommon for television shows to play on a sense of nostalgia in search of audiences. In the 1970s film and television producers demonstrated that nostalgia for the 1950s could be packaged and sold in movies such as *American Graffiti* (1973), and the television show *Happy Days*. The success of *Happy Days*, which began as a mid-season replacement show on ABC in 1974, and ran through 255 episodes to 1984 (and endless re-runs) demonstrated the marketing potential of what might loosely be called decade nostalgia. More recently *That '70s Show*, which debuted in August 1998 on the Fox Network and is pitched as 'a nostalgic and funny flashback to the "Me" decade', has shown that decade nostalgia's popularity has not waned (*Happy Days* website; *That '70s Show* website).

Both *Happy Days* and *That '70s Show* use watered down versions of easily discernible features of particular eras to set the situation of the comedy. In *Happy Days* ersatz rebel without a cause, Fonzie, meets 1950s apple pie-loving suburban America, in the form of the Cunninghams. In *That '70s Show* bored low-key rebellious teenagers meet working American conservative parents, the Formans, lost in a sea of change. The shows invite the audience to laugh at both the situation and potentially their own or their parents' past. The appeal of nostalgia in these shows probably works on at least two levels. First, it appeals to those who were there and see their own past somehow represented in the shows; second, it appeals to those who were not there, but who none the less want the memory. The humour derives from a sentiment of how innocent they/we were back then. This type of nostalgia can also be used in shows that are set in the here and now.

Numerous shows ranging from *Till Death Us Do Part* (Britain 1966–8, 1972–5), *All in the Family* (USA 1971–9), *My Name's McGooley – What's Yours?* (Australia 1966–8) and *Phua Chu Khan* (Singapore 1998–present) have used a version of nostalgia that relies on contrasting values of say the young and old, the newly rich, or class-mobile families who respond in different fashions to their situation. The comedy comes from the clash of values. In these shows one set of values is generally posed as old-fashioned, perhaps even retrograde, and the other as modern and sophisticated, perhaps even pretentious. In both *Till Death Us Do Part* and *All in the Family* the clash was between the conservative values of the father figure and the liberal values of the son-in-law. In *My Name's McGooley – What's Yours?* a couple with middle-class aspirations were saddled with the recalcitrant working-class father of the wife. In these three shows part of the appeal lay in laughing at the outmoded or reactionary thinking of the older figures. But at the same time some of the audience for these shows viewed the proclamations of the conservatives favourably.

In the USA debates over *All in the Family* concerned themselves with whether the show demonstrated a 'New Class' patronising working-class males or an institutionalised racism where even satire was received as affirmation of bigotry by sections of the audience (Adler, 1979; Lasch, 1983; Vidmar and Rokeach, 1974). In these debates the ability of audiences to view characters such as Alf Garnett and Archie Bunker, respectively the conservative protagonists of *Till Death Us Do Part* and *All in the Family*, as figures of nostalgia was not stressed. That is such characters represented a passing era, or an era segments of the audience wished past, and so the humour while perhaps patronising, as Lasch suggested, also figured as a means of disengaging the conservatism of such figures from current social norms and placing it in some version of the past. As a narrative structure this is a means of disengaging the past from the present by reducing it to nostalgia and so it becomes a means for either defusing or ignoring social tension.

The ability of television shows to create nostalgia for a past that still exists in the present can be seen most clearly in *Phua Chu Khan*, a Singaporean situation comedy that depicts the extended family of Phua Chu Khan, a building contractor who lives with his wife, mother, brother, sister-in-law, and the latter couple's son. Phua Chu Khan is an *Ah Beng*, a sort of Flash Harry character as played by George Cole in the St Trinian's movies. Chu Khan has gained wealth on the back of Singapore's prosperity and the demand for building contractors, but little social propriety. The short time in which Singapore has moved from Third World to First is represented in the character of Chu Khan's mother a former street vendor and his brother an Australian-trained architect who has a socially ambitious westernised wife. The series satirises many aspects of Singaporean society, but Chu Khan's Singapore is rapidly receding and he and it are already figures of nostalgia. His passing is close to being official government policy. For instance, his catchphrases of the first two seasons: 'use your *blain* [brain]' and 'don't *pray pray* [play]' have been eliminated by the government's fear that the popularity of the show would have university-educated students mimicking his patois and undermining the nation's world-class status (Goh Chok Tong, 1999; Lee Yock Suan, 2000).

The nostalgia of *Lois & Clark* has, like *Phua Chu Khan*, a certain presentness. At the same time though it exists as part of a larger narrative that informs its audience and shapes its desirability as a show to watch. This aspect too involves nostalgia, but it is nostalgia of a form and type beyond the common-sense use of the term.

Lois & Clark and nostalgia

When Hawker pointed to the 'timeless' nature of *Lois & Clark* she associated it with a conflation of a 'futuristic' and 'nostalgic' vision. Her review of 'That Old Gang of Mine' episode (the seventh episode from the second season: aired 27 March 1995 in Australia and 13 November 1994 in the USA) noted that the laboratory used by a DNA researcher looked like something out of the 1950s.[3] While the subject of DNA research might have been current the visualisation of it was more of futures past. That is, the futuristic look was a 1950s' version of futurism. *Lois & Clark* is nicely laden with this sort of retrospective styling, which Fredric Jameson has noted, the French term *la mode rétro* captures. Jameson discussed this mode in his analysis of pastiche films, such as *Body Heat*, which he saw as blurring the contemporary into some 'dehistorised' vision of the past (1983; 1984; 1991). As Jameson noted this blurring of time in movies and the creation of a visual pastness developed alongside a range of nostalgic movies such as *American Graffiti* (nostalgia for the 1950s), *Star Wars* (1978) and *Raiders of the Lost Ark* (nostalgia for 1950s' movie serials) and *Chinatown* (nostalgia for the moody ambience of film noir). The producers of *Lois & Clark* blurred time both through a use of visual pastness and by playing with the history of Superman as an icon of American culture making use of earlier comic-book, television and movie incarnations of the characters to create a pastiche of their own.

Deborah Joy LeVine, *Lois & Clark*'s original producer and creator, acknowledged the importance of Superman's history and read some 300 comic books as part of her preparation for the series. She also sought to emulate the 1970s' series of Superman movies staring Christopher Reeve and Margot Kidder, in which the sexual tension between the characters was a central theme (Westbrook, 1993). Another key source for *Lois & Clark*'s pastiche was the earlier television series *The Adventures of Superman* of which 104 episodes were made between 1951 and 1957 and referents to the earlier series cropped up in several early episodes of *Lois & Clark*. In using these three earlier versions of Superman the producers of *Lois & Clark* created a version of the character with diverse audience appeal because the deployment of earlier versions lent the series an authenticity as part of a broader narrative of Superman. As LeVine noted she owed it to the comic-book fans to know the history, and she knew them to be an important component of her audience even as she focused the show on the human relationship of the two title characters rather than the action-centred plots of the comic book (ibid.).

The premiere episode of *Lois & Clark* on 12 September 1993 introduced the main characters and the standard features of the Superman story. As in any retelling some aspects of the story varied. In *Lois & Clark* Superman's nemesis Lex Luthor was a suave businessman somewhat in the mould of Donald Trump, rather than the mad-scientist type of the comic book, or the buffoon figure of the 1970s' movies. Jonathan and Martha Kent were still alive in Smallville and Clark visited them for advice. Rather than exploding 'Great Caesar's Ghost' when astounded as Perry White had done in *The Adventures of Superman*, the new Perry proffered 'Great Shades of Elvis', which incidentally gave the series another dimension of nostalgia on which to play. The producers retained other incidental features from the 1950s' television series such as Perry White and Jimmy Olsen sparring and police Inspector Henderson a character not seen in other versions of Superman.

The producers originally set the series in the manner of the 1970s' movie version of Superman in which Lois was a woman of experience and Clark's a more naïve Smallville boy. In the first episode Lois confessed to Clark that a former colleague, with whom she had had an affair, had betrayed her. As the first season developed the producers played down the sexuality of Lois, and later dropped another character, Cat, played by Tracey Scoggins, whose main function was to increase the sexual tension, almost certainly because of the Sunday-evening family timeslot assigned by ABC (Cerone, 1994; Westbrook, 1993; Zoomway, 1997a).

The visual design of the series also helped create an aura of timelessness. The main set for the show, the *Daily Planet* newsroom with its heavy emphasis on wood, gilt-lettered names on doors and marginalisation of computers, looked more like a 1930s' newsroom, at least as depicted in movies such as *His Girl Friday* (1940). Although computers and the ubiquitous coffee pot and other such modern appliances were present, the overall visualisation of the show served to blur their presence. For instance, in the third episode broadcast when Lex Luthor checks the morning papers the front page of the *Daily Planet* is composed in a retro style with narrow columns and no photographs, at least above the fold. Luther is served by Asabi, a South Asian manservant reminiscent of Daddy Warbucks' 'mysterious oriental' servant, Punjab, in Harold Gray's 1920s' comic strip *Little Orphan Annie*. These visual devices are then set against Luthor's curiosity about Superman when he poses a set of questions using phrases from the 1950s' television show. Can Superman 'leap tall buildings in a single bound'? Is Superman say, 'more powerful than a locomotive'? Later Luthor discovers some answers: Superman is 'faster than a speeding bullet' and a 'man of steel'. The use of key phrases from previous incarnations of Superman was one means with which the producers gave *Lois & Clark* a timelessness. In the first episode spectators seeing Superman fly exclaim: 'Is it a bird? Is it a plane?' In the second episode Lois prompts Superman in an answer about what he means by helping people with 'like fighting for truth and justice'.

Other episodes added to the series' timelessness. In the sixth episode both Lois and Clark worked undercover in a nightclub owned by gangsters. Although the plot had the quasi-feminist sister of a gang boss forcing her brother out of the gang because his old-fashioned way of doing things did not match her MBA business skills, the nightclub had torch singers, dancing showgirls and cigarette-girl-like waitresses. Perhaps such clubs still exist in the USA somewhere, certainly casinos offer this type of entertainment, but they are considerably larger than clubs. Indeed if my years of living in Washington, DC, are any indication clubs with dancers are on the whole likely to be strip clubs. The nightclub's day came and went some time between the end of Prohibition in the 1930s and the 1960s. *Lois & Clark* sometimes appealed more directly to nostalgia. In the ninth episode about a heat wave Sonny Bono, then between jobs as mayor of Palm Springs and his later seat in the House of Representatives, appeared briefly as the mayor making references to his hit songs of the 1960s with 'and the heat goes on' about the heat wave and 'I got you babe' in answer to a question from Lois Lane. Phyllis Coates, who played Lois Lane in the first twenty-six episodes of *The Adventures of Superman*, appeared as Lois Lane's mother in the final episode of the first season. In the fourth season Jack Larson who had played Jimmy Olsen in the 1950s' series made a guest appearance ('I've Got A Crush On You' [24 October 1993]; 'The Man Of Steel Bars' [21 November 1993]; 'The House of Luthor' [8 May 1994]; 'Brutal Youth' [26 October 1996]).

The point of all this nostalgia was not so much an appeal to a past, but to some narrative of the past. For instance, in the sixth episode the evocation of an earlier nightclub era could not be accurately represented complete with cigarette-girls because the attitude to cigarette smoking is no longer the same and it could have been construed as an advertisement for smoking. Moreover smoking in places that sell food is banned in many American states. *Lois & Clark*'s producers did not always maintain the timelessness of the show. In the third episode reference was made to a 'drive-by shooting' and Lois Lane watched a television set that showed what appeared to be the infamous Rodney King video and footage of the Waco debacle of 1993.[4] Although only shown for a total of five seconds, and within the context of the need for heroes such as Superman, this 'reality' was a disconcerting intrusion into the visualisation and timelessness of the series and was not repeated in the fifty or so episodes I viewed.

The producers of the show created the nostalgic references more likely out of a desire to make the show popular and to thereby generate income rather than to engage in some sort of post-modernist project. They did however occasionally have to address the issue of Superman's longevity as a character and his commercial presence in American culture in a manner relevant to the series' storylines. For instance, in the fourth episode of *Lois & Clark* the producers used a storyline about merchandising Superman products from a 1938 comic book as a subplot. In the episode Clark/Superman struggled to find his true self as his fame resulted in numerous Superman products such as dolls and soft drinks. An agent, straight out of vaudeville, approached Superman with commercial endorsement offers including one to go to Cleveland – an in-joke recognisable to those aware that Jerry Siegel and Joe Shuster created Superman while teenagers living in Cleveland. Eventually Clark/Superman decided that he controlled his own destiny and no commercial product would affect his true self. None-the-less he agreed to the licensing of his name provided that the profits went to charity. The episode neatly fitted the developing narrative of *Lois & Clark* with the commodity status of Superman as a trademark and much-licensed product of the Time Warner conglomerate ('I'm Looking Through You' [10 October 1993]; *Action Comics*, November, 1938; Gordon, 1998; Gordon, 2001).

The narrative structure of *Lois & Clark*, that is the stories it told and the manner in which it told (visualised) those stories, was nostalgic. If we regard this as a failure to represent current experience at the popular level of a television show then we might want to join Jameson and see such a situation as 'an alarming and pathological symptom of a society that has become incapable of dealing with time and history' (1983, p. 117). Other social commentators have pointed to the ahistoricism of nostalgia. Indeed Christopher Lasch (1984) noted that both nostalgia and anti-nostalgia deny history, the former by romanticising it, and the latter by demanding that life be lived in the here and now. Susan Stewart (1984) has suggested that nostalgia is a construction that denies the past except as a narrative meditation. Svetlana Boym's (2001) concept of nostalgia acknowledges its ahistoricism and capacity, in an unreflective state, for producing monsters. But by reminding us of the utopian impulses within nostalgia and through an etymological dissection she recovers possibilities of human agency within nostalgia. Boym writes 'restorative nostalgia puts emphasis on *nostos* and proposes to rebuild the lost home and patch up the memory gaps' whereas 'reflective nostalgia dwells in *algia*, in longing and loss, the imperfect process of remembrance' (ibid., p. 41). Boym stresses that these two types of nostalgia are tendencies and not absolutes, but she does suggest that reflective nostalgia opens a playfulness in which the longing, or the consciousness of distance, is more important than any perceived homecoming. She sums this up nicely as 'a modern nostalgic can be homesick and sick of home at the same time'. All of which is to say that longing and critical thinking can go hand in hand (ibid., pp. 49–50). Was part of the appeal of *Lois & Clark* then that it allowed its audience or a segment of its diverse audience, to long for something lost and address that longing in a critical manner?

The internet offers ample evidence that *Lois & Clark* resonated deeply enough with a section of its audience that it engaged them in an active relationship with the series.

There are thousands of pages of *Lois & Clark* material on the web. This interaction with the series extends from scanned photographs of the stars, through episode guides and detailed summaries, to fan fiction. As of 15 August 2001, 1,564 fan-written stories centred on the *Lois & Clark* television series were available through the web-based *Lois & Clark* Fanfic Archives (www.lcfanfic.com). Stories have been added at regular intervals up to 12 August 2001. This site has received over half a million visits since May 1996. Fans have also written for the fifth season that never was and posted them on websites with twenty-four episodes appearing at <members.aol.com/thenando/eps.htm> and thirty-six episodes at <www.lcfanfic.com/thm-s5.htm>. There are also several thousand postings to various *Lois & Clark* bulletin boards at <www.zoomway.com/boards>. Although not all of this activity could be classed as critical thinking, diverse scholars, such as the anti-comic-book campaigner psychiatrist Fredric Wertham, and the feminist film theorist Constance Penley, have suggested that fan magazines (fanzines) and fiction (fanfic, slash) empower their creators since they lets them slip outside mass-mediated experience. Wertham empathetically noted that these fans refused to accept 'the processing and manipulation of people … in all of this there is definitely an implied social criticism' (Penley, 1992; Wertham, 1973, p. 132).

At the same time though the fans dedication to the series and their use of it for their own purposes has helped give *Lois & Clark* an afterlife on cable television. The series is currently shown at 8am Monday to Friday on the US cable TNT Network. The TNT website for the series (alt.tnt.tv/scifi/loisandclark) includes extensive links to fan sites. Given the legal actions of Viacom and 20th Century-Fox to shut down fan websites for series such as *The X Files*, *Millennium*, *The Simpsons* and *Star Trek* and the prior aggressive stance of DC comics and its parent company Time Warner in defence of their trademark property, Superman (Gaines, 1991; Gwenllian-Jones, 2002), and indeed the extensive legal notice elsewhere on the site, it is stunning to see the Time Warner-owned TNT cable network promoting such sites with only the minimal disclaimer 'external sites are not endorsed by TNT'. At very least this suggests that the fan activity, and the fan longing, feeds the commercial worth of *Lois & Clark*, and other Superman-linked products, in sufficient degree that the corporation must run the risk of undermining its legal claims to sole control of the character in order to market it better. Indeed the series *Smallville*, yet another incarnation of Superman, from yet another arm of Time Warner, the teenager/young adult-oriented WB Network has a webpage that lists fan sites and invites participation in a discussion forum and this was before the series had been telecast except for one episode in a few test markets.

The producers of *Lois & Clark* originally aimed it at a specific audience segment who enjoyed light romance. The series' US timeslot caused a rethink of format and the need to search for more diverse appeal. This appeal was created in part through nostalgia in all senses of the term. The series then sold the older segment of the audience its own memories. For the younger audience the series introduced a fictional narrative, which has existed in many versions over sixty years, and shaped communities. A large part of the series' appeal then lay in its ability to unite past and present, to elide history and offer a disembodied past in the form of a commodity for consumption. In Australia this helped the show to dramatic ratings success in its first two seasons. At the same time the use of nostalgia and *la mode rétro* opened possibilities for reflective nostalgia and creative engagement with the series. None the less even these aspects have been incorporated into the marketing of the series as 'must see TV' beyond its original broadcasts. In an era of increased audience segmentation, due in part to cable television, *Lois & Clark* demonstrated that timelessness has a diverse appeal and can draw audiences from outside a particular target segment.

Notes

1. My figure for media mentions of *Lois & Clark* and content of articles derives from my research in the Dow Jones Interactive online service, which provides content for some 6,000 newspapers, newswires and trade journals.

2. One other reason for *Lois & Clark*'s greater success in Australia might be the absence of cable television in that country in 1993 and as a result a higher potential viewership across the spectrum of age and gender.

3. All dates for *Lois & Clark* hereafter are original US airdates, although I viewed the series in Australia.

4. In 1991 the brutal treatment of Rodney King, an African-American pulled over on a traffic violation, by four officers of the Los Angeles Police Department, was captured on video tape by a nearby resident. The tape was broadcast across America. On 28 February 1993 the Bureau of Alcohol, Tobacco and Firearms raided the Branch Davidian's (a religious sect) compound in Waco, Texas. This failed raid was followed by a siege and a subsequent botched attack by the FBI on 19 April. Eighty Branch Davidians died. The events of 19 April were broadcast live in the USA. I saw portions in a car dealership waiting room in California.

Bibliography

Action Comics, nos 1–91 (June 1938–December 1945).

Adalian, Josef and Schneider, Michael, 'WB Network Flies with Superman', *Reuters Wire Service* (19 September 2000).

Adler, Richard P. (ed.) All in the Family: *A Critical Appraisal* (New York: Praeger, 1979).

Andrae, Thomas, 'From Menace to Messiah: The History and Historicity of Superman', in Donald Lazure (ed.), *American Media and Mass Culture: Left Perspectives* (Berkeley: University of California Press, 1987), pp. 124–38.

Associated Press Wire Service, 'List of Weekly TV Ratings' (1994–6).

Bark, Ed, 'Can CBS Win Over Younger Viewers and Still Keep Its Lead?', *Dallas Morning News* (10 September 1995), p. Q14.

Beck, Marilyn, 'Superman Set to Leap Tall Scripts', *Rocky Mountain News* (26 October 1994), p. D16.

Boym, Svetlana, *The Future of Nostalgia* (New York: Basic Books, 2001), pp. 49–50.

Brodie, Ian, 'A Modern Marvel', *The Australian* (20 November 1996), p. 47.

Buckle, Greg, 'Britain Claim Blue Riband at Penrith', in Rediff.com, <www.rediff.com/sports/2000/sep/24brit.htm> (accessed 3 February 2003)

Browne, Rachel, 'When Wedding Bells Sound the Knell', *Sun Herald* (3 November 1996), p. 112.

Business Wire, 'Warner Bros. Signs One Year Deal with America Online', *Business Wire* (11 December 1995).

Byrne, John, 'Superman: A Personal View', in John Byrne (ed.), *Superman: The Man of Steel* (New York: Ballantine Books, 1988).

Casimir, Jon, 'The Return Of Romance', *Sydney Morning Herald* (14 July 1994), p. 11.

Cerone, Daniel, 'TV's Superman Undergoing a Planetary Shift', *Los Angeles Times* (17 September 1994), p. H1.

Dale, David, 'The Tribal Mind', *Sydney Morning Herald* (26 April 1995), p. 24.

Daniels, Les, *Superman: The Complete History* (San Francisco: Chronicle Books, 1998).

Desai, Anita, 'The Writing Life', *Washington Post Book World* (28 May 2000), p. 8.

Dickinson, Greg, 'Memories for Sale: Nostalgia and the Construction of Identity in Old Pasadena', *Quarterly Journal of Speech*, vol. 83, no. 1 (February 1997), pp. 1–27.

Eco, Umberto, 'The Myth of Superman', *Diacritics*, vol. 2 (1972), pp. 14–22.

Elberg, Lynn, 'Man of Steel Likes to Be Man of Words', *San Francisco Chronicle* (5 December 1994), p. E1.

Entertainment Wire, 'Superman and Batman Join Forces with Arch-Rival Stan Lee for the Coolest Collaboration on the History of Comic Books' (12 April 2000).

Friedrich, Otto, 'Up, Up and Awaaay!!!', *Time* (14 March 1988), pp. 66–74.

Frow, John, *Time and Commodity Culture* (Oxford: Clarendon Press, 1997).

Gable, Donna, 'Superman Writes His Own Season's Greeting', *USA Today* (1 December 1994), p. D3.

Gaines, Jane M., 'Superman, Television, and the Protective Strength of the Trademark', in Jane M. Gaines (ed.), *Contested Culture: the Image, the Voice, and the Law* (Chapel Hill: University of North Carolina Press, 1991).

Geertz, Clifford, 'Ideology as Cultural System', in Clifford Geertz (ed.), *Interpretation of Cultures: Selected Essays* (New York: Basic Books, 1973), pp. 193–233.

Goh Chok Tong, 'National Day Rally Speech' (22 August 1999), <app10.internet.gov.sg/data/sprinter/pr/1999082202.htm> (accessed 30 January 2003).

Gordon, Ian, *Comic Strips and Consumer Culture, 1890–1945* (Washington, DC: Smithsonian Institution Press, 1998).

Gordon, Ian, 'Nostalgia, Myth, and Ideology: Visions of Superman at the End of the American Century', in Matthew McAllister, Edward Sewell and Ian Gordon (eds), *Comics and Ideology* (New York: Peter Lang, 2001).

Graham, Jefferson, 'Superman Shows His Ratings Steel', *USA Today* (13 April 1995), p. D1.

Grahnke, Lon, 'Lois Lane's Alter Ego', *Chicago Sun-Times* (2 March 1995), p. 43.

Gwenllian Jones, Sara, 'Web Wars: Resistance, Online Fandom and Studio Censorship', in Mark Jancovich and James Lyons (eds), *Quality Popular Television* (London: BFI, 2003).

Harris, Neil, 'Who Owns Our Myths? Heroism and Copyright in an Age of Mass Culture', in Neil Harris (ed.), *Cultural Excursions: Marketing Appetites and Cultural Tastes in Modern America* (Chicago: University of Chicago Press, 1990).

Hawker, Philippa, 'Cheerful Daft Plot in Timeless Cartoon', *Age* (27 March 1995), p. 15.

Holloway, Diane, '*Lois & Clark* Seduces Viewers', *Austin American-Statesman* (20 August 1995), p. 7.

Hornery, Andrew, 'TV Networks Spend Millions to Attract Younger Viewers', *Sydney Morning Herald* (5 October 1995), p. 34.

Huff, Richard, 'Latest Pose from the Queen of the Internet', *New York Daily News* (31 December 1995), p. 7.

Jameson, Fredric, 'Postmodernism and Consumer Society', in Hal Foster (ed.), *The Anti-aesthetic: Essays on Postmodern Culture* (Port Townsend, Washington, DC: Bay Press, 1983).

Jameson, Fredric, 'Postmodernism, or The Cultural Logic of Late Capitalism', *New Left Review*, no. 146 (July/August 1984), pp. 53–92.

Jameson, Fredric, *Postmodernism, or The Cultural Logic of Late Capitalism* (New York: Verso, 1991).

Jensen, Jeff, 'Stubborn CBS Refuses to Send in Punting Unit', *Advertising Age* (13 June 1994).

Kobler, John, 'Up, Up and Away! The Rise of Superman Inc.', *Saturday Evening Post* (21 June 1941), pp. 14–15, 70–8.

Lasch, Christopher, 'Archie Bunker and the Liberal Mind', in Les Brown and Savannah Waring Walker (eds), *Fast Forward* (Kansas City: Andrews and McMeel, 1983), pp. 165–70.

Lasch, Christopher, 'The Politics of Nostalgia', *Harper's* (November 1984), pp. 65–70.

Lawrence, Mark, 'Is It a Plane . . . Is It a Bird', *Age* (19 May 1994), Green Guide, p. 3.

Lee Yock Suan, 'Speech at the Colloquium on the Teaching and Use of Standard English' (26 May 2000), <app10.internet.gov.sg/data/sprinter/pr/2000052601.htm> (accessed 30 January 2003).

Lévi-Strauss, Claude, *Structural Anthropology* (London: Allen Lane, 1968).

Marshall, Leslie, 'Hatcher If You Can', *InStyle Magazine* (1 May 1996), p. 118.

Mifflin, Lawrie, 'Cable TV Continues Its Steady Drain of Network Viewers', *New York Times* (25 October 1995), p. 13.

Miller, Ron, 'Powerful Female Producers', *Salt Lake Tribune* (6 January 1995), p. Z1.

Moore, Frazier, 'Sunday Evening Rating Race Is Escalating', *Seattle Post-Intelligencer* (29 September 1995), p. 38.

Oliver, Robin, '"Lois" Makes a Super Debut', *Sydney Morning Herald* (31 May 1994a), p. 23.

Oliver, Robin, 'Superman Soars to the Top', *Sydney Morning Herald* (26 July 1994b), p. 23.

Oliver, Robin, 'Networks in Bidding War for US Shows', *Sydney Morning Herald* (5 August 1995a), p. 7.

Oliver, Robin, 'Nine out to Snare Teenage Market', *Sydney Morning Herald* (7 August 1995b), p. 4.

Oliver, Robin, 'Superman to Leap Nine's Ratings Slump', *Sydney Morning Herald* (14 August 1995c), p. 7.

Oliver, Robin and Passey, David, 'Sydney Warms Itself to a Man in Tights', *Sydney Morning Herald* (26 July 1994), p. 7.

Penley, Constance, 'Feminism, Psychoanalysis, and the Study of Popular Culture', in Lawrence Grossberg, Cary Nelson and Paula Treicher (eds), *Cultural Studies* (New York: Routledge, 1992).

People Weekly, 'The 50 Most Beautiful People in the World', *People Weekly* (8 May 1994), p. 123.

People Weekly, 'Classic Pinups', *People Weekly* (6 May 1996), p. 188.

Reed, J. D., 'Lois Lane: Download Pinup', *People Weekly* (19 December 1994), p. 35.

Rosaldo, Renato, 'Imperialist Nostalgia', *Representations*, no. 26 (Spring 1989), pp. 107–22.

Roush, Matt, 'Look! Behind the Cameras, It's Dean Cain', *USA Today* (3 June 1994a) p. D3.

Roush, Matt, 'Most of the Fittest Survive', *USA Today* (7 June 1994b), p. D3.

Roush, Matt, 'A Lovable Loony *Lois & Clark*', *USA Today* (26 April 1996), p. D3.

Russell, Lisa, 'Lois Common Denominator', *People Weekly* (22 May 1995), p. 98.

Sharkey, Betsy, 'Television: The Secret Rules of Ratings', *New York Times* (28 August 1994), p. S2-1.

Stewart, Susan, *On Longing: Narratives of the Miniature, the Gigantic, the Souvenir, the Collection* (Baltimore: Johns Hopkins University Press, 1984).

Storm, Jonathan, 'Behind the Scenes with *Lois & Clark*', *Salt Lake Tribune* (8 April 1994), p. Z2.

Tannock, Stuart, 'Nostalgia Critique', *Cultural Studies*, vol. 9, no. 3 (1995), pp. 453–64.

Thomas, Brett, 'Satire Takes a Bit of Everyone: Sexual Tension', *Sun Herald* (15 May 1994), p. 140.

Vidmar, Neil and Rokeach, Milton, 'Archie Bunker's Bigotry: A Study in Selective Perceptions and Exposure', *Journal of Communication*, vol. 24, no. 1 (1974), pp. 36–47.

Warneke, Ross, 'What Are You Looking at?', *Age* (1 June 1995), p. 10.

Weinstein, Steve, 'The Unsinkable Angela Lansbury', *Los Angeles Times* (21 May 1995), p. H1.

Wertham, Fredric, *The World of Fanzines* (Carbondale: Southern Illinois University Press, 1973).

Westbrook, Bruce, 'A Romance for Superman', *Houston Chronicle* (12 September 1993), p. T3.

Zoomway, 'How It All Began' [a history of Lois and Clark] (1997a), <www.neumedia.net/~sykes/lc> (accessed 30 January 2003).

Zoomway, 'I Only Have Eisner for You' [the demise of Lois and Clark] (1997b), <www.neumedia.net/~sykes/lc> (accessed 30 January 2003).

Television shows

Lois & Clark (*The New Adventures of Superman*).

'Premiere' (12 September 1993) Season 1, Episode 1. Written by Deborah Joy LeVine. Directed by Robert Butler.

'Strange Visitor (From Another Planet)' (26 September 1993) Season 1, Episode 2. Written by Bryce Zabel. Directed by Randall Zisk.

'Neverending Battle' (3 October 1993) Season 1, Episode 3. Written by Dan Levine. Directed by Gene Reynolds.

'I'm Looking Through You' (10 October 1993) Season 1, Episode 4. Written by Deborah Joy LeVine. Directed by Mark Sobel.

'I've Got A Crush On You' (24 October 1993) Season 1, Episode 6. Written by Thania St John. Directed by Gene Reynolds.

'The Man Of Steel Bars' (21 November 1993) Season 1, Episode 9. Written by Paris Qualles. Directed by Robert Butler.

'The House of Luthor' (8 May 1994) Season 1, Episode 21. Written by Deborah Joy LeVine and Dan Levine. Directed by Alan J. Levi.

'That Old Gang Of Mine' (13 November 1994) Season 2, Episode 7. Written by Gene Miller and Karen Kavner. Directed by Lorraine Senna Ferrara.

'Brutal Youth' (26 October 1996) Season 4, Episode 5. Written by Tim Minear. Directed by David Grossman.

Information from Jeff Skyes, 'The Original Internet Lois and Clark Episode Guide', <www.neumedia.net/~sykes/lc>

Websites

All in the Family website, <www.geocities.com/televisioncity/set/8663/episode.html> (accessed 25 September 2000).

Happy Days website, <www.sitcomsonline.com/happydays.html> (accessed 25 September 2000).

Lois & Clark Bulletin Boards website, <www.zoomway.com/boards> (accessed 13 July 2001).

Lois & Clark Fanfic Archives website, <www.lcfanfic.com> (accessed 15 August 2001).

Lois & Clark Fifth Season websites, <members.aol.com/thenando/eps.htm> and <www.lcfanfic.com/thm-s5.htm> (accessed 13 July 2001).

Smallville website, <www.thewb.com/Shows/Show/0,7353,||126,00.html> (accessed 30 January 2003).

That '70s Show website, <www.that70sshow.com> (accessed 25 September 2000).

TNT *Lois & Clark* website, <www.tnt.tv/Title/Display/0,5918,307664~Series,00.html> (accessed 30 January 2003).

11

Web Wars: Resistance, Online Fandom and Studio Censorship

Sara Gwenllian Jones

'Resistance' – meaning all sorts of grumbling, multiple interpretation, semiological inversion, pleasure, rage, friction, numbness, what have you – is accorded dignity, even glory, by stamping these not-so-great refusals with a vocabulary derived from life-threatening political work against fascism – as if the same concept should serve for the Chinese student uprising and cable TV grazing.

Gitlin, 1990, p. 191

It has become something of an orthodoxy for scholars to elevate television fans to the status of modern-day Robin Hoods, folk heroes busily snatching back 'our' popular cultural texts from the greedy global conglomerates who claim to own them. This version of fandom implicitly constitutes 'resistance' as a condition inherent to fandom itself, one that manifests as an excess devotion that recalls Baudrillard's proposed 'fatal strategy' of wilful over-consumption as a response to capitalism (1990). Notions of resistance are to be found everywhere in studies of media fans. Thus, for John Fiske, fandom is 'an intensification of popular culture which is formed outside and often against official culture' (1992, p. 34), while for Henry Jenkins fans are rakish, misunderstood outsiders engaged in the transgressive practice of 'textual poaching' (1992). Jimmie L. Reeves, Mark C. Rodgers and Michael Epstein go even further, explicitly constituting postmodern cult television series as cynical devices that 'commodify oppositional reading and cash in on viewer resistance to commercial culture' (1996, p. 34).

The political framework into which so many scholarly accounts have organised fandom and fan practices is essentially binaric. It assumes the mutual exclusivity of the culture industry and fan culture, constructing an antithetical relationship in which the former is constituted as unequivocally exploitative and the latter as a species of resistant folk culture. Fan practices, this reasoning goes, involve 'unauthorised' readings and the production of unauthorised tertiary texts; they are therefore oppositional. But fan 'politics', insofar as one can even impose such a monolithic concept upon fandom, are enormously problematic and complex. Despite scholarly interventions, television fandom's primary characteristic remains a slavish devotion to a television series, a textual fetishism that very often has much more to do with the hedonistic pleasures of the imagination than it does with critiquing or challenging commercial culture. Many fan-produced texts are adoring or whimsical and exhibit little in the way of politicised engagement with their beloved cult object. K'Tesh's Klingon Recipe Pages, for example, include culinary trivia from the various *Star Trek* series and detail some interesting recipe ideas for those in search of the ultimate in exotic cuisine. But extra-terrestrial gastronomy surely does not qualify as 'resistant'. All too often, the activities of fans become oppositional only when subjected to the alchemy of academic analysis. Unsurprisingly, many fans have seized upon and perpetuated this ennobling of their activities as inherently politically consequential and renegade. Such interpretations are a preferable alternative to the mainstream's stigmatisation of fans as nerds, losers and potential stalkers. But the fact that many fans prefer to see themselves as representatives of a radical cultural underground doesn't make this description uniformly accurate.

This is not to suggest that television fan cultures are *never* politicised, *never* 'resistant'. There are many instances where fans recruit television texts in order to interrogate, critique, evade or oppose aspects of mainstream culture. Elsewhere, I have discussed how the playful constructions of genders, sexualities and histories in the series *Xena: Warrior Princess* (1995–2001) are used by many fans as a resource for rethinking cultural inscriptions of, especially, lesbian and bisexual identities (see Gwenllian Jones, 2000). Cult television characters such as Lieutenant Uhuru, Xena, Buffy, Cisco and Seven of Nine are complex ciphers that provide opportunities for challenging orthodoxies about race and gender in ways that have been, and continue to be, widely and thoughtfully discussed by fans and scholars alike. Online, it is easy to find countless instances where fans debate issues of identity and otherness or integrate them into fan fiction and cultural criticism. Other fan practices that might be broadly described as 'resistant' are often personal and hidden, allied to individuals' interior engagements with characters and storylines and rarely publicly stated. The popular T-shirt that bears the slogan 'What would Xena do?' articulates an empowering question that fans of the series no doubt ask themselves upon occasion, but such uses of television texts are mostly private and invisible. Importantly, however, such politicised engagements very rarely 'resist' the cult text itself; rather, the cult text is recruited as an ally to oppose wider sociocultural forces. Fandom is a profoundly liminal occupation, one that takes place neither within nor outside commercial culture, creative but also derivative, a celebration of consumerism as well as a maverick mode of consumption. In the heated debate around studio censorship of fan websites, the sweeping and often uncritical valorisations of 'the television fan' that occur in so many academic accounts meld into an explicit construction of the fan as an unlikely folk hero championing freedom of expression against the might of the media corporations that own and control popular culture.

In common usage, the term 'cult television' has a variety of different meanings. It may refer to series that have nostalgic appeal (such as certain defunct children's programmes, or programmes associated with a particular decade); series considered to have an offbeat or risqué appeal (*Absolutely Fabulous, Beavis and Butthead, South Park*); or series that fall into the 'so bad, it's good' category (*Sunset Beach*). In this chapter, I use the term to refer to those television series that accrue substantial active fan cultures that engage in creative and interpretive practices such as writing fan fiction or producing fan art. Such series usually (though not always) belong to one or other of the fantastic genres of science fiction, fantasy, horror and the supernatural. They constitute an extreme form of 'must see TV' or, to use the industry vernacular, 'appointment viewing' where viewers schedule the programme into their weekly routine and make every effort to ensure that they watch it. But cult television series seek audiences composed not just of regular viewers but also including a high proportion of avid viewers. They seek a significant following of fans so devoted that they will not only watch every episode but also tape and archive it *and* buy official video releases as well, who will purchase a range of spinoff products, and who will participate in loyal fan cultures that promote and 'support' the series in a variety of ways. Unlike cult film, which usually caters to minority tastes and interest groups, fantastic genre cult television series are very often mainstream programmes with high production values; series such as *Buffy the Vampire Slayer* and *The X Files* appeal to both a mass general audience and to a dedicated fan base. Distinctions between the so-called 'general audience' and so-called 'fandom' have become increasingly blurred as cult series become franchises; today, shops such as *Forbidden Planet* selling series-related merchandise can be found on the high streets of most provincial cities, catering not to hardcore fans but to a mainstream market that increasingly resembles fandom.

The evolution of fandom, the mass audience and the marketing strategies of cult television producers sits uncomfortably alongside intellectual property laws that are based upon outdated models of production and consumption, texts and readers. In this chapter, I suggest that if online cult television and film fan cultures do need to be saved from corporate and legal tyranny (and there remains some considerable doubt as to whether, in fact, they do), then their defence requires a critical understanding of the culture industry and fandom that does not rely on notions of opposition. Instead, fandom needs to be understood as a liminal, fetishistic and highly engaged consumer culture that is both born of and fully implicated in the cultural processes it supposedly 'resists'. Fandom, I argue, is a mode of interactivity as well as a mode of consumption, and the fictions it dedicates itself to are modelled accordingly.

'Must see TV' and how to make fans

Until the early 1990s, television fan culture was the barely visible terrain of a tiny minority of the television audience. Only the most dedicated fans participated and its most tangible expressions were paper fanzines and conventions. The fanzines were mostly obscure, amateurish and available only by subscription. Conventions involved travel and expense and were usually attended by only a few hundred fans. Not only were television fan cultures difficult to find and access but they were also blighted by the profoundly unappealing stereotypes of fans circulated by the media and exemplified by portrayals of 'Trekkies' as 'nerdy guys with glasses and rubber Vulcan ears' (Jenkins, 1992, p. 9). To most outsiders, television fans seemed like a bunch of harmless obsessives whose eccentric activities were of little or no consequence. If the derivative texts they produced – fanzines, fan fiction, fan art, 'filk' music – involved copyright infringements (and they usually did), then the production studios who owned the copyright either didn't notice or were content to turn a blind eye as long as fans weren't producing them for profit. Usually, fans produced their own texts only to share them with other fans; their distribution was too small and their quality too poor to merit any censorious response from the studios that held copyright on the original works from which they derived.

Over time, fandom has become a significant source of extra revenue for production studios. The multimedia success of the *Star Trek* franchise provides ample demonstration of the long-term financial rewards that can accrue from a series that evolves a substantial fan following. A thriving fan culture can ensure a high public profile for a series that might otherwise quickly vanish into the wastes of television history. It constitutes a lucrative, ready-made and ongoing market for an array of official spinoffs such as novels, episode guides, photographs, posters, models, videos, collectors' cards and, in *Star Trek*'s case, four more series (to date) and a succession of movies. Together with the fragmentation of the television audience effected by multi-channel cable, satellite and digital technologies, the consumption habits of fans have helped ensure that niche audiences which include high quotas of avid viewers have become a highly desirable market for an increasingly intermedial culture industry. The development of *Twin Peaks* (1990–1) reflects, Jim Collins notes, 'a fundamental change in the way the entertainment industries now envision their publics' not as 'a homogeneous mass but rather as an amalgamation of microcultural groups' (1992, p. 342). From 1990 onwards, a number of television series have been produced and marketed precisely in order to attract particular microcultures and to foster within them not just regular viewers but also a high proportion of fans. Series such as *The X Files, Babylon 5, Xena: Warrior Princess, Buffy the Vampire Slayer, Dark Angel, Farscape* and *Witchblade* employ a range of textual and narrative devices that make an explicit address to the immersive, interpretive and interactive viewing practices that characterise fandom. Intertextuality, metatextuality, self-referentiality, story-arc and stand-alone episodes within the same series, an exaggerated play of fracture and textual excess and generic interconnections with wider subcultures (science-fiction, fantasy, horror, conspiracist, ufological) are knowingly employed to seduce viewers into intense engagements with the fictional worlds and fantastic logics of the cult television series' diegesis. The wide open, producerly texts of these series appeal not so much to their audiences' desire to be entertained as to its need to be imaginatively involved.

This is world-building for profit. The cult television builds fictions that are not confined to a single medium but rather sprawl across a variety of different media and texts that are connected not by any linear master narrative but rather contribute to a fantastical, populated and coherent cosmology. The cult series simultaneously encourages and supplies fans' hunger for what Janet H. Murray describes as 'a psychologically immersive experience ... that takes over all of our attention, our whole perceptual experience' (1999, p. 98). Here, the contingencies and pleasures of willed hallucination, rather than the surface pleasures of ordinary viewing or the jarring self-consciousness of resistant reading, become apparent. Fans' devotion to official texts, their seemingly insatiable appetite for merchandise, their need to share their fascination and ardour with other fans, their production and consumption of derivative texts, bespeak not opposition but a deep-seated compulsion to build, enter and uphold a virtual reality. The 'must see' status of cult television series stems from this compulsion. Fans seek to reinforce and expand the fictional cosmology by continually gathering new information about its characters, geographies, backstories, plots and themes. They eagerly anticipate new episodes, watching, taping, re-viewing and analysing them. After a new episode has been aired, fan mailing lists, messageboards and chat rooms throng with activity as fans exchange opinions and interpretations. The fantasy is at once individuated and shared, the product both of myriad unique imaginings and of collaboration. As Murray notes, when we enter a fictional world we 'do not suspend belief so much as we actively *create belief*' (ibid., p. 110). For fans, part of creating belief involves seeking out or creating tangible objects – images, literature, sounds – that function as semiotic shields against everyday reality in order to reinforce the fictional world. By providing the raw materials for this process, in the form of both primary and secondary texts, the culture industry creates, feeds, directs and profits from a desire for immersion and interactivity that can never be fully satisfied because it can never be fully achieved.

Interactivity here is not of the same variety that characterises computer games or the fictional technology of the holodeck. The television text itself cannot be interacted with; it has no facility for material intervention and exists unalterably unassailable from opening sequence through to closing credits. But the fiction that it generates, and which vastly exceeds containment by any discrete text, is a different matter. The fiction consists not only of textually explicit and implicit information from the series itself but also of exterior constructions, whether officially or unofficially produced. It is accumulative and forever incomplete; every new text contributes to and subtly reshapes it. The cult fiction, unlike the cult television text in which it originates, is interactive. It is this fiction that fans engage interactively with when they write stories of their own based on characters, events and topographies drawn from the series. Interactivity here occurs not as a material process involving physical interventions but as an imaginative one.

In his essay 'The Poachers and the Stormtroopers', Henry Jenkins suggests that the production and marketing of cult television's 'rich, multilayered texts' is symptomatic of 'a more powerful cultural industry which co-opts fan politics and defuses its threat to corporate power' (1998, website). The culture industry tailors and packages its fictions in order to make cult objects of them and produces and markets merchandise so that it can further cater to and capitalise upon fans' hunger for immersion in the imaginary world of the text. Of course, this is part of the ordinary logic of capitalism, and media fans are media consumers *par excellence*. As Janelle Brown points out,

> extreme fandom is Hollywood's dream come true – consumers so devoted to Xena and Leia and Spock and Luke that they'll consume every *Star Wars*-branded product, watch every *Xena* episode, proudly display their *Star Trek* pins on dirty back-packs.
>
> 1997, website

The merchandising industry that surrounds cult television series imitates the text-producing practices of fans. Instead of fan-authored trivia files and cultural criticism, commercial culture produces episode guides and glossy magazines. Instead of 'filk' music, it produces CDs of soundtracks. Instead of fan fiction, it produces novelisations, comics and, sometimes, spinoff series that extend the metatextual logics of fan readings. It sells fans shinier versions of their own texts, all stamped with an official seal of approval.

Supply, demand and the world wide web

During roughly the same period that the Hollywood studios started to fully realise and exploit the voracious consumerism of fans, the arrival of the world wide web complicated the straightforward transactions of supply and demand. Digital and internet technologies facilitate the production and dissemination of high-quality fan-produced texts and 'steals' from source texts in ways that were previously unimaginable. Digital production and dissemination profoundly alters the unwritten contract between the culture industry as the producer and distributor of popular cultural texts and fans as merely passive consumers. Online, a few mouse clicks are all it takes to access video and sound files, fan fiction archives, galleries of photographic images, graphics and fan art, professional-quality screensavers and wallpapers, fan-produced e-journals, chat rooms, mailing lists and messageboards. Where a successful fanzine in the 1970s might have reached a few hundred fans, today a successful fan website can accumulate thousands, even millions, of hits.[1] Fandom's move onto the web has effected a massive increase in the numbers of avid viewers actively engaged in fan culture as producers, distributors and consumers of tertiary texts. In the series-derived metaverses of online fandom, fans achieve and share something of the immersive participation in fictional cosmologies which is the root of their fandom. At the same time, the distinction between the 'narrowcast' texts of fan culture and the 'broadcast' texts of official culture that John Fiske described in 1992 (p. 39) has, to a limited extent, become eroded. The possibilities opened up by the web mean that 'narrowcast' no longer need indicate circulation among a select few who are already in the know.

Online fandom's accessibility, imaginative richness and diversity haven't only seduced more of the television audience into active fandom. These characteristics have also meant that online fandom has attracted substantially more attention from journalists, scholars and, crucially, the culture industry itself. As the 'shadow culture industry' of fandom (Fiske, 1992, p. 30) has become significantly less shadowy, so too have many Hollywood studios become increasingly uneasy about online fandom's conspicuous and widespread flaunting of intellectual property laws. Since the mid-1990s, there have been a succession of legal actions by studios attempting to limit fan culture to those pursuits that do not constitute major infringements of copyright. In 1996, lawyers for Viacom were among the first to act, sending out stern 'cease and desist' letters to *Star Trek* fans whose websites made unauthorised use of copyrighted materials. As a result, dozens of fan websites were shut down almost overnight by webmasters fearful of being sued.

Since then, similar actions have been taken by lawyers acting for, among others, 20th Century-Fox against fan sites devoted to *The X Files*, *Millennium*, *The Simpsons* and (on behalf of Warner Bros., for whom they produce the series) *Buffy the Vampire Slayer*.

Even more controversially, LucasFilm has attempted to censor *Star Wars* sites carrying material (especially faked pornographic images of characters and slash fiction) considered by the company to be detrimental to the 'family-friendly' image of the *Star Wars* brand name (see Tushnet, 1997, website). To fans, whose primary motivation is their love for a particular popular cultural text, such actions often seem to represent a betrayal of their loyalty, enthusiasm, and emotional and creative investments in their cult objects. They have responded to studio censorship by organising petitions, letter-writing campaigns, boycotts of studio products, and a twenty-four-hour protest blackout of fan websites. Online, they have co-ordinated their own anti-censorship campaigns, founding groups such as 'The Online Freedom Federation' (website) and 'X-Factor – X-Philes For Abolishing Censorship Threatening Our Rights' (website).

Fans' opposition to studio censorship coheres around two main strands of argument. First, many fans stress that their activities are non-profit-making and benign, pointing out – with some justice – that they complement rather than detract from the commercial value of their favoured cult object. Bret Rudnick, graphics editor of the fan-produced *Xena: Warrior Princess* e-journal *Whoosh!*, claims that fan sites,

> are, overwhelmingly, the equivalent of placing posters in your room, stickers on your locker
> or notebook, or pictures on your refrigerator. The Internet is the means by which you can
> invite others into your room or school or kitchen. For the vast majority of fans who create or
> visit fan sites, it's simply a venue to share your interest with others world-wide, rather than
> just in your immediate neighbourhood.
>
> 2000, website

Second, many fans argue that studios' attempts to restrict their activities represent an infringement of fans' rights to creative and critical expression. Moreover, they suggest that the 'textual poaching' that underlies and structures their own imaginative engagements differs from the studios' own practices of toll-free cultural appropriation only insofar as fans do not poach for profit. As Jesse Walker says,

> When the government tells us that we can't use those scraps without permission from Disney,
> Fox or the Sherwood Anderson Trust, it constrains our creativity, our communications and
> our art. It tells us that we cannot draw on pop songs the way we once drew on folk songs, or
> on TV comedy the way we once drew on Vaudeville; it says that we cannot pluck pieces from
> *Star Wars* the way George Lucas plucked pieces from foreign films and ancient legends.
>
> 2000, website

It is in these two areas – the fiscal innocence of fandom and fan appropriations as a legitimate species of 'fair use' – that the tensions and uncertainties of the transforming relations between the culture industry and fan cultures are at their most emphatic and complex. As the culture industry recasts and commodifies both folk culture and fan culture as commercially produced popular culture, so too does fandom recast popular culture as a contemporary manifestation of traditional folk culture (see Jenkins, 1998).

For fans, the ubiquity and public character of popular culture makes it in some respects unownable. By this rationale, once a popular cultural text enters the public domain it becomes, to an extent, public property. It acquires the same status as mythology and fairytales, and may be similarly and legitimately disarticulated and reworked by anyone who chooses to do so.

Myths and assimilations

John Fiske and John Hartley have described how television serves a 'bardic function' in contemporary western society, relaying and mediating our common cultural resources. Television, like traditional bards, 'composes out of the available linguistic resources of the culture a series of consciously structured messages which serve to communicate to the members of that culture a confirming, reinforcing version of themselves' (1978, pp. 85–6). In his essay 'Digital Land Grab', Henry Jenkins makes a similar argument and extends it to issues of ownership:

> For most of human history, the storyteller was the inheritor and protector of a shared cultural tradition . . . The great works of the western tradition were polished like stones in a brook as they were handed off [sic] from bard to bard. This process of circulation and retelling improved the fit between story and culture, making these stories central to the way a people thought of themselves . . . Contemporary Web culture is the traditional folk process working at lightning speed on a global scale. The difference is that our core myths now belong to the corporations, rather than to the folk.
>
> 2000, website

However, part of the complexity of the legal issues involved in studio censorship of fan sites arises from the fact that the ownership of popular cultural texts by corporations is not as clearcut as it seems. Kristen Baldwin points out that, by taking legal action against fan sites, studios are not necessarily acting in their own interests. They also have a legal responsibility to protect the creative works of their employees: 'Guild contracts require them to negotiate permission with a show's actors, directors, musicians, and writers every time an episode is aired – even if that "airing" is a grainy 2-by-2 inch image on a PC screen' (2000, website). Intellectual property laws must address and accommodate a variety of competing interest groups, including the studios, their employees, other producers of cultural texts, fans and the wider public.

Just as legally inscribed notions of popular cultural texts as 'intellectual property' need to be interrogated, so too does their apposite construction as a contemporary manifestation of traditional folkloric or mythopoetic practices. What exactly is meant by descriptions of texts as 'folklore' or 'myth'? Even in their more traditional applications, these terms are notoriously difficult to define. Professor K. K. Ruthven articulates his own problems with the term 'myth' by quoting Saint Augustine's meditation on time: 'I know very well what it is, provided that nobody asks me; but if I am asked and try to explain, I am baffled' (1976, p. 1). Nevertheless, we might venture to say that a text may be considered 'mythic' or 'folkloric' if it draws heavily upon, and contributes to, a shared cultural lexicon of archetypal figures, themes, gestures, encounters and collisions. And of course this is precisely the sort of text that the culture industry produces over and over again. Iconic characters such as Xena, Luke Skywalker, Kirk and Spock recall a variety of archetypal figures drawn from history, myth, folklore, literature and other cultural texts, and many of the storylines in which they are engaged again recall or re-enact the major moments and movements of older storytelling traditions.

Even so, questions and problems remain. Do all popular cultural texts qualify as folkloric or mythic, or just some? Are the criteria for such classifications to be based on circulation, particular media, textual strategies and subject matter, the ways in which consumers read and use such texts, or some combination of these? Who decides? Can a popular cultural text be considered 'folkloric' in its entirety, or is such a definition viable only when limited to certain textual elements (for example, storylines and themes but not *verbatim* scripts; characters' names and histories but not screen captures)? Are some fan practices better described as part of a legitimate 'folk' cultural process than others? Do photographic, video and audio files lifted directly from the source text and circulated without further creative intervention have the same claims to 'folkloric' status as do, say, fan fiction, cultural criticism and art? What about pornographic fake images of characters, which use actors' bodies to visually mediate a double fantasy, a fiction born of a fiction but fixed in the photographically reproduced materiality of real bodies?

The point here is not that the notion of popular culture as a species of folk culture is wrong but rather that, if it is to be effective, a rather more precise notion of what constitutes legitimate folk culture and folk practices is required. Preferably, this should be one that does not implicitly conflate the concepts of 'folk culture', 'fan culture' and 'opposition' or 'resistance' to commercial culture. It is neither accurate nor enough simply to constitute fans as Everyman avatars of a heroic resistance, pitted against a ruthless culture industry which harvests and sells back to us our collective myths and dreams. What is overlooked in this simple binary formula is any sense of the extent to which fans, as the culture industry's most voracious consumers, are complicit in the very processes they are supposedly resisting. For the most part, relations between the culture industry and online fan cultures are more symbiotic than they are antagonistic. The culture industry not only produces popular cultural texts but also constitutes their fan cultures, and it does so in order that it may profit from them by selling them its television series, its films and its merchandise. A fan culture is not an independent phenomenon that spontaneously attaches itself to a cultural artifact that has some particular meaning for it. Rather, fandom is a construct, not really a 'culture' at all but a nodal gathering of disparate individuals who may well have little in common beyond a shared love for their cult object. The stability and coherence indicated by the nominations 'fan culture' and 'fandom' are largely artificial; the terms describe a set of consumer practices, modes of intense engagement, not a discrete, consistent or homogeneous consumer population.

Paradoxically, fan culture's slippery, liminal status makes it, in legal terms at least, both difficult to defend and difficult to prosecute on much more than a case-by-case (or rather 'fan practice-by-fan practice') basis. For example, US intellectual property laws distinguish between the uncopyrightable 'idea' of a work and its copyrightable 'expression'. This legal distinction was invoked when 20th Century-Fox and LucasFilm famously sued the makers of the television series *Battlestar Galactica* (1978–9) on the grounds that it closely resembled the *Star Wars* films. Ultimately, Fox and LucasFilm lost the case because copyright ownership does not protect the 'idea' of a work. In the interests of free creative enterprise, copyright laws cannot be used to 'prevent the creation of another film which includes a dashing hero who saves a princess in the midst of numerous space battles set in the future' (Radcliffe, 1996, website). In an exhaustive analysis of how existing intellectual property laws relate to fan-produced texts, copyright expert Rebecca Tushnet argues that much the same distinction can be applied to fan fiction. Fan fiction, Tushnet suggests, 'transforms' rather than 'copies' characters, and 'the extent of protection for characters independent of the works in which they appear is unclear' (1997, website). At the same time, fans do not profit from fan fiction and neither does fan fiction seem to detract from the sales of broadly similar official spinoffs such as novels. For these reasons, a strong case can be made in favour of fan fiction's exemption from ordinary copyright law on the grounds that it constitutes 'fair use' of its source material. Furthermore, Tushnet argues that,

> If a line is not drawn at noncommerciality when it comes to creative re-use of characters, then a fan's daydream is theoretically as illegitimate as the story she posts on the Web. The regime implied by this interpretation would clearly be impossible to enforce and equally difficult to respect.
>
> Ibid.

But Tushnet's careful appraisal of how various intellectual property laws relate to fan fiction is less easily extended to other, non-literary fan practices. Though fan fiction and cultural criticism would seem to merit a legal defence based on the concept of 'fair use', screen captures, sound files and scratch videos (which are composed of re-edited extracts from episodes, usually overlaid with a music soundtrack), though also non-commercial, are less easily defended in these terms. They are explicit appropriations of the 'expression' rather than the 'idea' of the copyrighted work, straightforward 'steals' involving little or no original creative input from fans.

Money talks

Ultimately, the issues of intellectual property ownership and studio censorship are likely to resolve themselves in terms of the economics rather than the 'politics' of fandom. The resolution will probably be favourable to fans simply because, far from threatening the capitalist machinery of the culture industry, online fan culture encourages and participates in its commercial operations. Profitable symbiosis, not altruism or legal difficulty, is the main reason why – despite all the scare stories to the contrary – only a tiny percentage of the tens of thousands of copyright-infringing fan websites have provoked 'cease and desist' letters from studios. Toby Miller notes how 'corporations sell merchandise (often directly) thanks to fan web sites, and the free advertising and public relations that keep "their" commodity in the public eye amount to a classic free ride in economic terms' (forthcoming). These factors, Miller suggests, underlie the studied ambiguousness of many of the 'cease and desist' letters sent to webmasters whose sites carry unauthorised materials. A letter sent out by Fox lawyers demonstrates this careful balancing of legal objection and 'all rights reserved' tolerance. First of all, the letter unambiguously instructs the webmaster to 'remove all wallpaper, screensavers, desktop themes, fonts, skins, audio and video clips and the image galleries relating to "Buffy the Vampire Slayer" from your website'. But then the blow is softened by a cagey and conditional statement of limited tolerance:

> In addition, we note that your site contains "Buffy the Vampire Slayer" stationary-frame
> images on other pages of the web site besides the image galleries. We must inform you that
> the unauthorised display and distribution of such images constitutes a copyright violation.
> While we are not asking you to delete these images at this time, we must nonetheless request
> that you revise your legal notice and disclaimer and prominently display the following on
> every page of your site exhibiting any "Buffy the Vampire Slayer" images.
>
> 20th Century-Fox, 1999, website

LucasFilm has taken this logic of circumscription much further. In an attempt to contain and police online *Star Wars* fandom without eradicating it, LucasFilm offers fans free homepages with a highly desirable domain name at 'starwars.com'. But, in order to establish and maintain their sites in the official *Star Wars* domain, fans must first agree to be bound by an exhaustive list of terms and conditions. These, of course, prohibit the unauthorised use of copyrighted materials, which are defined as 'all logos, characters, artwork, stories, information, names, and other elements associated thereto . . .' (website). Clause 2 of the 'Terms of Use' agreement states that,

> The creation of derivative works based on the materials contained herein including, but not
> limited to, products, services, fonts, icons, link buttons, wallpaper, desktop themes, on-line
> postcards and greeting cards and unlicensed merchandise (whether sold, bartered or given
> away) is expressly prohibited.
>
> Website

As Elizabeth Durack rightly points out, 'the sort of deeply-engaged fans who create and visit fan websites are prime consumers of *Star Wars* merchandise' (2000, website). The point, then, for Hollywood studios, is not to erase or overly compromise online fan culture, not to antagonise fans, but rather to assimilate them into what are (again, for the studios) acceptable, authorised zones of activity. For Henry Jenkins, such tactics are a strategy of co-optation (see Jenkins, 2000, website). And indeed they are. But, however galling it may be to admit it, fan culture is already co-opted from the moment it comes into being. By definition, fandom is an effect of the culture industry; it is commercial culture's adoring and irreverent offspring, not its nemesis. The battle that is being enacted in this slow and half-hearted choreography of legal parries and fan feints is as much a boardroom negotiation as it is a civil liberties debate. At heart, this is not a conflict about freedom of expression but rather a redrawing of the increasingly blurred boundary between production and consumption, and a redefining of the relations between 'texts' and 'readers'. As I have argued elsewhere, the text-reader relationship does not adequately describe how contemporary cult television fictions are produced and marketed to fans (Gwenllian Jones, 2001). Intellectual property laws assume the imperviousness and fixity of the television text but ignore its function as the untidy generator of a much larger virtual reality. The market value of these multimedia cult fictions lies in precisely the fact that they are neither impervious nor fixed but rather mechanisms for immersive and interactive engagements with a fictional world. In short, then, the culture industry is producing and marketing cult television series as interactive fictions while, in some instances, prohibiting the very practices that are intrinsic to their appeal.

While the big Hollywood studios retain a conventional corporate attitude towards their properties and the limited rights of consumers of their products, the fact that legal actions against fan websites have been few and far between is indicative of a gradual shift in the studios' understanding of their products, marketing strategies and customers. But this shift is most marked in the example of the independent Hollywood production studio Renaissance Pictures. Founded by Sam Raimi, Rob Tapert and Bruce Campbell, whose creative and business alliance began when they were college students, Renaissance Pictures' first production was the low-budget cult horror film *The Evil Dead* (1982), directed by Raimi, starring Campbell and produced by Tapert, and this was followed by other cult-oriented film productions including *Darkman* (1990) and *Timecop* (1994). The company's forays into television similarly reflect its creators' interest in fantasy genre cult fare. *American Gothic* (1995–6) is a supernatural horror series set in small-town America. *Hercules: The Legendary Journeys* (1995–9) is a fantasy action adventure set in the world of classical mythology and populated with gods and monsters. From *Hercules* came the more successful spinoff series *Xena: Warrior Princess (XWP)* , set in the same mythological cosmos. *XWP*'s diegesis and marketing is indicative of its producers' deliberated address not just to a general audience but to an audience of potential *fans*. The series employs to excess all of those textual devices beloved of avid viewers – campy humour, insider gags, a coherent and well-populated fictional world, deep backstory, offbeat and charismatic major characters, metatextuality, 'mythic' themes and plots and the extension of the cult fiction across a full range of media and merchandise products. Like *The X Files* before it, *XWP* demonstrates its producers' awareness of what constitutes a 'cult' fiction and how fandom is not a matter of passive consumption but rather one of interactive imaginative engagement.

This understanding has been extended to the series' vast and prolific online fandom. *XWP*'s release in 1995 coincided with the rapid growth in internet usage that occurred in the early to mid-1990s, following the development of the user-friendly world wide web interface. From the outset, its fandom was a predominantly online affair, rapidly evolving into a rich multimedia phenomenon across thousands of websites. It consists of photographic stills, desktop themes, fan-created graphics, scratch videos, short streamed extracts from episodes, screensavers, vast archives of fan fiction, sound files, 'filk' music, episode guides, critical essays, e-journals, galleries of fan art, and an extensive 'Encyclopaedia Xenaica' with entries on every conceivable aspect of the series. Transcripts of interviews and articles from magazines and newspapers appear online within hours of publication. Fans interact with each other via Internet Relay Chat, dedicated message-boards and mailing lists. Online fandom reflects the depth of critical and creative engagement of fans, endlessly extending the world of the series into innumerable per-mutations and elaborations that each, in turn, feed back into a vast fiction that has long since dissolved the boundaries that might define it as a 'text'. Dynamic, diverse and – as often as not – slickly professional-looking, the online Xenaverse seduces less ardent fans of the series into more devoted modes of fandom, presenting a range of attractive possibilities for deep engagement with the cult fiction that is its inspiration. Part virtual temple, part cosmology in and of itself, part community, part arena for creative enter-prise, and part unofficial advertising campaign, it represents not just a response to but the manifestation of logics already implicit to the diegesis and marketing of the cult fiction.

Renaissance Pictures' dealings with fans tacitly acknowledge that the creations and appropriations of online fandom represent not copyright theft but are rather legitimate manifestations of interactive imaginative engagement with the cult fiction, an engage-ment which is pleasurable for the fans and profitable for the studios. Far from detracting from sales of official spinoff products, online fandom seems to increase them by deep-ening audience interest and promoting everything relating to the series to a wide body of fans; fans buy official products *as well as*, rather than instead of, accessing and creat-ing unofficial ones. As a result, Renaissance Pictures has not followed the lead of the major studios in their attempts to curtail and control online fan practices. Bret Rudnick of the online fan journal *Whoosh!* describes a symbiotic relationship with the company:

> Renaissance have known about fan sites from Day One. They certainly know about WHOOSH! and have been very cooperative with us. Several representatives of Renaissance have told me personally that they appreciate what we and others like us do for the shows. Our relationship has generally been quite good. There have been times when they have asked us to remove sensitive information from our site and we have complied. They have been quite responsive to us in the past regarding requests for information, making it available when possible.
>
> 2000, website

Only in those rare instances where fans attempt to profit from their unauthorised series-related creations has Renaissance Pictures taken legal action, warning off one fan who was selling audio tapes of *XWP* fan fiction stories.

It is not difficult to shut down fan websites carrying illicit copyrighted materials. They are easy to locate, and most ISPs will refuse to host sites if they can be shown to be in breach of the law. Studios show restraint because most recognise, to some extent, that it is in their financial interests to nurture rather than to eradicate a thriving fan culture.

This leaves fans vulnerable, their activities dependent upon the tolerance of the studios, but the conditions of the cult television phenomena also provide fertile new directions for both legal and academic argument in defence of fan practices, for if cult television fictions are produced and marketed as species of interactive multimedia entertainment, as I have argued, then fans who use them as such surely should not and cannot be prosecuted for doing so.

Note

1. For example, 'Tom's Xena Page' (website) had registered 5.5 million hits in October 2001.

Bibliography

Baldwin, Kristen, 'Rebuffed', *Entertainment Weekly* (21 January 2000),
    <www.ew.com/ew/report/0,6115,275214~6~~,00.html>.

Baudrillard, Jean, *Fatal Strategies*, translated by Philip Beitchman and W. G. J. Niesluchowski, edited by Jim Fleming (London: Pluto Press, 1990).

Brown, Janelle, 'Fan Fiction on the Line', *Wired News* (11 August 1997),
    <www.wired.com/news/business/0,1367,5934,00.html>.

Collins, Jim, 'Television and Postmodernism', in Robert C. Allen (ed.), *Channels of Discourse, Reassembled* (London: Routledge, 1992), pp. 327–53.

Durack, Elizabeth, 'fans.starwars.con', *Echo Station* (12 March 2000),
    <www.echostation.com/editorials/confans.htm>.

Fiske, John, 'The Cultural Economy of Fandom', in Lisa A. Lewis (ed.), *The Adoring Audience: Fan Culture and Popular Culture* (London and New York: Routledge, 1992), pp. 30–49.

Fiske, John and Hartley, John, *Reading Television* (London: Methuen, 1978).

Gitlin, Todd, 'Who Communicates What to Whom, in What Voice and Why, about the Study of Mass Communication?', *Critical Studies in Mass Communication*, vol. 7 (1990), pp. 185–96.

Gwenllian Jones, Sara, 'Histories, Fictions and *Xena: Warrior Princess*', *Journal of Television and New Media*, vol. 1, no. 4 (November 2000), pp. 403–17.

Gwenllian Jones, Sara, 'Conflicts of Interest? The Folkloric and Legal Status of Cult TV Characters in Online Fan Culture', Society for Cinema Studies Conference, Washington, DC (26 May 2001).

Jenkins, Henry, *Textual Poachers: Television Fans and Participatory Culture* (New York and London: Routledge, 1992).

Jenkins, Henry, 'The Poachers and the Stormtroopers', transcript of talk presented at the University of Michigan, posted to *Red Rock Eater Digest* (1998),
    <commons.somewhere.com/rre/1998/The.Poachers.and.the.Sto.html>.

Jenkins, Henry, 'Digital Land Grab', *Technology Review* (March/April 2000),
    <www.technologyreview.com/articles/jenkins0300.asp>

K'Tesh's Klingon Recipe Pages, <www.klingonfood.com>

Miller, Toby, 'Train-spotting *The Avengers*', in Sara Gwenllian Jones and Roberta E. Pearson (eds), *Worlds Apart: Essays on Cult Television* (Minneapolis: University of Minnesota Press, forthcoming).

Murray, Janet H., *Hamlet on the Holodeck: The Future of Narrative in Cyberspace* (Cambridge, MA: MIT Press, 1999).

The Online Freedom Federation, <www.off-hq.org>.

Penley, Constance, 'Brownian Motion: Women, Tactics and Technology', in Constance Penley and Andrew Ross (eds), *Technoculture* (Minneapolis: University of Minnesota Press, 1991), pp.135–61.

Penley, Constance, *NASA/Trek: Popular Science and Sex in America* (London and New York: Verso, 1997).

Radcliffe, Mark F., '*The Law of Cyberspace for Non-Lawyers*', <www.gcwf.com/articles/cyber/primer.html>.

Reeves, Jimmie L., Rodgers, Mark C. and Epstein, Michael, 'Rewriting Popularity: the Cult *Files*', in David Lavery, Angela Hague and Marla Cartwright (eds), *Deny All Knowledge: Reading* The X Files (London: Faber, 1996), pp. 22–35.

Rudnick, Bret, 'The Night of the Boggling Blackout', Editor's Page, *Whoosh! The Online Journal of the International Association for Xena Studies*, no. 44 (May 2000), <www.whoosh.org/issue44/editor44.html>.

Ruthven, K. K., *Myth* (London: Methuen, 1976).

starwars.com, 'Terms of Use', <www.starwars.com/copyright.html>.

Tom's Xena Page, <www.xenafan.com>.

Tushnet, Rebecca, 'Legal Fictions: Copyright, Fan Fiction, and a New Common Law', *Loyola of Los Angeles Entertainment Law Journal*, no. 17 (1997), reprinted online at: <www.schrag.info/tushnet/law/fanficarticle.html>.

X-Factor, <www.kiva.net/~muggs/xfiles.html>.

Walker, Jesse, 'Copy Catfight: How Intellectual Property Laws Stifle Popular Culture', *Reason Online* (March 2000), <www.reason.com/0003/fe.jw.copy.html>.

Afterword

12

What Is Television for?

Alan McKee

'Television is for appearing on, not looking at', says Noel Coward (Institute, 1993, p. 436). Many academics seem to subscribe to a similar dictum – although it might more accurately be formulated as: 'Television is for writing about, not looking at.' Catharine Lumby notes that:

> Dr Jocelynne Scutt, a prominent Australian feminist barrister and an opponent of degrading images of women in the media ... has spoken and written so frequently on the subject of sexism in the media [that] she is often invoked as an expert on the media by the media. It came as something of a shock to learn she didn't own a television set.
>
> 1997, p. ix

As Lumby notes: 'television watching is a guilty secret' – still, in the twenty-first century, 'something to be engaged in sparingly and in private' (ibid., p. x). Indeed, John Hartley has characterised this mode of engagement with television – to comment as an expert on it without actually watching it – as 'the intelligentsia mode of television reception' (Hartley and McKee, 2000). And although not all academics are members of the intelligentsia, in this sense, I have also noticed that many of my colleagues, teaching Media Studies, strongly organise their viewing schedules around public service broadcasting at the expense of commercial programming. Of course, this is not in itself problematic – unless the academics in question then begin to speak as experts about all television. At this point, a refusal to actually watch the medium being discussed seems, to me at least, to be a little odd.

Indeed, the majority of academic writing about television has shown little interest in television programmes. David Marc suggests that:

> Questions of authorship, genre and discourse were almost completely ignored in post-war mass media studies. Indeed, specific television programs are not even mentioned in such seminal television-era works as Macdonald's *A Theory of Mass Culture*, or Marcuse's *One-Dimensional Man*.
>
> 1995, p. 89 [or, we might add, in McLuhan's *Understanding Media* (1964)]

Similarly, Lynn Spigel notes that: 'broadcast history has continually framed its object of study around questions of industry, regulation and technological invention' (1992, p. 5). Of course, there are many honourable exceptions to these generalisations. We must note Howard Newcomb's *TV: The Most Popular Art* (1974) as a groundbreaking piece of writing on television as a source of programmes; as is Raymond Williams' *Television: Technology and Cultural Form* (1974). (Although it is interesting to note that probably the most lasting impact of that book was to introduce the term 'flow' into television studies: a term which has been used to avoid discussing particular programmes by suggesting that television's overall stream of programming is more important. That this was emphatically not Williams' point in his own use of the word is merely ironic.) John Fiske and John Hartley's *Reading Television* (1978) is a third important germinal book in this tradition. Indeed, when you add in the BFI's television monographs – Richard Dyer's *Light Entertainment* (1973), Colin McArthur's *Television and History* (1978), Dyer *et al.*'s *Coronation Street* (1981) – and the many gorgeous books on television programmes which have been published in the last decade – my favourites include Corner's *Popular Television in Britain* (1991), Jane Shattuc's *The Talking Cure: TV, Talk Shows and Women* (1997), Lynn Spigel and Michael Curtin's collection *The Revolution Wasn't Televised: Sixties Television and Social Conflict* (1997) and John Hartley's *Uses of Television* (1999) – you might wonder what Marc, Spigel – and myself – are going on about. There's plenty written on television programmes, surely?

I don't want to fall into simple statistical claims – I am sure that an absolute majority of writing on television remains uninterested in programming, but this is not necessarily relevant – as I am more interested in the ways it is possible for writing about television to conceptualise the medium. Take the case of *Australian Television Culture* and *Australian National Cinema*. These two books, magisterial accounts of Australian media cultures, are very different. The first offers 'a picture of Australian television', the second analyses (according to its cover blurb) 'the distinct and diverse nature of Australian cinema'. The books share an author (Tom O'Regan, 1993, 1996). Despite this, their objects of study are constituted very differently. The first mentions almost no programmes and those that are addressed are mentioned in passing: there is no analysis of any particular television text. The second is replete with examples of particular films, analyses of their representational strategies, and links to the social context of production.

The difference between these books cannot be explained in terms of authorial fickleness: rather, it represents the different ways in which television and film have been constructed as objects of study. While film has a recognised canon and a tradition of close textual analysis, in the study of television the programmes themselves have tended to vanish – as they do in *Australian Television Culture*. It is still possible – indeed, I would argue, normal – to study television without even thinking about programming. This is not the case with other media that are researched by academics: cinema, books, visual arts. And I am interested in what it means for the topic of this book – 'must see TV' – that for much of the history of academic study of television, programmes have been largely absent from the writing. In particular, to what extent can we argue that 'must see TV' is a recent phenomenon, and to what extent must we realise that it might rather be the case that the 'must see TV' that came before has simply vanished because it was invisible – like all television programming – to the academics who have studied television?

My specific discussion here will be of Australian television. It is important to acknowledge the specificity of this study: Australia is not America, nor is it Britain. For example, in terms of drama programmes, approximately 105 Australian series were produced in Australia up to 1993 (Moran and Pinne, 1993). This is not very many compared to, for example, the number of series produced in the UK, or the USA. In the UK, audiences expect that most evenings will offer a choice of different local drama production on several terrestrial channels. By contrast, the largest number of first-run local drama series presented in a given week on any Australian television channel in 1999 was two. So Australian television relies on a disproportionately large amount of imported programming to complete its schedules, particularly drama and sitcoms. These imported programmes are often relatively successful, but rarely top the ratings.

But even acknowledging this specificity, the comments of Marc and Spigel suggest that a similar process of academic misrecognition has occurred in academic study of television in Australia and in other countries and that comments on the Australian situation might be relevant when thinking about the UK and the USA.

Constructing television

Reading through the material which has been published on Australian television, political economy appears to be the most popular approach taken by academics interested in the medium (see, for example, Jacka and Johnson, 1998). Particularly important for such work is the Australian public broadcaster, the ABC (as in Inglis, 1983). The only genre of television which justifies continued critical attention is news and current affairs (for example, Bell, Boehringer and Croft, 1982 – although a decidedly worrying recent trend sees 'high-culture' television programmes becoming canonised as an object of study, be that 'serious' one-off plays or adaptations of literary novels, see Bignell, Lacey and Macmurraugh-Kavanagh, 2000; Caughie, 2000; Giddings and Selby, 2001; Jacobs, 2000). For these approaches to Australian television, politics is more interesting than television programmes: both the politics of television and the televising of politics. A third approach to the study of television – although one which is less prominent in Australia than in other countries – is medium theory (Morris, 1998, p. 114; see also Innis, 1991 [1951]; Meyrowitz, 1985). A fourth approach to Australian television avoids discussing programmes by addressing television's 'effects' (see Silberstein, 1983, for a particularly impressive example of this trend). A fifth discusses the production of programmes, more interested in the industrial and institutional constraints of what is made than in the texts which are finally broadcast (Burke, 1984; Moran 1982; Tulloch and Moran, 1986).

These approaches to thinking about television, about the form it takes as an object of study, what is important about it – ultimately, what it is *for* – share one common aspect. In any of these approaches, it would be quite feasible to write a history of Australian television without ever seeing an episode of any programme that has been broadcast on the medium.

These are not the only approaches to television in Australian academia. There has also been some fascinating writing on the programmes that have been broadcast. Tulloch and Turner's *Australian Television: Programs, Pleasures and Politics* (1989), Cunningham and Miller's *Contemporary Australian Television* (1994) and collections such as *Australian Screen Comedy* (McKie and Turnbull, 1996) and *Tomorrow Never Knows* (Bowles and Turnbull, 1994) bring together much useful writing on particular programmes. Also important is the work of Graeme Turner (1989), John Hartley (1996) and John Docker (1983, 1988). But such work has certainly not formed the dominant approach to the understanding of television in academia. It seems to me that this has less to do with the industry and the kinds of programmes being broadcast than with our academic paradigms and the way we think of what television is for. Underlying many of our theories of television, and our research into it remains, I suspect, a distaste for this messy, downmarket medium – a distaste which means that the very concept of distinction between programmes becomes almost literally unthinkable.

'Must see TV'

Such critical paradigms lead to a situation where, in Australia at least (and, as Spigel and Marc suggest, perhaps in other contexts), although we know a lot about television industries, policies, productions, and even reception, comparatively little has been written about the history of television programmes. But this does not mean that television until recently was indeed a simple flow, with guaranteed audience loyalty and unthinking viewership. Writers in this book examine the ways in which industrial changes have led to the promotion of 'must see TV' as an important part of the television schedule – emphasising the importance of factors such as the emergence of new channels and technologies, and new forms of corporate organisation. It is undoubtedly the case that a shift has taken place, from what industry analysts call 'TVI' to 'TVII'. 'TVI' describes 'network era television':

> once [the three networks] commanded over 90 per cent of the audience, today the major network audience has decreased to about 60 per cent . . . CBS's 'rural purge' in 1971 [saw] the cancellation of highly rated shows . . . because they did not attract segments of the population that were most valued by advertisers . . . 'Popularity' came to mean high ratings with the eighteen to forty-nine-year old urban dweller rather than popularity with the older rural audience.
>
> Jane Feuer, quoted in Reeves, Rodgers and Epstein, 1996, p. 30

However, this should not lead us to think that the 'cult television' Reeves, Rodgers and Epstein are discussing, or the 'must see TV' which is the focus of this book, did not exist before the industrial changes described. Rather, it seems to me, their presence had simply not been detected because of the ways in which academics have studied television. It is my contention that 'must see TV' has existed, in Australia at least, since the beginning of broadcasting. Since its inception, television has supported what can be called, to use a later coinage, 'watercooler shows'. Such programmes passed beyond the boundaries of the text to become more widely circulated, to become programmes which even non-viewers knew about. Not simply watched by large audiences, they also became part of the culture in which they were broadcast. An imperative existed, if not necessarily to watch these shows (although many did), then to know about them as part of the condition of living in a public culture.

It is possible to look outside of traditional academic paradigms in order to get some sense of the 'must see TV' that has always existed on Australian television. Thomas McLaughlin takes up the term 'vernacular theory' from the work of Houston Baker in order to describe the kind of 'theoretical practice [that] is widespread in the culture', noting that the theoretical work practised in everyday situations by people outside of the academy, 'does not differ in kind from academic theory, and that academic theory should therefore be thought of . . . as a rigorous and scholarly version of a widely practiced analytical strategy' (1996, p. 6). He goes on to argue that:

> theory is not the elite activity that both its enemies and defenders claim it to be. It is an integral and crucial element in everyday culture . . . I have always been sceptical of the academy's easy conflation of genteel cultural style and intellectual skills.
>
> Ibid., p.29

Looking at the wider mediasphere, it is quickly obvious that television in Australia has always had its 'must see' programmes. Looking beyond academic writing to the vernacular theory of the popular media, it is obvious that for television itself (and for writers in newspapers and magazines) television is constructed as quite a different object of study. While, for academics, television has overwhelmingly been a medium with spatio-temporal effects, a regulated medium, a produced medium, and so on, in vernacular theory, it has been quite a different object. It has been a medium that broadcasts programmes. It has been a medium which has continually presented 'must see TV'. These programmes are not part of a 'flow' of endless broadcasting, but have become part of a public archive of the important moments and programmes in Australian television history. It is thus possible to recover them.

It is interesting to note that the writers in Australia who have paid most attention to television *programmes* are often those writing in journalistic or popular modes, rather than academic ones. Adrian Martin, for example, writes about: 'indelible TV memor[ies]' (1994, p. 57), a concept almost unimaginable for those interested in legislation and the adequacy of news coverage of political events. Similarly Morris Gleitzman's account of Australian television is one which is focused on its programmes (1992).

In the mediasphere, it is clear that television programmes are neither ephemeral nor amnesiac. Newspapers, magazines, radio shows, popular books and television itself are continually involved a project of working out, restating and negotiating a public archive of Australian television. Dozens of texts can easily be cited in the Australian context. On television itself, see for example *30 Years of Television* (Wilton, 1994); *40 Years of Channel 9 Unplugged* (Anon., 1999a) and *35 Years of Television* (Vikingur, 1991); 'Simply

The Best's' programme on 'the best TV show of the century' (Anon., 1999b, p. 114); and *Today Tonight*'s item on 'TV's Top 100 Moments' (1999); *Our Century*'s account of television's history (1999), *Homicide: 30 Years On* (Lee and Bladier, 1994) and *The Homicide Story* (Anon., 1970); the last, tribute episode of *Hey Hey It's Saturday* (1999). In newspapers and magazines, see 'The 25 All Time Best Australian TV Shows' (Elder, 1995, p. 6S); or '40 Years of Channel 7' (Anon., 1999c p. 3); 'The 50 Most Influential Shows on Australian Television' (Dale, 1998); *TV Week*'s 'Great Moments on Australian Television' (Anon., 1999d, p. 31) or the '100 Greatest Moments in Television' (Anon., 1999e); and in the publications of the Australian Television Appreciation Society, including its magazine, *TV Eye* (Keating, 1993). In advertising, take the examples of television promos presenting 'Perth's own TVW Channel 7 – 40 years in the making'; and advertising series promoting 'Great Moments in Television', featuring such moments as '*A Country Practice*: Lucy and Matt's Wedding' (Norman, 1999, p. 29). Such archival accounts of television's own past have recently become extremely visible, particularly in British culture (take, for example, 'I Love the 1970s' – or at least, the television from the 1970s). These programmes are not a new phenomenon – as the citations above suggest – but their current visibility suggests that television's public archive is increasingly visible in the mediasphere.

Of course, for many commentators, such programmes are worthless and trivial, demonstrating the lack of original thought in popular culture. It is easy simply to dismiss all of this popular work in creating and negotiating an archive of television's greatest moments. It is not, after all, academic writing. It is not refereed, nor published by university presses. Following Simon Frith and Jon Savage's comments on *The Modern Review*, we could describe popular culture's construction of television's archive as 'self-serving nostalgia' (1997, p. 14), and worry that television is imploding, feeding off itself, with nowhere left to go.

Such dismissals do not, it seems to me, demonstrate a familiarity with the cultural objects they discuss. These programmes, one could argue, are a sign of the emptiness of post-modern culture, its reliance on pastiche rather than parody, its dearth of originality. But to make this claim would be to ignore the fact that such programmes have existed for decades, and would be to make a value judgment as to their archival purposes which is, from the perspective of this viewer at least, unnecessarily nasty.

There are other, more respectful ways of approaching the increasingly visible television tributes which form this public archive. For after all, nobody has ever attacked a retrospective festival of art films, or season of Shakespearean performances, as being 'self-serving nostalgia'.

Lynn Spigel describes:

> . . . two ways of thinking about the past – one properly 'academic' and the other conventionally 'popular'. As opposed to the professional ideals (if not always practices) of exhaustive data gathering, accuracy and conclusive analysis, the histories told in the texts of popular culture simplify the complexity of historical events . . . [P]opular memory . . . is a form of storytelling through which people make sense of their own lives and culture . . . [it]

acknowledges its subjective past and selective status . . . [and it is] less concerned with historical 'accuracy' than it is with the uses that memory has for the present.

1995, p. 21

Spigel argues that both forms of archive are worthwhile; each can illuminate the other. It seems obvious upon viewing and reading the accounts of Australian television's archive of 'great moments' which is negotiated in popular culture that they are not simply 'nostalgia': in the sense of 'weren't things great then, aren't they worse now'. Most of the histories mentioned above are involved in quite specific projects of storytelling; tracing the place of national identity in Australian television, for example; or struggling to place Channel 0–10 at the centre of the Australian mediasphere. But we need not dismiss them because of their specificity. Rather, this contributes to their interest. Rather than 'self-serving nostalgia', we can name these genealogies as part of 'popular memory' about Australian television. To understand them in this way – or using related terms such as 'cultural memory' (Jancovich, 1996, p. 169), 'social memory' (Scannell, 1996, p. 91), 'collective remembering' (Middleton and Edwards, 1990, p. 1), 'collective television unconscious' of the nation (Gitter, Anapol and Glazer, 1999, back cover); or even 'shared television memories' (Bianculli, 1996, p. 16) – points towards the work done by these texts in helping to work out which programmes are important in the history of Australian television broadcasting. The term I favour to describe these texts is the 'public archive' of television programmes in Australia; this term, I hope, avoids the confusing implications of subjective experience which the term 'memory' might imply, insisting that this is not simply an idiosyncratic account of Australia's television history, but one which survives in the mediasphere, and is available to all citizens of that sphere (Hartley, 1996).

Australia's public archive of 'must see TV'

In a recent research project, I attempted to map a genealogy of Australian television's 'great moments': to present the public archive of 'must see TV' since the medium's beginnings in Australia (1956) (McKee, 2001). Many of these, I would contend, were moments of 'must see TV': even though the Australian television system has never really progressed beyond TVI. I gathered information for this history from a variety of sources: popular histories of Australia's television programmes, mentions (usually brief) in academic histories of television, contemporary coverage of television in other media, my own experiences as a television viewer in Australia, suggestions from other media academics, letters solicited on radio and in newspapers from viewers answering a general question about their favourite television memories and fan coverage of programmes on the internet and in fanzines. From these sources, it was relatively easy to build a picture of 'must see TV'. There survives a stable archive of programmes whose importance has remained, and whose position in 'cultural memory' is stable. There is not enough space in this chapter to look at the archive for the whole of Australian television history. However, a summary of some of the important programmes of the first two decades of the medium makes clear that, long before the industrial changes which have resulted in some countries in a shift to 'TVII', 'must see TV' was a part of Australia's television.

In Melbourne Tonight (1957–70, 1972–5)

One of the most important of the early programmes was *In Melbourne Tonight* (IMT), a variety show hosted by Australia's first television star, Graham Kennedy. One correspondent for my research states that:

> I am 73 years of age, and can honestly say that in my lifetime the person who gave me the most pleasure and laughter . . . is Graham Kennedy, *In Melbourne Tonight*. What he used to do with advertisements was hysterical and they stuck in your mind – still do actually.

This programme survives in popular memory in Australia. Channel 9's *Our Century* (18 April 1999) includes clips of the programme; the figure of Kennedy appears in programmes such as *The Australian Image*, where the claim that 'In the early days, it was variety shows that gave us our Australian heroes' is illustrated with a performance from Kennedy (Brookman, 1989). A later episode of the same series claims that 'Graham Kennedy is one of the great comic figures of Australian television' and illustrates this with another clip (Thompson, 1989).

Written histories of the medium – in newspapers, magazines, popular books and academic writing – insistently lay claim for Kennedy as a 'legend' (Hugh Stuckey, quoted in Johnson and Smiedt, 1999; p. 140), a 'star' (Hutchinson, 1986; p. 255); 'Australia's first television personality' (ibid., p. 257), 'a household word throughout Melbourne [and] . . . the first great television star to emerge in Australia' (Anon., undated, p. 5). Indeed, he is Australian television royalty: 'King Gra-Gra . . . the most famous man in Australian television and, after 35 years, its longest reigning and most victorious protagonist' (O'Grady, 1989, p. 22). Evidence from the period of the show's broadcast suggests that such estimates of Kennedy's importance are not overstated. Certainly in Melbourne, his star status can be seen quickly emerging. Within weeks of *IMT* premiering on Melbourne television, Kennedy had reached star status in that city. His first appearances in the television/radio magazine *Listener In-TV* are recognisably generic – a front-cover appearance on the 4 May 1957 promotes *IMT*'s first appearance on Australian television, while his place in the photos of 'Stars of the Week' in the 12 December issue of the same publication reeks of the casual use of the term 'star' that continues in gossip magazines to the present day.

But by the start of 1958, Kennedy's status in the mediasphere is palpably changing. In the 23 January issue of *TV-Radio Week*, a columnist complains:

> Whoa people! I'm being swamped with letters from eager fans of Graham Kennedy who want to meet him following the paragraph last week offering to arrange for the person who gave the best reasons for wanting to do so to have dinner with Graham.
>
> Lever, 1958, p. 4

In the same vein, this publication manages to stage a front-page stunt that suggests the interest Kennedy holds for Melbourne television viewers: a fake wedding for the 'star'. The next issue of the magazine (30 January 1958) presents a front-cover photograph of

Kennedy and a masked bride, with the caption 'Who will she be?' It is no longer simply advertising the show: Kennedy is of interest as a celebrity in his own right – presumably to those 'eager fans' who are so keen to dine with him. To me, the passion evinced by these viewers suggests that Kennedy's show was, for them, 'must see TV'.

This marks the beginning of a remarkable career for Kennedy in such magazines. In the late 1950s, publications like *TV-Radio Week* and *Listener In-TV* present a picture of the mediasphere which is dominated by radio, and where television consists of only three types of programmes: those imported from America; sport; and variety. Over the next few years, stories about variety programmes, about *IMT* in particular, and about Kennedy especially, dominate the vision of what television is in these Melbourne publications. Television is – variety programmes. Television is – Graham Kennedy. In 1959, Kennedy got the Gold Logie television award as Star of the Year, and retained the Logie for Best Male Personality in 1966 and 1967 (Beilby, 1981, p. 29). In 1967, the programme topped the ratings in Channel 9 Sydney (under its NSW guise of *The Graham Kennedy Show*) (Johnson and Smiedt, 1999, p. 169). Indeed, as *TV Week* notes in 2000, Kennedy is the 'all time champ' in the Logies department (eight Gold Logies, thirteen altogether).

Four Corners (1961–present)

Many writers – both academic, and journalistic – have placed the Australian Broadcasting Corporation's current affairs documentary series *Four Corners* at the centre of Australia's mediasphere. It is 'the flagship of ABC public affairs sessions' (Semmler, 1981, p. 156); and 'Nothing since has matched the profound effect on production attitudes or the nation's viewing habits' (Courtis, 1981, p. 98). It is '[t]he prototypal Australian television documentary (or current affairs) program' (Breen, 1997, p. 128).

For many writers, the moments which make *Four Corners* so important are those which have resulted directly in changes in the practice of governments in Australia. The programme is often celebrated – again both by academic and journalistic writers – for 'causing Royal Commissions and resulting in public figures being jailed . . .' (Masterson and Patching, 1990, pp. 189–90). For example, a 1985 programme on indigenous deaths in custody resulted in a Royal Commission (Pullan, 1986, p. 152; Mickler, 1998, p. 174). 'The most frequently cited example' (Gibson, 1997, p. 628) of *Four Corners'* reach in party politics is the effect of the 1987 episode 'The Moonlight State'. This led to the Fitzgerald Inquiry, the jailing of the state's police commissioner, and the National Party Government losing power after more than twenty years in office (Gerry Teekman, quoted in Bowden, 1990, p. 72). In a further instance:

> A 1963 program on the Returned Serviceman's League (RSL) . . . stirred controversy for
> showing members of the organisation in casual dress drinking at a bar, rather than exclusively
> in the context of formally structured studio debate . . . The story on the RSL directly
> challenged the organisation on its claim to political neutrality.
>
> Gibson, 1997, p. 628.

This last moment has certainly been written into Australia's public archive, and the public controversy it created suggests something of its 'must see' status. On the flyleaf of his autobiography, Ashbolt highlights 'the famous *Four Corners* report on the RSL' (1974); Semmler notes that the 'item critical of the Returned Serviceman's League . . . evoked fierce public and political controversy . . .' (1981, p. 24); Blain notes that it 'brought about [Ashbolt's] removal' (1977, p. 123); and the documentary 'Four Corners: 25 Years' (Manning, 1987) proudly covers the controversy with a series of clips. This programme has never been a ratings hit in Australia, but for a certain small group of society – the 'knowledge class' (Frow, 1995) – it has been 'must see TV'.

Homicide (1964–76)

On the 20 October 1964, the first episode of the Australian cop show *Homicide* was broadcast and rated thirty-three (33 per cent of available television sets were tuned to the programme [Anderson ratings]). It was the first popular Australian television drama.

Homicide is a police show, shot in Melbourne. It centres around the Homicide Squad of the Victorian police, and each episode deals – as the title suggests – with a murder. The first three stars of the programme (fifteen detectives appeared in the programme's thirteen-year run [Harrison, 1994]) were Detective Sergeant Frank Bronson (Terry McDermott), Detective Fraser (Lex Mitchell) and Inspector Connolly (John Fegan). Its importance is metonymically remembered as the first time that viewers heard Australian accents in television drama. Although this is not strictly true – it was the first *successful* Australian drama series, not the first ever – it is true that until this point all prime-time drama on Australian television had been imported, usually from America. It is not surprising that the importance of hearing Australian accents emerged quickly in the public sphere, and has been attached to the programme ever since. Its success, and the massive public discussion of how important that success was for Australian national identity, ensured its status as 'must see TV'. From its first broadcast in Melbourne in 1964, it was in the top five programmes; and starting in Sydney in 1965, it proved just as popular. During 1966, its Melbourne ratings reached the fifties; in 1970 and 1971, it was the number one show in both Melbourne and Sydney. When the show was cancelled, it was still rating in the forties in Melbourne. In the all-time Australian top ten of programmes on Australian television, it is the highest Australian drama show (Beilby, 1981, p. 185).

The programme has also survived well in the public archive. Documentaries such as *Homicide – 30 Years On* and *The Homicide Story* have written it into Australian television history; as have documentaries such as *30 Years of Television*; and *35 Years of Television*, and the work of the Australian comic group the D-Generation has brought *Homicide* to a whole new generation, sharing clips from the programme with irreverent voice-overs which draw attention to the characters' 'brown suits'.

The Mavis Bramston Show (1964–8)

On the 21 July 1965, *The Mavis Bramston Show* rated over fifty in Sydney, and became the number two-rating national programme of the year (Beilby, 1981, p. 1). This was unheard of. Even *Homicide* did not reach the top five programmes in Australia until later in its run. *Mavis Bramston* brought a new form to Australian television, and made it central to the mediasphere: that form was called 'satire'. The programme introduced political commentary, entertainingly presented, to Australian television.

The place of *The Mavis Bramston Show* in Australian television history is assured, with historians giving it an important place in their accounts of the medium (Davies, 1981, p. 125). The programme was a 'sensation' – a word that many commentators have used to describe its success, and that might fairly be related to 'must see TV' – once rating an unheard-of fifty-nine in Sydney (ibid., p. 126). *Mavis* makes *Who Weekly*'s list of '100 Greatest Moments in Television' at number twenty-five (Anon., 1999e, p. 60); and for Graeme Turner, it is part of his genealogy of 'transgressive television' in Australia (1989).

The programme debuted in 1964. Presented by three hosts – Carol Raye, Gordon Chater and Barry Creyton – its format was a mixture of comedy sketches and songs, performed by the stars and a variety of guests. Many of these sketches and songs commented directly on political and social issues of the day. The first episodes were shown only in Sydney. From the sixth episode, it was also shown in other cities. It created many moments of fond cultural memory. For example, the 'Flower arrangement' sketch:

> became a short-lived legend . . . [reading from] an innocent book on flowers . . . Gordon
> Chater and Carol Raye wrung every last double entendre and risqué nuance from the book's
> instructions on how to arrange flowers, from stamen to stem, from pistil to bloom.
>
> Davies, 1981, p. 126

Mavis Bramston focused on topical issues – even to the exclusion of humour, rather than as a focus for it – and this marks it as a turning point in Australian television. It rated up to fifty-nine, and it created public 'sensation' – once again, 'must see TV'.

Number 96 (1972–8)

Number 96 was a nightly half-hour soap opera dealing with the lives of a group of characters living in a Sydney block of flats. It was a vital part of Australian television in the 1970s; and of everyday culture in Australia during this time. It was the number one-rated programme in Australia in 1973 and 1974 (Jones and Bednall, 1980, p. 32), and number nine in the top ten of most popular programmes ever on Australian television, until 1981 (Beilby, 1981, p. 185). It has also provided many moments of 'must see TV' – fondly remembered by several interviewees for the research project in the form of childhood memories of sneaking downstairs after they had been put to bed in order to watch the programme through a crack in the doorframe. Many of the programme's storylines were amusingly excessive and sex-obsessed. In one, characters were menaced by the 'pantyhose murderer', a killer who strangled unfortunate victims with women's underwear. This made it to number nine of Channel Ten's 'Ten's Top 10 Moments' in 1996, and was mentioned by correspondents for the research project as one of the great moments of Australian television history. In another storyline, the menace came from the 'knicker-snipper': a criminal who spent his time lurking under beds and cutting the elastic in ladies' undergarments: again, mentioned by correspondents as a great moment. Perhaps the single most remembered incident from the programme was the bomb blast in Aldo Godolfus's delicatessan: mentioned by correspondents, appearing in public discussions of Australian television history (Robbins, 1999; p. 95); appearing at number seven in *Who Weekly*'s '100 Greatest Moments' (Anon., 1999e, p. 50); and topping the top ten list in the Channel Ten documentary mentioned above (www.magna.com.au/ ~lindsay/info/Preface4.html). Several of these great moments were repeated on the Foxtel *Number 96* Anniversary season in 2000 ('the pantyhose murderer – a different victim every night!' [www.magna.com.au/~lindsay/temp/Foxtel]). When *Number 96* was launched: 'Channel Ten's publicity chief, Tom Greer, organised a skilful promotional campaign, promoting the premier episode as "The Night Television Lost Its Virginity"' (Oram, 1988, p. 24). This slogan has survived as a description of *Number 96*'s importance in bringing sex to Australian television. Hilary Kingsley introduces her comments on the programme using the phrase (1989, p. 262); as does Chris Keating (1999).

The single aspect of *Number 96* which has survived most strongly in television's public archive is the fact that it had sex in it. The programme was explicitly commissioned to be 'controversial' (Oram, 1988, p. 23); indeed, 'Sexuality . . . had been part of the brief' (Day, 1981, p. 147); 'to break new ground' and be 'a bit more sexy' (Brookman, 1989). It was 'the first show to repeatedly depict full-frontal nudity' (Keating, 1999). It covered 'such subjects as . . . abortion, [and] homosexuality' (Reid and Groen, 1977, p. 88), and 'incest . . . adultery, attempted rape . . . wife and lover-swapping, run-of-the-mill affairs, and for a brief and seamy period, witchcraft culminating in the ritual sacrifice of two naked virgins' (Radic, 1973, p. 8). It presented 'permissiveness' (Jones and Bednall, 1980) and included 'sex and humour' in a 'daring' way (Kingsley, 1989; p. 6). It showed 'a see-through blouse with nipples and aureoles on the other side' (Anderson, 1972, p. 40). In fact, *Number 96* was 'full of sex' (Peach, 1992, p. 152). It is no surprise that 'These days people remember it for its nudity' (Kingsley, 1989, p. 262).

Particularly central in the public archive of *Number 96* is the character of Bev, played by the surnameless 'Abigail'. This figure condenses for many writers exactly what *Number 96* was about: 'the big-bosomed Abigail' (Peach, 1992, p. 152). She was 'the actress who just couldn't seem to keep her clothes on' (Kingsley, 1989, p. 262); 'its major star and sex symbol':

> Time was whenever Abigail dropped her bra, half of Australia would sit up and take notice. And if you happened to miss the disrobings of Abigail's Bev Houghton, the newspapers kept you in touch as never before with headlines that captured even more followers.
>
> Hohensee, 1978, p. 24

With all of this sexuality unleashed on the Australian television-viewing public in 1972, it is unsurprising that the programme was not only massively popular, but entered public debate, and has survived in Australian cultural memory as a particularly vital example of 'must see TV'.

Changing paradigms

These programmes were 'must see TV', in the sense of events that stepped outside Williams' 'flow' of television. They were all broadcast in a national television system which largely remains in the 'TVI' phase of production, and has not really produced its own 'cult' programmes (even *Prisoner [Cell Block H]*, which has become a cult overseas, was originally a mainstream hit in Australia). The reason that they did not receive a substantial amount of academic attention is due not to the fact that 'must see TV' did not exist in earlier decades of television: but because academic approaches to the medium did not imagine such a thing to be a possibility.

Will 'must see TV' exist in the future? Do recent developments – particularly the increasing number of television channels available to viewers – challenge the concept?

My object of study in visiting this archive is 'Australian television'. A necessary fiction is at the heart of such a project – the idea that there is such a thing as 'Australia', a simple object, where television is watched by 'Australians', who all know the same programmes and remember the same things. Of course, this is not true – if I asked what might be the public archive of television for Indigenous Australians, for example, or for Queer Australians, it would produce quite a different list. Or, in a federated country such as this one, what might be the archive for Victorians? South Australians? New South Welsh-people?

And yet, this 'imagined community', this 'necessary fiction' of the nation still has some use as a tool for thinking about culture. We still often think about television at a national level (see the discussions of the perceived importance of television for national representation in Buscombe, 2000), even as more channels mean that audiences for individual programmes are not always as large as they were during the period of 'TVI'. Some writers have worried that the introduction of these channels leads to 'fragmentation' of national culture (see, for example, Graham Murdock in ibid.). Such concerns strike me not only as being misinformed, but also as presented in bad faith. The writers who mourn the supposed loss of a common culture are the same ones who tend to react in horror to the examples of large popular audiences (for 'mass', 'popular' culture) which can still demonstrably be shown to exist. More than a decade after regular satellite broadcasting was introduced in the UK, *EastEnders* can still gather together massive audiences of British viewers on a regular basis; and *Big Brother* can become a phenomenon – 'must see TV', a rapidly archived moment of common culture that must be added to the public archive ('I love blinking, me'; 'Demons!'). I suggested above that the texts of 'must see TV' do not exist in isolation: they are moments that spread out into culture more generally. Thus, even though audiences for particular channels may decline, the great moments of 'must see TV' can spread through the mediasphere, in newspapers, magazines, radio shows, other television programmes, and still reach vast audiences. When dealing with culture – ultimately with human beings and the ways they express themselves – we can never make accurate predictions. I would merely say – based on my own observations of the historical and continuing production of moments of 'must see TV' – that we can look forward to a common culture of shared moments of television. And, sadly, that most academics writing about television will continue to ignore or dismiss such a history because of their own distaste for popular culture – and for the people who like it. Against such Coward-ly prejudice I can only insist that television – all television – is, in fact, for watching – for the vast majority of citizens. If we fail to understand this in our writing on the medium, then we fail to understand television itself.

Bibliography

Anderson, D., 'Rotton Forbidden Fruit', *The Bulletin* (1972), p. 40.

Anon., *The Homicide Story* (Melbourne: Crawfords Australia, Channel Seven, 1970).

Anon., *40 Years of Channel 9 Unplugged* (Sydney: Channel 9, 1999a).

Anon., 'Simply the Best' (1999b), pp. 114–15.

Anon., 'Channel 7: 40 Years of Television', *Channel 7: 40 Years of Television Supplement with the West Austrialian* (1999c), pp. 3–17.

Anon., 'What's Your Most Memorable Australian Television Moment?', *TV Week* (1999d), p. 31.

Anon., '100 Greatest Moments in Television', *Who Weekly* (1999e), pp. 44–94.

Anon., *The Graham Kennedy Story: From Birth to Stardom in Words and Pictures* (Melbourne: Southdown Press, undated).

Ashbolt, A., *An Austrialian Experience: Words from the Vietnam Years* (Sydney: Australasian Book Society, 1974).

Ashbolt, A., 'The ABC in Civil Society: The Relationship with Institutions and Audiences', in T. Wheelright and K. Buckley (eds), *Communications and the Media in Australia* (Sydney: Allen and Unwin, 1987), pp. 97–116.

Beilby, P. (ed.), *Australian TV: The First 25 Years* (Melbourne: Thomas Nelson, 1981).

Bell, P., Boehringer, K. and Croft, *Programmed Politics: A Study of Australian Television*, (Sydney: Sable Publishing, 1982).

Bianculli, D., *Dictionary of Teleliteracy: Television's 500 Biggest Hits, Misses and Events* (New York: Syracuse University Press, 1996).

Bignell, J., Lacey, S. and Macmurraugh-Kavanagh, M., *British Television Drama: Past, Present and Future* (Basingstoke: Palgrave, 2000).

Blain, E., *Life with Aunty: Forty Years with the ABC* (Sydney: Methuen of Australia, 1977).

Bowden, T., *The Backchat Book* (Crows Nest, NSW: ABC Enterprises, 1990).

Bowles, K. and Turnbull, S. (eds), *Tomorrow Never Knows: Soaps on Australian Television* (South Melbourne: Australian Film Institute, 1994).

Breen, M. P., 'Australian Programming', in H. Newcomb (ed.), *Museum of Broadcast Communications Encyclopedia of Television* (Chicago and London: Fitzroy Dearborn, 1997), pp. 126–31.

Brookman, C., *The Australian Image: 'The One-Eyed Monster'* (Canberra: Capital Television/National Film and Sound Archive, 1989).

Burke, J., *Survey of Australian Television Program Production* (Melbourne: Australian Broadcasting Tribunal Research Branch, 1984).

Buscombe, E., (ed.), *British Television: A Reader* (Oxford: Clarendon Press, 2000).

Business Wire, 'Warner Bros. Signs One Year Deal with America Online', *Business Wire* (11 December, 1995).

Caughie, J., *Television Drama: Realism, Modernism and British Culture* (Oxford: Oxford University Press, 2000).

Corner, J. (ed.), *Popular Television in Britain: Studies in Cultural History* (London: BFI, 1991).

Courtis, B., 'News and Documentaries', in P. Beilby (ed.), *Australian TV: The First 25 Years* (Melbourne: Thomas Nelson, 1981), pp. 90–109h.

Cunningham, S. and Miller, T., *Contemporary Australian Television* (Sydney: University of New South Wales Press, 1994).

Dale, D., 'The 50 Most Influential Shows on Australian Television History', *The Guide, Sydney Morning Herald* (1998), pp. 4–5.

Davies, B., *Those Fabulous TV Years* (North Ryde, NSW: Cassell Australia, 1981).

Day, C., 'Drama', in P. Beilby (ed.), *Australian TV: The First 25 Years* (Melbourne: Thomas Nelson, 1981) pp. 134–59.

Docker, J., 'Unprecedented in History: Drama and the Dramatic in Television', *Australasian Drama Studies*, vol. 1, no. 2 (1983), pp. 47–62.

Docker, J., 'Popular Culture and Bourgeois Values', in *Constructing a Culture: A People's History of Australia since 1788* (Victoria: McPhee Gribble/Penguin, 1988), pp. 241–58.

Dyer, R., *Light Entertainment* (London: BFI, 1973).

Dyer, R., Geraghty, C., Jordan, M., Lovell, T., Paterson, R. and Stewart, J., *Coronation Street*, (London: BFI, 1981).

Elder, B., 'The 25 All-Time Best Australian TV Shows', *The Guide Magazine, Sydney Morning Herald*, (1995), p. 6S.

Fiske, J. and Hartley, J., *Reading Television* (London: Methuen, 1978).

Frith, S. and Savage, J., 'Pearls and Swine: Intellectuals and the Mass Media', in S. Redhead (ed.), *The Clubcultures Reader* (Oxford: Blackwell, 1997).

Frow, J., *Cultural Studies and Cultural Value* (Oxford: Clarendon Press, 1995).

Gibson, M., 'Four Corners', in H. Newcomb (ed.), *Museum of Broadcast Communications Encyclopedia of Television* (Chicago and London: Fitzroy Dearborn, 1997), pp. 627–9.

Giddings, R. and Selby, K., *The Classic Serial on Television and Radio* (Basingstoke: Palgrave, 2001).

Gitter, M., Anapol, S., and Glazer, E., *Do You Remember TV?* (San Francisco: Chronicle Books, 1999).

Gleitzman, M., *Gleitzman on Television: Just Looking* (Sydney: Sun/Macmillan, 1992).

Harrison, T., *The Australian Film and Television Companion* (East Roseville, NSW: Simon and Schuster Australia, 1994).

Hartley, J., *Popular Reality: Journalism, Modernity, Popular Culture* (London: Arnold, 1996).

Hartley, J., *Uses of Television* (London: Routledge, 1999).

Hartley, J. and McKee, A., *The Indigenous Public Sphere* (Oxford: Oxford University Press, 2000).

Hey Hey It's Saturday (Melbourne: Channel 9, broadcast 20 November 1999).

Hohensee, M., 'TV's Success Story – the Soaps', *TV Times, Melbourne*: (1978), pp. 24–5.

Hutchinson, G., 'The Funny Melbourne Television Phenomenon', *Meanjin*, vol. 46, no. 2 (1986), pp. 254–66.

Inglis, K., *This Is the ABC: the Australian Broadcasting Corporation 1932–1983* (Carlton, VIC: Melbourne University Press, 1983).

Innis, H., *The Bias of Communication* (Toronto: University of Toronto Press, 1991 [1951]).

Institute, P. L. (ed.) *21st Century Dictionary of Quotations* (New York: Dell, 1993).

Jacka, E. and Johnson, L., 'Australia', in Antony Smith (ed.) *Television: An International History, 2nd Edition* (Oxford: Oxford University Press, 1998), pp. 208–23.

Jacobs, J., *The Intimate Screen: Early British Television Drama* (Oxford: Clarendon Press, 2000).

Jancovich, M., *Rational Fears: American Horror in the 1950s* (Manchester: Manchester University Press, 1996).

Johnson, R. and Smiedt, D., *Boom-Boom: A Century of Australian Comedy* (Sydney: Hodder and Stoughton, 1999).

Jones, C. and Bednall, D., *Television in Austrialia: Its History through Ratings* (Sydney: Australian Broadcasting Tribunal, 1980).

Keating, C., 'Australian Television Drama: A Brief Overview', *TV Eye: Journal of the Australian Television Appreciation Society*, vol. 1 (1993) pp. 24–6.

Keating, C., Interview (1999).

Kingsley, H., *Soap Box: The Australian Guide to Television Soap Operas* (South Melbourne: Sun Books, 1989).

Lee, D. and Bladier, J., *Homicide: 30 Years On* (Melbourne: Crawfords Australia, 1994).

Lever, R., 'Fine Tuning', *TV Radio Week* (1958), p. 4.

Lumby, C., *Bad Girls: The Media, Sex and Feminism in the 90s* (St Leonards, NSW: Allen and Unwin, 1997).

Manning, P., '*Four Corners*: 25 years' (Sydney: Australian Broadcasting Corporation, 1987).

Marc, D., *Bonfire of the Humanities: Television, Subliteracy and Long Term Memory Loss* (Syracuse: Syracuse University Press, 1995).

Martin, A., *Phantasms* (Ringwood, VIC: McPhee Gribble, 1994).

Masterson, M. and Patching, R., *Now the News in Detail: A Guide to Broadcast Journalism in Australia* (Victoria: Deakin University Press, 1990).

McArthur, C., *Television and History* (London: BFI, 1978).

McKee, A., *Australian Television: A Genealogy of Great Moments* (Oxford: Oxford University Press, 2001).

McKie, D. and Turnbull, S., (eds), *Australian Screen Comedy, Continuum*, vol. 10, no. 2 (1996).

McLaughlin, T., *Street Smarts and Critical Theory: Listening to the Vernacular* (Madison: University of Wisconsin Press, 1996).

McLuhan, M., *Understanding Media: The Extensions of Man* (London: Routledge and Kegan Paul, 1964).

Meyrowitz, J., *No Sense of Place: The Impact of Electronic Media on Social Behaviour* (New York: Oxford University Press, 1985).

Mickler, S., *The Myth of Privilege: Aboriginal Status, Media Visions, Public Ideas* (Fremantle, WA: Fremantle Arts Centre Press, 1998).

Middleton, D. and Edwards, D., *Collective Remembering* (London: Sage, 1990).

Moran, A., *Making a Television Series: The Bellamy Project* (Sydney: Currency Press, 1982).

Moran, A. and Pinne, P., *Moran's Guide to Australian TV Series* (North Ryde, NSW: Australian Film, Television and Radio School, with Allen and Unwin, 1993).

Morris, M., *Too Soon Too Late: History in Popular Culture* (Bloomington: Indiana University Press, 1998).

Newcomb, H., *TV: The Most Popular Art* (Garden City, NY: Anchor Press/Doubleday, 1974).

Norman, H., 'Great Moments in Television. Featuring *A Country Practice* ', in *TV Week* (10–16 April 1999), p. 29.

O'Grady, S., 'Lone Star: the Private Life of King Gra-Gra', *Sydney Morning Herald, Good Weekend Magazine* (1989), pp. 22–6.

O'Regan, T., *Australian Television Culture* (Sydney: Allen and Unwin, 1993).

O'Regan, T., *Australian National Cinema* (London and New York: Routledge, 1996).

Oram, J., *Neighbours: Behind the Scenes* (North Ryde, NSW: Angus and Robertson, 1988).

Our Century, Sydney, Channel 9 (broadcast 18 April 1999).

Peach, B., *This Day Tonight: How Australian Current Affairs TV Came of Age* (Sydney: ABC Enterprises, 1992).

Pullan, R., *Four Corners: Twenty Five Years* (Sydney: ABC Enterprises, 1986).

Radic, L., 'Sex in the Suburbs Adds up to Number 96', *The Age*, Melbourne, (1973), p. 8.

Rees, L., *A History of Australian Drama Volume 2: Australian Drama in the 1970s* (Melbourne: Angus and Robertson, 1978).

Reeves, J. L., Rodgers, M. C. and Epstein, M., 'Rewriting Popularity: The Cult Files', in D. Lavery, A. Hague and M. Cartwright (eds), *Deny All Knowledge: Reading* The X Files (Syracuse: Syracuse University Press, 1996).

Reid, D. and Groen, F.d. (eds) *Zoom In: Television Scripts of the Seventies* (South Melbourne: Macmillan Australia, 1977).

Robbins, M., 'Critics Choice', *Who Weekly*, (1999), p. 95.

Scannell, P., *Radio, Television and Modern Life: A Phenomenological Approach* (Oxford: Blackwell, 1996).

Semmler, C., *The ABC – Aunt Sally and Sacred Cow* (Melbourne: Melbourne University Press, 1981).

Shattuc, J., *The Talking Cure: TV, Talk shows and Women* (New York and London: Routledge, 1997).

Silberstein, R., *Electroencephalographic Responses of Children to Television* (Melbourne: Australian Broadcasting Tribunal, 1983).

Spigel, L., *Make Room for TV: Television and the Family Ideal in Postwar America* (Chicago: University of Chicago Press, 1992).

Spigel, L., 'From the Dark Ages to the Golden Age: Women's Memories and Television Reruns', *Screen*, vol. 36, no. 1 (1995), pp. 16–33.

Spigel, L. and Curtin, M., (eds), *The Revolution Wasn't Televised: Sixties Television and Social Conflict* (London and New York: Routledge, 1997).

Thompson, W., *The Australian Image* (Canberra: Capital Television/National Film and Sound Archive, 1989).

Tiffen, R., *News and Power* (St Leonards, NSW: Allen and Unwin, 1989).

Today Tonight (broadcast 16 April 1999).

Tulloch, J. and Moran, A., *A Country Practice: Quality Soap* (Sydney: Currency Press, 1986).

Tulloch, J. and Turner, G., (eds), *Australian Television: Programs, Pleasures and Politics* (Sydney: Allen and Unwin, 1989).

Tunstall, J. *The Media Are American* (London: Constable, 1977*)*.

Turner, G., 'Transgressive TV: From In Melbourne Tonight to Perfect Match', in J. Tulloch and G. Turner (eds), *Australian Television: Programs, Pleasures and Politics* (Sydney: Allen and Unwin, 1989), pp. 25–38.

Vikingur, M., *35 Years of Television* (Australia: Nine Network, 1991).

Williams, R., *Television: technology and cultural form* (London: Fontana, 1974).

Wilton, N., *30 Years of Television* (Melbourne: Channel 10, 1994).

Index

Names of persons and TV programmes are indexed at every mention in the text, studios and corporations only where they are singled out for special comment. *n* = footnote; *t* = table